A Study of the

Minor Prophets

Chad Sychtysz

© 2025 Chad Sychtysz.
All rights reserved. No part of this book may be reproduced in any form without the written permission of the publisher.

Published by
Spiritbuilding Publishers
9700 Ferry Road, Waynesville, Ohio 45068

A STUDY OF THE MINOR PROPHETS
By Chad Sychtysz

ISBN: 978-1-964-80517-7

Spiritbuilding
PUBLISHERS

spiritbuilding.com

Table of Contents

Introduction to the Minor Prophets 1
Introduction to Obadiah 23
Overview of Obadiah 25
Introduction to Joel 30
Overview of Joel 33
Introduction to Jonah 40
Overview of Jonah 44
Introduction to Amos 53
Overview of Amos 56
Introduction to Hosea 71
Overview of Hosea 74
Introduction to Micah 90
Overview of Micah 93
Introduction to Zephaniah 105
Overview of Zephaniah 107
Introduction to Nahum 116
Overview of Nahum 120
Introduction to Habakkuk 129
Overview of Habakkuk 132
Introduction to Haggai 144
Overview of Haggai 147
Introduction to Zechariah 154
Overview of Zechariah 158
Introduction to Malachi 195
Overview of Malachi 198
Sources Used 212
Endnotes 214

Unless otherwise noted, Scripture taken from the NEW AMERICAN STANDARD BIBLE®
Copyright 1960, 1962, 1963, 1968, 1971, 1972, 1973, 1975, 1977, 1995
by The Lockman Foundation. Used by permission.

The author can be contacted at chad@booksbychad.com.

Cover design by Larissa Lynch.

Introduction to the Minor Prophets

One of the major categories of books of the Hebrew Bible (what we call the "Old Testament") is that of the Prophets (Mat. 5:17, 22:40, Luke 16:29, 24:44, etc.). The Israelites regarded the Prophets, as a division of sacred literature, as the most important of their ancient writings after the Law of Moses itself (i.e., the Pentateuch, or the first five books of the Old Testament). Within the category of "the Prophets" were the major prophets (*Isaiah, Jeremiah, Ezekiel,* and sometimes *Daniel*) and the minor prophets (the final twelve books of the Old Testament, from *Hosea* to *Malachi*).

The greatest difference between "major" and "minor" prophets was the size of the books themselves. The abundant text of the major prophets provided a far more detailed message, and thus often made a more significant impact upon the Israelite community than that of the minor prophets. We should not, however, diminish the importance of the minor prophets simply based upon their written length. Significant New Testament [NT] citations (and theological concepts) came out of the minor prophets. For example, "The righteous {man} shall live by faith" (Rom. 1:17) is a quote from *Habakkuk* (Hab. 2:4), one of the shortest Old Testament [OT] books. This serves as the basis for most of the book of *Romans* and is also used significantly in Heb. 10:36–38. Another example is God's quote in the book of Hosea ("I will say to those who were not My people, 'You are My people!' And they will say, 'You are my God!'"—Hos. 2:23) which serves as a major theological point in Rom. 9:25–26 as well as 1 Peter 2:10.

Definition of a "Prophet": The ancient prophets were God's human mouthpieces. The Hebrew word for prophet can be translated "seer," suggesting the visionary character of the prophet's message (see 1 Sam. 9:9). God did not always merely dictate His message to the prophet; in one way or another (i.e., through actual visions or figurative explanations), God often *showed* it to him and thus he *saw* it.[1] "Prophet" covers a broad spectrum, from general applications (as in the case of Abraham in Gen. 20:7) to those who are specifically recognized as prophets (in the case of Samuel, 1 Sam. 3:20; "Nathan the prophet," 2 Sam. 7:2; "the prophet Gad," 2 Sam. 24:11; etc.).

In essence, any man served as a prophet in some sense if he communicated a divine message *from* God *to* another person, people, or nation. Sometimes even singers are referred to as "prophets" (see 1 Chron. 25:1–7), in that they spoke the word of God in their songs, often set to music. This may give us a better understanding of Miriam's identification as a "prophetess" (Exod. 15:20) and Saul's experience "among the prophets" (1 Sam. 10:5–11). In some cases, music itself was used as an accompaniment to the very act of prophesying (2 Kings 3:15). "Under the law [i.e., Law of Moses—MY WORDS] there were at least five classes of speakers: Moses, the lawgiver; the wise men, who gave counsel; priests, who taught the law; prophets, through whom God spoke His word; and psalmists, who were the singers or poets in Israel."[2] It appears that some of the earlier prophets formed guilds or schools to instruct certain prophets how to best conduct themselves, present their oracles, and/or serve as assistants to the prophets. Thus, "sons of the prophets" (2 Kings 4:38) likely refers to those who sat at the feet of great prophets like Elisha for this kind of instruction (see also 1 Sam. 10:5 and 19:20). Men like Gehazi (2 Kings 4:12) and Baruch (Jer. 36:4) are in this category. However, such men are not always presented in a favorable light (see 2 Kings 2:15–18, for example), indicating that they may have been only assistants to the prophets rather than genuine prophets themselves.

Moses served as the prophetic prototype—a model for all prophets to come. He spoke the words of God; the people came to him with questions *for* God; and he interceded for the people. Yet, since Moses, "no prophet has risen in Israel…whom the LORD knew face to face, for all the signs and wonders which the LORD sent him to perform in the land of Egypt…, and for all the mighty power and for all the great terror which Moses performed in the sight of all Israel" (Deut. 34:10–12). Moses and Elijah together represented *all* the OT prophets in their appearance with Jesus on the mountain of transfiguration (Mat. 17:1–5).

Even so, Jesus was to receive the title of "Prophet" in the fullest and most deserved sense (see John 1:19–27). Moses himself predicted that "The LORD your God will raise up for you a prophet like me from among you, from your countrymen, you shall listen to him" (Deut. 18:15). Indeed, God Himself said *through* Moses, "I will raise up a prophet from among their countrymen like you, and I will put My words in his mouth, and he shall speak to them all that I command him. It shall come about that whoever will not listen to My words which he shall speak in My name, I Myself will require it of him" (Deut. 18:18–19). While this might apply in the most general sense to all prophets after Moses, God clearly had His Son in mind when He said this, since Peter quotes this passage in Acts 3:19–26 and attributes it to Christ.

To speak *for* the Lord is to prophesy His word (Ezek. 6:2, 11:4, 13:2, 17, etc.).[3] While God is the source of the message, the prophet is His mouthpiece (Jer. 26:12). Just as Aaron served as a "mouth" or "prophet" for Moses (Exod. 4:16 and 7:1), so the prophet served as a "mouth" for God. In doing so, the prophet also served as a representative of God, much in the same way that Jesus' apostles did for Him. Thus, God sent Jonah, for example, to Nineveh not only with a message to speak but also as His own representative. (This should give greater weight to our role as proclaimers of the gospel: we not only carry a *message* of God; we are also to take on the proper *character* of such a messenger.) This works in the opposite way as well: not only does the prophet take on the character of God, but in his prophecies, God reveals *His* character to all people. We know more about God's personal nature—because God *reveals* this in His own words—through the written record of the prophets than we do anywhere else in Scripture.[4]

The Bible offers little in the way of explanation as to how God calls a man to serve as a prophet. Samuel's dramatic call is evident (1 Sam. 3), as is Isaiah's (Isa. 6:1–10). In most cases, however, a man simply identifies himself as a prophet (e.g., Hag. 1:1) or declares that God's word "came" to him (e.g., Hos. 1:1, Joel 1:1, Mic. 1:1, etc.). In both the Old and New Testaments, we see men (and a few women) who are what we might call "career" prophets, and those who simply have one thing to say (or, at least, one thing that is recorded), and nothing more. While the Bible itself does not make these distinctions, it seems clear to us all the same. Compare, for example, the prophetic *career* of Isaiah with the few words of Haggai. Isaiah prophesied throughout his entire lifetime; Haggai spoke (late in life) only for a brief period, as God needed him. Yet, in both cases, God used *both* men to communicate His message and fulfill His objective. (This presents another parallel to the Christian perspective: a preacher may have influence over many people during a lifetime; another person may win only one soul to the Lord. Yet, *both* are doing God's will, and *both* are communicating His message.)

> Sometimes a distinction has been made between the prophetic office and the prophetic gift. Such a distinction has no foundation in the Bible or in any ancient writing. Strictly-speaking, the work of a prophet is not the fulfilling of an office, but the performance of a function. It would appear that God on several occasions selected a man to give one or two messages and never again used him as His mouthpiece. On other occasions the Lord used a man as a prophet over a long period. The prophetic position is entirely a matter of relationship to God and cannot be enhanced or decreased by any human agency.[5]

"Thus says the LORD" is a common and appropriate expression among the prophets: while it is a *man* who spoke the words, it is *God* who "says"—authors, dictates, and originates—the message. This helps us to understand the concept of divinely "inspired" literature. The act of prophesying is a verbal manifestation and activity of the Holy Spirit of God (Joel 2:28). This is especially clear in the NT where the words of David, Jeremiah, and others are in fact attributed to the Holy Spirit (Mat. 22:43, Acts 1:16, 4:25, Heb. 3:7, 10:15, etc.).

The Messages of the Prophets: The prophets' messages were often referred to as "oracles" or "burdens" (Nah. 1:1, Hab. 1:1, Zech. 9:1, 12:1, and Mal. 1:1), signifying a great moral or spiritual weight of responsibility that the prophet carried in serving *as* a prophet (consider James 3:1 and 1 Peter 4:11 in connection with this, in principle).

The prophets' messages were called the "word" (Heb. *dābār*) of God, an "oracle" or "utterance" (*neʾum*) of Yahweh, or a "burden" (*maśśāʾ*) from God. God's word delivered by the prophets revealed the divine personality and will; it was creative and authoritative because of the sovereign wisdom and power of God. The phrase, "the word of the LORD came to me") occurs over two hundred times in the OT as a technical formula for prophetic revelation.[6]

The prophets communicated these messages orally, had them written down on a scroll, or both. (Many of Isaiah's prophecies, for example, appear to have been written down, not spoken to anyone in person; however, in Isa. 7:3 and 39:5–8, he did speak directly to King Ahaz and King Hezekiah, respectively.) In the case of Jeremiah, for example, his prophecies were often spoken first, then written down. Sometimes there does not seem to be a specific audience to a prophet's discourse, except by implication. At other times, the prophets spoke to the "people," meaning the nation of Israel or Judah (Hos. 5:1, Amos 3:1, Micah 1:2, 3:9, etc.). In some cases, the audience was only *certain* people, as when Ezekiel was told to prophesy to the "shepherds of Israel" (Ezek. 34:1ff), even though the message was meant for *everyone* to hear.

Prior to the prophets who wrote books, there were a number of lesser-known prophets (Nathan, Shemaiah, Ahijah, Jehu [not the king], Iddo, Oded, etc.). Elijah and Elisha, however, are very well-known prophets, yet they do not appear to have written anything down (or, what they *did* write down has not survived). There are even several unnamed prophets (such as the anonymous prophet in Judg. 6:8, the "man of God" who spoke to Jeroboam in 1 Kings 13, and the "man of God" who spoke to Amaziah in 2 Chron. 25:7–9). (Incidentally, "man of God" is the most common title for a prophet other than the word "prophet" itself. Elisha, for example, was called a "man of God" nearly 35 times in 2 Kings.) Some of these men were considered court seers who spoke directly to, and were consulted by, various kings. This included, for example, Gad (2 Sam. 24:11), Iddo (2 Chron. 9:29, 12:15), Hanani (2 Chron. 19:2), and other, unnamed prophets (2 Chron. 33:18).

These prophets, and the literary prophets as well, provided messages for kings, for "the people," or in response to certain events. Yet they also contributed to the spiritual stability of Israel and Judah. Their function was not *only* as mouthpieces, but to remind the people that they were a people *of God* and not simply a nation with their own private identity. God called them out of Egypt to *be* His people (Exod. 19:5–6); the prophets' messages constantly drove this point home in numerous ways.

In this role, the prophets were not creators of "new doctrine" for Israel, as though providing supplements or additions to the Law of Moses. Rather, they were spokesmen for Jehovah God—the same God who delivered them out of bondage *and* brought them into the Promised Land. "The prophets did not call for the abolition of the temple worship, nor did they claim to be creating a new system of spiritual values. Instead they called their people back to the traditions ... that God had instituted early in the nation's history."[7] Parallel to this thought, Keil remarks:

> Prophecy opened a way for that which was an impossibility to the law; namely, for renewing the hearts of the people, for kindling and inflaming the love of God with all their heart and all their powers. ... The prophets do not at all stand above the law, in the sense of the law ceasing to be the absolute binding will of God ... Yet they do open up a higher spiritual conception of the law, in which obedience to His word appears as the true sacrifices well pleasing to God (1 Sam. 15:22).[8]

In this role, the prophets simply reiterated what Israel and Judah were to have already learned from the Law. They drew attention not only to what the Law *said*, but also to when (and how) the people *digressed* from it. Thus, they often addressed some moral defect, unethical behavior, and/or direct violation of specific laws. In so doing, they reminded the people of God's promised curses for disobedience *and* His blessings for obedience. While the curses (in particular) may seem like they were being invented or newly introduced by a prophet (or, his prophecy), the truth is that they were simply an application of what was already in the Law (see Lev. 26, Deut. 4:5–40, and chapters 28 and 29). The blessings and rewards for obedience (in the Law of Moses) included:

- renewal of Jehovah's favor and presence (Deut. 4:29–31).
- renewal of the covenant.
- restoration of Jehovah worship.
- population increase.
- agricultural abundance.
- restoration of general prosperity, well-being, and health.
- return from exile to the Promised Land.
- reunification (Deut. 30:3–4).
- power over enemies.
- freedom from any further destruction (brought about by disobedience).

Punishment and curses for disobedience (in Law of Moses) included:

- inciting God's anger and the removal of special providence and protection.
- rejection and destruction of their temple (Lev. 26:31).
- the incidents, horror, and ravages of war—and siege in particular (which was particularly brutal; Deut. 28:52–57).
- psychological fear—of God, their enemies, and impending death (Deut. 28:66–67).
- futility (working hard, but "in vain"), helplessness, and stumbling (Deut. 28:20–41).
- occupation and oppression by their enemies.
- agricultural disaster and unproductivity (through drought, crop pestilence, and other destructive factors; see Lev. 26:20).
- wasting away or destruction of herds and flocks (Deut. 28:18).
- starvation and famine.
- sickness, pestilence, and contamination.
- desolation—of cities, towns, and the land (Lev. 26:32–35).
- attack from predators (wild animals) (Lev. 26:22, Deut. 32:24).
- decimation of family, cattle, and the general population.
- exile and captivity—of the people and of the king.
- idolatry forced upon them in exile (Deut. 4:23–28).
- dishonor and humiliation (Deut. 28:37).
- loss of possessions; loss of family; impoverishment.

- loss of peace.
- denial of burial.
- death and destruction.
- general distress, calamities, and disasters.

Again, we should not regard the prophets' predictions of some kind of punishment or disaster for God's disobedient people as something altogether new. Rather, these are simply the activation of the terms and conditions of God's covenant with Israel from the beginning. God warned in the covenant, in essence, "If you disobey Me and chose to serve idols, this is what will happen." His prophets only reiterated this message, then predicted its historical application.

Prophets of Hope and Encouragement: But the prophets were not only voices of doom and gloom. They were also the voices of encouragement, promises, and hope. After nearly every prophecy of discipline, punishment, or disaster, God offered a window into the future regarding restoration, prosperity, and hope. The book of Amos, for example, is almost entirely a series of divine condemnations against Israel and Judah (and neighboring nations). Yet, in Amos 9:11–15, God speaks of Israel's glorious future "in that day" of restoration; "days are coming" when His people will no longer bear the agony of divine wrath, but will enjoy the peace, warmth, and abundance of divine fellowship. (See also Hos. 14:1–9, Joel 2:18–32, Mic. 4:1–7, etc.) Such prophecies, however, were not meant for a literal interpretation—there is no record that they had any historical fulfillment—but *spiritually*, in the context of God's fellowship with Christ's church. Thus, God looks forward to the making of a "new covenant" with His people that will supersede the covenant He made with Israel (compare Jer. 31:31–34 and Heb. 8:8–12). Initially, however, this is all expressed in a purposely obscured manner in the words of the prophets since it was not yet the "fullness of the time" (Gal. 4:4) for God to unveil His Son and His universal gospel message to the world. "The prophets were aware of this part of their work [i.e., as foretellers of the Son of God's entrance into the world], but they often realized that they themselves knew only a small part of the truth that God planned eventually to reveal."[9] To this point, Peter says (1 Peter 1:10–12):

> As to this salvation, the prophets who prophesied of the grace that would come to you made careful searches and inquiries, seeking to know what person or time the Spirit of Christ within them was indicating as He predicted the sufferings of Christ and the glories to follow. It was revealed to them that they were not serving themselves, but you, in these things which now have been announced to you through those who preached the gospel to you by the Holy Spirit sent from heaven—things into which angels long to look.

Thus, the role of prophet was not only to recall the past (in reminding the Israelites of their Law), but also to foretell the future (the anticipation of a glorious restoration).[10] "The future" means not only the historical future (i.e., things limited to the secular world, dealing with the rise and fall of nations, calendar events, etc.), but also an otherworldly future—i.e., the shift from the *physical* land, people, and sacrifices to their *spiritual* counterparts, which requires no geographical location (John 4:23–24), no special ethnicity (Rom. 10:12–13), or animal sacrifices (Heb. 10:10–14). The Jews of the later OT times, in the post-exilic period (which refers to the time *after* the 70–year captivity of Judah in Babylon, but *before* the coming of Jesus), saw themselves as participants in the "last days" of human history. In this final era, they believed that God would make them the center of the world, Jerusalem the capital of the world, and their Messiah the king of the world (for example, try reading Isa. 60:1–22 through the eyes of these Jews). They did not recognize, or possibly ignored, that the "in that day" phraseology often indicated not merely a certain time on calendar, but the changing terms of covenant fellowship between God and His people, often introduced by some upheaval in the present system (as in Acts 2:14–21, quoting Joel 2:28–32). The prophecies concerning these "last days" became known as apocalyptic [Greek, *apokalupsis*, "revealing" or "uncovering"] in nature, since they revealed Israel's role in the end-of-time events.

> Both apocalyptic and prophetic books claimed to be the result of revelation by dreams, visions, or direct speech; both used symbolism and had a pessimistic view of the world situation

apart from God; both were universalistic in outlook and saw history as the outworking of God's determined plan; and both looked forward to the Day of Yahweh [Jehovah] when God would miraculously redeem His people and judge the evil nations. ...[A] distinguishing feature that sets apocalyptic apart from prophecy is the apocalyptic search for a solution to the world's problems through a divine intervention outside of history in another aeon [age].[11]

The Cosmic (Big Picture) Perspective: Unfortunately, the Jews of the post-exilic period read the prophets in terms of political, national, and historical fulfillment rather than in a spiritual context. Thus, they assumed that Messiah would come and *literally* revive the David- and Solomon-era glory that Israel once enjoyed, and that He would be a *political* King for all the world. (See John 6:15, Luke 19:11, and Acts 1:6 for examples of this.) Few Jews understood that God had a spiritual King and a spiritual kingdom in mind, as Jesus clearly indicated in Luke 17:20-21 and John 18:36-37.

In speaking to nations other than Israel or Judah, the prophets presented God as the highest authority that existed—the Divine Personage to whom *all* nations give account (regardless of their own beliefs). Their messages named Israel's God as *their* God and summoned all other nations to honor God as *the* God—the One greater than any of their own pagan gods. In the so-called major prophets, we see a great deal of attention given to prophecies against foreign nations (Isa. 13—23, Jer. 46—51, and Ezek. 25—32). Specifically, these are nations that surround Israel and Judah and have contributed to the moral decline of God's people. Even in the so-called minor prophets are messages to foreign nations; in fact, the books of *Obadiah*, *Jonah*, and *Nahum* are to nations other than Israel and Judah.

As honorable as the role of a prophet was to God, such men were not always honored by those to whom they prophesied. This makes sense, to a degree, if the message the prophet brought was against them, or was exactly the opposite of what the people wanted to hear. Thus, many of the ancient prophets were viewed with contempt and rejection (Amos 7:10–13); some were imprisoned (1 Kings 22:26–28, Jer. 37:11–16); others were threatened with death or even killed (1 Kings 19:1–2, 2 Chron. 24:20–22). Likely, Heb. 11:37–38 refers to OT prophets: "They were stoned, they were sawn in two, they were tempted, they were put to death with the sword; they went about in sheepskins, in goatskins, being destitute, afflicted, ill-treated (men of whom the world was not worthy), wandering in deserts and mountains and caves and holes in the ground."

Not only this, but God's authentic prophets often were challenged by—and forced to respond to—the false prophets among the people. This refers to any man "who speaks a word presumptuously in My name which I have not commanded him to speak, or which he speaks in the name of other gods"; such a man was to be executed (Deut. 18:20; see also Deut. 13:1–5). Such men "prophesied by Baal and led My people Israel astray" (Jer. 23:13) or claimed to "[see] false visions and divining lies for them, saying, 'Thus says the Lord God,' when the Lord has not spoken" (Ezek. 22:28; see also Jer. 23:25–32). Certainly, financial gain, in one form or another, was a motive behind some false prophecy (Mic. 3:11). Other men simply spoke what the people wanted to hear (to gain popularity, and probably an honorarium), or spoke what the king wanted to hear (to save their own necks). In either case, a wicked spirit incited the false prophets to speak. This was either their own wicked spirit (Jer. 14:14) or a demonic influence (1 Kings 22:22). God clearly denounced all false prophets (Ezek. 13:9). "Wherever there is something good, counterfeits are apt to appear."[12]

Emphasis on the Covenant: While the prophets wrote about kings, politics, social problems, mistreatment of the poor and helpless ("widows and orphans," etc.), or the threat of war from some foreign enemy, the real issue was always the same: the people's relationship to Jehovah God through covenant. While the Law of Moses dictated sacrificial requirements and legal commands, the covenant went far beyond this. The Law spelled out the terms of covenant, but the Law was *not* the covenant. Covenant defines the relationship and provides for the mutually beneficial function of all its parties. Thus, the two parties can have fellowship through the terms stipulated in that agreement. God, as Sovereign over all the earth, provides these terms and conditions; Israel agreed to them (Exod. 24:3–8). The Law (or simply, "law") was not given to God to obey, but Israel; essentially, God's "law," is His own righteousness and holiness that He cannot violate or deny. God always honored His side of the covenant; Israel and Judah often failed to honor theirs. God was always faithful to His people; His people were often unfaithful to Him.

Moral issues are always at the heart of a covenant relationship with God. The Law described how Israelites were to live while *in* a covenant, but the covenant dictated what kind of *heart* they should have toward God. Thus, Moses said, "Moreover the Lord your God will circumcise your heart and the heart of your descendants, to love the Lord your God with all your heart and with all your soul, so that you may live" (Deut. 30:6). This is not something Law can do; this is something God did for those faithful to His covenant with them. (See Col. 2:10–12 for a parallel thought for those in a covenant relationship with God through Christ.)

Good hearts will always seek truth, justice, righteousness, and God Himself. Wicked hearts will seek idolatry, the corruption of Jehovah worship, immorality, and chronic sinful behavior. Since wicked hearts have no place in a holy covenant with God, the Lord sent prophets to warn the people to repent of their sins, remove their idols from their land, and return to the covenant. Sadly, both Israel and Judah had become insensitive to God's spokesmen. "Self-satisfied, enjoying life, and hardened by sin, the majority of God's people settled for the sensual pleasures of idolatry and rejected the calls of a loving, compassionate God who wanted a relationship with people He called His own."[13] For example, the prophet Amos wrote (Amos 5:14–24, bracketed words added):

> Seek good and not evil, that you may live; and thus may the Lord God of hosts be with you, just as you have said! Hate evil, love good, and establish justice in the gate! Perhaps the Lord God of hosts may be gracious to the remnant of Joseph.

… [God says,] "I hate, I reject your festivals, nor do I delight in your solemn assemblies. Even though you offer up to Me burnt offerings and your grain offerings, I will not accept them; and I will not even look at the peace offerings of your fatlings. Take away from Me the noise of your songs; I will not even listen to the sound of your harps. But let justice roll down like waters and righteousness like an ever-flowing stream."

Likewise, the prophet Micah wrote (Mic. 6:6–8):

With what shall I come to the Lord and bow myself before the God on high? Shall I come to Him with burnt offerings, with yearling calves? Does the Lord take delight in thousands of rams, in ten thousand rivers of oil? Shall I present my firstborn for my rebellious acts, the fruit of my body for the sin of my soul? He has told you, O man, what is good; and what does the Lord require of you but to do justice, to love kindness, and to walk humbly with your God?

Obedience and sacrifices are required by Law; love, compassion, and humility are required by covenant. One describes legal and ritual procedures; the other, the disposition of one's heart. God takes no pleasure in those who come to Him only "procedurally" by going through the motions of religion without coming to Him in humility and submission. (See James 4:7–10 for a parallel thought in the Christian's covenant with God.) John the Baptist, another prophet of God, was sent to Israel "in the spirit and power of Elijah, to turn the hearts of the fathers back to the children and the disobedient to the attitude of the righteous, so as to make ready a people prepared for the Lord" (Luke 1:17; compare Mal. 4:6).

Jesus—the greatest Prophet who ever lived—centered His entire so-called sermon on the mount (Mat. 5—7) on one great theme: get your heart right with God, and then you will live in fellowship with Him. This was no different than the messages of the prophets but is more succinct, and it anticipated the fulfillment of God's relationship with Israel and the establishment of His church. The prophets, John the Baptist, and Jesus all spoke to the same people: Israelites who were in a covenant relationship with God. Unfortunately, the Israelites often focused more on ritual observances of Law than on their heart condition.

The World of the Prophets: When we read the prophets, we must do our best to see their world through their eyes rather than attempting to interpret it through our 21st-century point of view. Israel lived under a theocracy—a God-governed nation—not a monarchy, democracy, or dictatorship. While certainly Israel had kings to govern the people and protect the land, God *owned* the land and reigned above the kings as the highest authority *in* the land. This is a far different situation than what we know today; God has no covenants with *nations* today, only with a called-out or "chosen" *people* (1 Peter 2:9). Even though we may refer to America as "one nation, under God," this sentiment is not at all comparable to ancient Israel—a nation that belonged to God as His own possession (Exod. 19:5–6) and had agreed to a written *covenant* with Him. Therefore, we must guard against trying to impose modern democratic principles, modern methods of justice, and modern views on social issues (i.e., race, slavery, women's rights, capital punishment, war, etc.) upon a situation in which these things were seen entirely differently or were altogether irrelevant.

When we read the prophets, we are not to think that these men were simply giving their religious opinions, however pious or right those might have been, to God's people. A prophet is not merely a wise man who dispenses good advice. Wise men *can* give good advice, to be sure, but only a *prophet of God* will speak the Lord's revealed will. Prophets, left to their own understanding, are prone to error. Consider, for example, Samuel's assumption that Eliab (David's elder brother) was a fit choice to be king of Israel; but God corrected him and chose David instead (1 Sam. 16:6–12). In another example, David wanted to build a temple for God, and Nathan the prophet spoke on his own accord and gave his blessing to the project. That night, God corrected the prophet in a dream and told him that He did *not* want David to build His temple (2 Sam. 7:3–16). A genuine prophet does not speak from his own heart but speaks only what the Lord tells him to say. It is not even necessary that the prophet understand the message, but only that he communicates it and does so accurately. "The prophet was not omniscient, and he was not an automaton. The Lord increased his understanding, but He also gave him commands and messages to be presented in exactly the form in which they were given."[14] Thus, "God … spoke long ago to the fathers in the prophets in many portions and in many ways …" (Heb. 1:1).

As stated earlier, God gave His message(s) to the prophets, and thus they spoke these message(s). (Contrast this with modern commentators or theologians who may comment on or expound upon what God's prophets said, but certainly have no new revelations *from* Him.) God—the One who provided and oversaw His covenant with Israel—had every right to tell His people what they needed to know, to correct their misunderstandings, or even to punish them for their sins.

> The interpreter must remember the limited perspective of the prophet. The prophets were not all–knowing but all–telling—that is, they told what God had told them to tell. Prophecy has a progressive character. One must seek to read prophecy in light of its whole, deriving partial insight from different prophets. Prophecy must also be read in its historical context. Particular attention must be paid to the intention of the prophet.[15]

Prophecy may also have more than one fulfillment. Many prophecies are what is known as "telescopic" in nature. To describe this, imagine an old–style collapsing telescope that can be fully extended to utilize its intended potential. It may magnify things up close, but (when extended) can also see things far away. In a similar manner, some prophecies pointed to a limited or physical fulfillment, but at the same time looked far ahead in time to a permanent and spiritual fulfillment. The several "day of the Lord" prophecies, for example (see Obad. 1:15–17, Zeph. 1:1–18, etc.), predicted a divine judgment that was in the relatively near future, yet the full realization of the "day of the Lord" culminated in the foundations-of-the-earth-shaking revelation of the kingdom of God under the reign of the Messiah. In the ultimate sense, although this went beyond the scope of OT prophecy, it foresaw the great Judgment Day when all of humanity stands before the Creator and Judge (2 Cor. 5:10, Rev. 20:11–15). Likewise, the prophet Joel predicted a reversal of all the damage caused by a terrible locust invasion (Joel 2:18–27), but clearly the full implications of that prophecy pointed to a *spiritual* prosperity enjoyed only by those who are "in Christ"—still some eight centuries in Joel's future (compare Joel 2:28–32 and Acts 2:16–21).

A Challenging but Important Study: All said, the study of the prophets—and the minor prophets in particular—is one which Christians ought not to avoid. Admittedly, this is not always easy: there are difficulties in understanding language, historical context, cultural references, ancient names and places, etc. At the same time, we should not think that we are reading a newspaper article, an op-ed piece, or a novel. We are reading what Almighty God said to those who would give answer to Him—a situation that is no different than our own.

God is not only the source of the prophets' messages, but He is also the One who made sure that these messages were written down, canonized (i.e., formally collected into a single, divinely-inspired work), and preserved for all these centuries so that we could read and learn from them. As Paul said, "For whatever was written in earlier times was written for our instruction, so that through perseverance and the encouragement of the Scriptures we might have hope" (Rom. 15:4). In other words, while this kind of study may be challenging, require more reading, and take more time, it is what God expects us to do. Furthermore, we should not overlook the unique and exceptional nature *of* what we are reading: there is nothing else in all literature or human history that is *like* these books. Homer Hailey says it well:

> Among the writings of the prophets are to be found some of the most beautiful, majestic, and artistic expressions of all literature. Although the prophet was inspired and spoke as the Spirit directed, Jehovah allowed the personality and background of each man to shine through his message, making the book throb with both the life of the man and of God.[16]

There are important overall lessons that we can (and should) learn from a study of the prophets:

- **First**, the moral, social, and economic conditions of God's people are unsettlingly mirrored in today's increasingly godless and immoral society. Prosperity, complacency, moral indifference, and intellectual laziness (especially toward God's word) made His people soft, undisciplined, and unfit to serve God. The more we study the prophets, the more our eyes are opened to *how* and *why* the ancient nations—and particularly Israel and Judah—fell from power, were punished by God, and/or disappeared altogether. We also learn how to *avoid* what happened to them (1 Cor. 10:11–12).
- **Second**, God's dealings with the ancient nations parallels how He continues to deal with nations today, as well as with individual people. While our secularized and humanistic society has tried to etch God out of existence, He is still very much in control, and we (nations *and* people) are most certainly under His authority.
- **Third**, just as God called repeatedly for repentance in the ancient world, so He is calling for it today (Acts 17:30–31, 2 Peter 3:9). God's mercy and patience are evident in the prophetical writings, but so are the limitations of these divine reprieves. His love is unconditional and never-ending; His patience, however, will not continue in the face of chronic impenitence (Amos 2—3, for example).
- **Fourth**, God will most certainly punish wicked nations and wicked people. Just because He does not do so immediately, or when righteous people want (or expect) Him to, does not mean that anyone will escape His ultimate divine justice.
- **Fifth**, we see the door slowly but steadily opening for a glimpse into God's answer to sin and hopelessness through the development of the "eternal purpose which He carried out in Christ Jesus our Lord" (Eph. 3:11). The foreshadowing of the Messiah and His work begin not in the NT gospel accounts, but in the writings of the prophets. The prophets say, in so many words, "God is coming to His people—*prepare* for Him!" When God's Son *does* finally come, He does not simply crack the door open a bit further, but blows it off its hinges, so to speak.

The so-called "major prophets" are *Isaiah, Jeremiah,* and *Ezekiel.* The "minor prophets" include *Hosea, Joel, Amos, Obadiah, Jonah, Micah, Nahum, Zephaniah, Habakkuk, Zechariah, Haggai,* and *Malachi.*[17] Some prophets have very specific political or historical references, so that we can know the timeframe in which they prophesied. Others (such as *Obadiah* and *Joel*) offer no specific detail by which to date them. While the chronological order of the minor prophets may vary from one source to the next, what follows is a conservative placement of the prophets in history:

Minor Prophet	Estimated Dates (BC)	Intended target of prophesies	Historical References (I = king of Israel; J = king of Judah); general message
Elijah	872–850	Israel	Ahab (I); 1 Kings 17:1—2 Kings 2:12; sought Israel's return to Jehovah (vs. Baalism)
Elisha	850–795	Israel	Ahab— Jehoram (I); 1 Kings 19:16—2 Kings 13:20; proved that a prophet of God was in Israel, despite widespread Baalism
Obadiah	845	Edom	Joram (J) (2 Chron. 21:8–20) (?); predicted divine judgment against Edom
Joel	830–800	Israel	Jehu (I); predicted a devastating plague of locusts as a divine punishment against Israel
Jonah	795–750	Nineveh (Assyria)	Jeroboam II (I) (2 Kings 14:25–27); predicted the fall of Nineveh, unless they repented
Amos	760–755	Israel (and Judah)	Jeroboam II (I); Uzziah (J); blasted Israel's arrogance and mistreatment of the poor

Hosea	750–725	Israel	Jotham—Jeroboam II (I); Uzziah, Hezekiah (J); denounced Israel's infidelity to God's covenant
Isaiah	740–700	Israel and Judah	Jotham, Uzziah, Ahaz, Hezekiah (J); Pekahiah, Pekah, Hoshea (I) [Israel exiled to Assyria, 721]; 2 Kings 19:2—20:19
Micah	735–700	Israel and Judah	(same kings as Isaiah); predicted Israel's ruin for oppressing the helpless, and its wickedness
Nahum	625–612	Nineveh (Assyria)	Josiah (J); graphically predicted the fall of Nineveh (612)
Zephaniah	630–625	Judah	Josiah (J); predicted judgment against Judah
Habakkuk	620–600	Judah	Josiah—Jehoiakim (J); predicted that Judah would fall to the Chaldeans (i.e., Babylonians)
Jeremiah	626–580	Judah	Josiah—Zedekiah (J) [Judah exiled to Babylon, 586]; predicted the fall of Jerusalem and Judah
Ezekiel	592–570	Judah	Jehoiachin—Zedekiah (J); prophesied while in Babylonian exile with many Jews; predicted the fall of Jerusalem and Judah
Daniel	605–536	Judah (in exile); Nebuchadnezzar (Babylon)	Demonstrated that God was still with His people (even while they were in captivity) especially to King Nebuchadnezzar of Babylon

Haggai	520	Post–exile Judah	Prodded the Jews to finish rebuilding God's temple in Jerusalem
Zechariah	520–518	Post–exile Judah	Installed Zerubbabel as governor, Joshua as high priest; received several visions concerning Israel's future glory
Malachi	450–430	Post–exile Judah	Chastised the priests and Jews for "robbing" God and failing to trust in Him

In the original Hebrew Bible, the minor prophets were collected as one book.[18] Since then, this single "book" (or, roll) has been broken out into the twelve different prophetical books we know today. This study will follow (what is believed to be) a chronological sequence of the minor prophets, not how they appear in the OT canon. A comparison of the two:

Order of the Minor Prophets in the Canon	Chronological Order of the Minor Prophets
Hosea	Obadiah
Joel	Joel
Amos	Jonah
Obadiah	Amos
Jonah	Hosea
Micah	Micah
Nahum	Zephaniah
Habakkuk	Nahum
Zephaniah	Habakkuk
Haggai	Haggai
Zechariah	Zechariah
Malachi	Malachi

Depending on how one wishes to chart OT history, there are basically three periods of time that the prophets—both "major" *and* "minor"—cover:

- **Pre-Assyrian invasion of (the northern tribes of) Israel:** The Assyrian Empire did not grow overnight, and the looming threat of their invasion into Palestine was years in the making. However, this nation did finally come from the north and invaded Israel (and other neighboring nations), inflicting catastrophic damage. This happened in 722/721 BC, culminating in the siege against Samaria (2 Kings 17:1–6). The minor prophets that ministered in this timeframe were (chronologically): Obadiah, Joel, Jonah, Amos, Hosea, and Micah. (Obadiah and Jonah did not speak against Israel specifically but did prophesy in the pre-Assyrian period.)
- **Pre-Babylonian invasion of Judah:** While Assyria did invade Judah, they could not take Jerusalem because God intervened on behalf of King Hezekiah and the prophet Isaiah (Isa. 36—37). Even so, Jerusalem/Judah did not show gratitude for this deliverance and sank even deeper into idolatry than had the northern tribes of Israel (Ezek. 16:46–59, where "Samaria" is Israel and "Sodom" identifies with Judah). God sent prophets to warn the Jews of their contempt for His covenant, but they did not listen. As a result, God sent Babylon, under the direction of King Nebuchadnezzar, against Jerusalem and he destroyed it *and* its temple in 586 BC. The minor prophets that ministered in this timeframe were (chronologically): Nahum, Zephaniah, and Habakkuk. (Nahum did not speak to Judah directly but did prophesy in the pre–Babylonian period.)
- **Post-exilic period:** Those Jews who survived the Babylonian invasion of their land were exiled to Babylonia for 70 years, according to Jeremiah's prophecy (Jer. 25:11–12, 29:10; see also 2 Chron. 36:15–21). After 70 years, the Persian emperor Cyrus proclaimed a release of these captives, allowing them to return to their homeland and rebuild it and their temple (see Isa. 44:21—45:3). This was a time of great difficulty and disruption for these captives, as they returned to a ruined city and a destroyed temple. God sent prophets to encourage them to rebuild, however, as well as men like Nehemiah to rebuild the city wall and Ezra to teach the people of God's laws. Specifically, God commissioned the Jews with rebuilding His temple in Jerusalem—a monumental task with formidable obstacles. The minor prophets that spoke in this timeframe were (chronologically): Haggai, Zechariah, and Malachi.

General timeline of OT History:

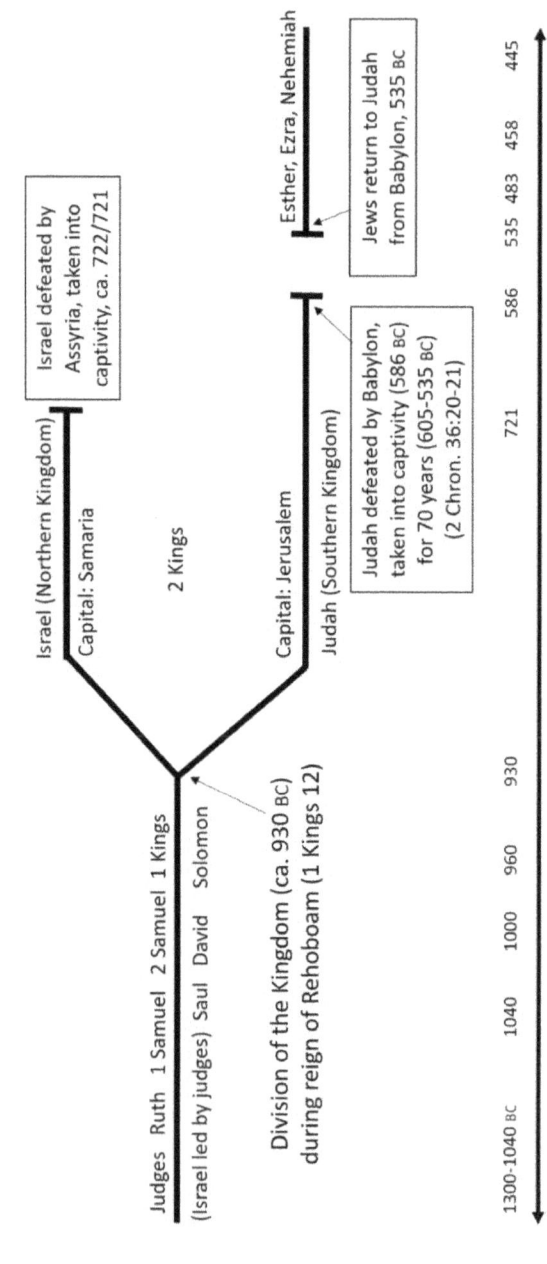

Introduction to *Obadiah*

Authorship: "Obadiah" means "servant" or "worshiper of Jehovah."[19] Nothing else is known about this prophet except for his name, which is shared by twelve other men in the OT. It is very possible that he is the Obadiah mentioned in 1 Kings 18, who hid one hundred prophets in caves to protect them from King Ahab and Jezebel. Incidentally, the book of *Obadiah* is the shortest book in the OT.

Date and Place of Writing: Fixing a date for Obadiah is very difficult since the information needed to do so is scant or non–existent. Conservative scholars tend to place it early (ca. 845 BC), likely during the time of King Jehoram (Judah) (2 Chron. 21:8–20).[20] This would make the prophet a contemporary with Elisha the prophet, making Obadiah the earliest of all the prophets. The absence of any mention of Assyria or Babylon, or the actual exiles of Israel or Judah, is also conspicuous. Liberal critics tend to place it late in time (586 BC), possibly even after the Jews' return from exile. These dates can vary by as much as six centuries. "The prophecy is elastic enough in its fulfillment to embrace all of the times of Edom's destruction, whether by the Chaldeans who laid Edom waste (Jer. 49:7ff, Ezek. 35:chapter)," or subsequent devastations.[21]

Purpose and Character of Writing: This entire one–chapter oracle records a divine judgment against the nation of Edom for their treatment of Israel, their blood–brothers. (Edom and Israel are related through Esau and Jacob, respectively, the sons of Isaac; see Gen. 25:19–34.) Edom, as the descendants of Esau, have long carried a simmering grudge against Israel, the descendants of Jacob. Jacob not only deceived Esau out of his first–born status birthright (Gen. 27), he also stole Esau's future blessings and prosperity. The Edomites are quick to gloss over their own patriarch's (Esau's) disregard for anything sacred but have held Israel responsible for robbing them of the Promised Land which, they reasoned, should have been rightfully theirs.

Given all this animosity, Edom naturally wished harm on their relatives. During some foreign invasion of Judah (or Israel, or both), Edom apparently "gloated" over the demise of their distant relatives, and even used the opportunity to inflict their own violence against them (1:10–14). Edom has been a thorn in Israel's side since they refused to let the children of Israel pass through their territory while on their way to claim the Promised Land (Num. 20:14–22). Later, David conquered them and set up military garrisons in their land (2 Sam. 8:14); they remained under Solomon's control as well (2 Chron. 8:17–18).

Circa 129 BC, John Hyrcanus (one of the Maccabees) forced many of the remaining Edomites to be circumcised and accept the Law of Moses; "thus, they became nominal Jewish proselytes [converts]."[22] During the Persian Empire, the land of Edom became known as the province of Idumea, and the Idumeans crossed paths with the Jews for centuries to come. Herod the Great was an Idumean, which is one of the reasons why he never completely won the Jews' favor, even though he built a grand temple for them in Jerusalem. "The loss of their [the Idumeans'] national independence, which they thereby sustained, was followed by utter destruction at the hands of the Romans" for their complicity in the Jewish Wars. By the end of the first century AD, coinciding with the Roman overthrow of Jerusalem and the land of Judea, the Edomites vanished completely.

The character of this prophecy is dark, especially when dealing directly with God's pronouncement of judgment against Edom. God has reached the end of His patience with Edom (see Isa. 34:5–6, Mal. 1:2–4). However, the final section (1:15–21) does speak gloriously of Israel's future—while still maintaining that "the house of Edom will be as stubble" (1:18). It is an emotional prophecy, and often repeats its expressions in different ways (known as Hebrew parallelism) to heighten its passionate message.

Overview of *Obadiah*

Obad. 1:1 "The vision [prophecy] of Obadiah"—this is all the personal information we know of the prophet. "Thus says the Lord God [lit., *Adonai Yahweh*] concerning Edom…"—indicating that God is speaking through the prophet. In other words, this is a divine revelation, not the prophet's own words. "Arise, let us go against her for battle"—"her" is most likely Edom. In other words, a divinely commissioned "envoy" or messenger (literal or figurative) has been sent out to the heathen nations that calls for the destruction of Edom.

Obad. 1:2–9 God reveals Edom's arrogance: they think they are safe by hiding and dwelling in the cliffs and therefore are unassailable and invincible (1:2–4). "The Edomites were justifiably proud of their fortress stronghold in the rocky vastness of Mt. Seir, the rugged country south of Palestine and extending to the gulf of Aqabah. Their principal city was Petra [a.k.a. Sela], one of the most spectacular fortresses of the entire ancient world."[24] Yet, God promises to bring them down—not just literally (from their cliff-cities), but also figuratively (from their self-exaltation). "Throughout the writings of the prophets Edom stands as a symbol of the earthly, non-spiritual people of the world."[25]

When thieves plunder a nation, they only take what they want, and leave everything else alone. Likewise, even grape-gatherers leave gleanings behind. Yet, God promises to lay waste to Edom, so that there will be nothing left when He is through with them (1:5–9). In other words, this will not be just another robbery by a foreign invader, but a devastation of divine vengeance. Even though Edom will promise to rebuild, God will not allow them to prevail (Mal. 1:2–4). "[O]n that day" (1:7)—a typical phrase denoting not a specific *time* as much as a future *event* (and the certainty of its coming)—Edom's allies by covenant will turn against the Edomites. Their "allies" likely include Moab, Ammon, Tyre, Sidon, and possibly some of the nomadic Arab tribes in the wilderness area.[26] "Teman" is the southernmost of Edom's two principal cities (the other being Petra/Sela), renowned for its wise men. (For example, Eliphaz, one of Job's counselors, was from Teman—Job 2:11.) God says that the wisdom of Edom's own wise men will not save the nation from certain disaster.

In all, God promised that Edom would fall because of their:

- intense pride (1:3–9)
- location (1:3–4)
- money or wealth (1:5–6)
- alliances (for trade and protection) (1:7)
- own wisdom and strength (1:8–9)

Obad. 1:10–14 Here, God provides the reason for His pronouncement of judgment: Edom's malicious and heartless treatment of Israel's own foreign invasions. "Jacob" is another name for Israel (Gen. 32:24–28) and reminds Edom of their blood relationship with the Israelites. While Israel (which may literally refer to Judah, or Israel, or both) was being slaughtered and plundered, Edom stood aloof—not only refusing to help but also applauding and gloating over the success of Israel's invaders (compare Psalm 137:7).[27]

Not only this, but the implication (1:13) is that Edom took full advantage of Israel's weakened situation and took plunder for themselves and killed their "fugitives in the day of their distress" (1:14). In other words, as the Israelites were running for their lives from a foreign invasion, the Edomites mercilessly struck them down on their own.

Obad. 1:15–21 The "day of the Lord" indicates a "day" (i.e., event, time, or series of calamities) of great trauma, upheaval, and (often) punishment. Edom's "day" is just one of several divine judgments against the nations surrounding Israel (see Isa. 13—24 for a full scope of these prophecies against foreign nations). "As Edom had desecrated the holy mount of Jehovah, whether by a drunken carousal on its sacred precinct at the time the inhabitants [Jews] were being carried away, or figuratively in the desecration of God's holy city and people by his violence done toward Jacob, so Edom would be swallowed up of his own ungodliness [1:16]."[28] In this section, God essentially says, "Israel will be glorified in the future, but you, Edom, will be debased and forgotten." Jacob (Israel) will be holy, will possess, and will survive; Edom will be ruined, lose all possessions, and "become as if they had never existed" (1:16). In fact, Israel will become the judges (i.e., by comparison, and for faithfulness to God) of Edom (see Mat. 12:41–42 and 1 Cor. 6:2). "Mount Zion" literally refers to one of the mountains (hills) upon which the city of Jerusalem sits. As it is presented in the prophetic context, however, it refers to the future glorification of God's people as represented in the reign of His Messiah. Consider this prophecy in Isa. 2:2:

> Now it will come about that in the last days the mountain of the house of the LORD will be established as the chief of the mountains, and will be raised above the hills; and all the nations will stream to it. And many peoples will come and say, "Come, let us go up to the mountain of the LORD, to the house of the God of Jacob; that He may teach us concerning His ways and that we may walk in His paths." For the law will go forth from Zion and the word of the LORD from Jerusalem.

Looking back, especially with our knowledge of Christ and His gospel (and how it did "go forth" from the Jews, and from Jerusalem in particular—see Acts 1:6–8), we can see the ultimate fulfillment of this prophecy in the church age.

In the figurative and often purposely exaggerated language of the messianic prophecies, Israel will reclaim their original territory and then some. Their borders will no longer be limited as before, but they will encompass other peoples and lands. (The church context fulfills this thought, in that it is comprised of people from every nation; see Rev. 7:9, for example.) "Joseph" (1:18) is another name for Israel, specifically the northern tribes (Ephraim and Manasseh were the two sons of Joseph), but generally the entire two-kingdom nation. "Negev" (1:19) [Hebrew, *Negeb*] is the wilderness area to the south of the land of Judah; "Shephelah" refers to the low–lying plains in that region. "Gilead" (1:19) is a general term for the entire area east of the Jordan River, which was occupied by the tribes of Gad, Reuben, and East Manasseh upon the apportioning of the Promised Land by Joshua. "Zarephath" (1:20) is near the city-state of Sidon, on the Mediterranean coast, the city to which Elijah was sent to stay at the home of a widow and her son (1 Kings 17:8–10, Luke 4:25–26). All attempts to accurately define "Sepharad" are disappointing.

Questions on *Obadiah*

1.) What do you think are some of the main lessons taught in *Obadiah*?

2.) The Edomites put more trust in the wise men of Teman than they did in God. How is this still happening today in the unconverted world? Does this happen even among Christians—and if so, how?

3.) Is God's condemnation of Edom's treatment of their own "brothers" (the Israelites) comparable to NT condemnations of one Christian's ill-treatment of his "brother" in Christ? Please explain, and provide supporting passages, if possible.

4.) God told the Edomites, "As you have done, it will be done to you. Your dealings will return on your own head" (1:15). Today we say, "What goes around comes around" (see Mat. 26:52) or "You shall reap what you sow" (see Gal. 6:7).

    a. Are these principles still true?

    b. Does this work *positively* as well as it does *negatively*?

Introduction to *Joel*

Authorship: Our only knowledge of this prophet is that he was "the son of Pethuel." His name ("Joel") is a combination of the names Jehovah and Elohim; thus, "Jehovah is my God." (There are thirteen other men in the OT who have this name.[29])

Date and Place of Writing: It is difficult to date this book since it has within it no definite time stamps or historical markers. The absence of any mention of Nineveh (Assyria), Babylon, or even Damascus (Syria) is conspicuous; likely, it is prior to any of these nations' invasions into Israel or Judah. Likewise, we are not even certain of the place from where this book was written. The prophet Joel does speak of Jerusalem, the temple, the Levitical priests, and the ritual ceremonies of the Law with what appears to be great familiarity, likely associating him with Judah more so than Israel. The absence of any mention of idolatry is also conspicuous, predating an advanced stage of this problem (as we see in other prophets' writings).

Purpose and Character of Writing: Joel's writing is emotional, dramatic, and rich in imagery and vivid characterizations. "Joel's style is pre–eminently pure. It is characterized by smoothness and fluency in the rhythms, roundness in the sentences, and regularity in the parallelisms. With the strength of Micah it combines the tenderness of Jeremiah, the vividness of Nahum, and the sublimity of Isaiah."[30] Much of his prophecy concerns an enormous locust swarm that comes upon the land (of Judah?). This swarm is described as a judgment from God for the nation to wake up from its complacent, spiritually–dull, and even intoxicated state of being.[31] Yet, Joel describes this literal swarm in terms of a potential military invasion from a foreign nation—a harbinger, of sorts, of what really *would* happen if the people did not respond properly (1:1–13, 2:1–11). His description of the locusts, their marching formation, and the devastation they wreak upon the crops is incredibly graphic, "the grandest description in all literature of such a plague."[32]

The recipients of Joel's message are told to petition God through repentance, fasting, and prayer to remove the locust plague from their land (2:12–17). God promises to remove the locusts swarm—literally, to cast it into the sea (2:20)—if the people do so, since their change of heart is what He seeks. Furthermore, He promises to restore the nation's crops, vineyards, orchards, and fortunes if they humble themselves before Him. (Keep in mind that this restoration is promised *before* the devastation even occurs.) "Thus you will know that I am in the midst of Israel, and that I am the LORD your God, and there is no other" (2:27)—an indication that the people had lost sight of this or had not been honoring Him properly. This refusal or neglect on their part is what warrants the punishment of the locust invasion.

The most famous passage in *Joel* is 2:28–32, since Peter quotes it in his first sermon to the Jews in Acts 2:17–21.[33] In the first section (1:1—2:18), Joel the prophet speaks; in the second section (2:19—3:21), God Himself speaks. "[T]he day of the LORD" is a time of great upheaval, judgment, and change—all of which characterize the ending of the Mosaic age, the introduction of the gospel of Christ, and the pending destruction of Jerusalem—all of which are in the background of Peter's discourse. Joel uses typical apocalyptic-style language to describe such a "day"; this language is hyperbolic (i.e., purposely exaggerated), purposely cosmic in scope ("the sun will be turned into darkness," etc.), and has great historical implications. Obviously, such language is not to be taken literally, but the seriousness of God's word *is* to be taken literally. On one hand, God will safeguard those who are faithful to Him, no matter what happens in history; on the other hand, the same God will destroy those who resist Him—not with locusts, but with a much greater calamity. "[W]hoever calls upon the name of the LORD will be delivered" (2:32) is an unprecedented and (from Joel's perspective) yet-distant promise that will not be fulfilled until Acts 2. The implication is that "whoever" is not limited to the Israelites, but will be available to all people, regardless of nationality or ethnicity (as in John 3:16 and Rom. 10:11–13).

Thus, "the day of the LORD" in Joel actually has a dual meaning: first, that "day" will come upon the land in the form of a devastating locust swarm; second, that "day" that will change the course of history forever with regard to God's people—a time when God will "pour out My Spirit on all mankind [lit., flesh]" (2:28), something that had never been done before and will mark a permanent change in God's relationship with people. There is a third implication of the "day of the LORD," and that is the day of the Final Judgment (Rev. 20:11–15), yet only in the context of the NT can we draw this latter conclusion. Nowhere is a final judgment of the world depicted in the OT prophetic writings.

In chapter 3, God challenges the Phoenicians (Tyre and Sidon) and Philistines—nations that have afflicted, invaded, and (to some extent) plundered His people—to come against Him in "the valley of Jehoshaphat" (3:2, 12). (This likely has no reference to Jehoshaphat the king, but merely describes a meeting place between God and His enemies.) In other words, these nations think they are simply dealing with Israel, yet He informs them that they are in fact contending with Israel's all-powerful God. And God will, He says, avenge His people and humiliate their oppressors "in those days and at that time" (3:1)—i.e., not yet, but for certain in the future. These foreign nations, whose "wickedness is great" (3:13), will indeed be judged and destroyed, but "Judah will be inhabited forever and Jerusalem for all generations" (3:20)—not literally or historically, but spiritually (through Christ and His church).

Overview of *Joel*

Joel 1:1–3 These opening verses serve as a preamble to the prophecy of the locust invasion. Joel introduces himself, however briefly, as one who bears "the word of the Lord"—a divine revelation. "Hear this" means pay special attention—not just to *what* will happen, but also *why*. This is not a prophecy concerning things the people already know, but of something altogether previously undisclosed. Locust plagues *themselves* are not new, but the one that is about to come upon the land is unprecedented in size, timing, and devastation. It will be one that will be remembered for generations.

Joel 1:4–13 Any agrarian society that depends entirely upon the produce of the land for its health and survival will especially fear a locust plague.[34] This invasion will come in waves or stages, wiping out everything from tender young plants to stripping the bark off tree limbs and trunks. Joel mentions the four stages of a locust's lifespan (1:4). **First**, there is the "gnawing" (or palmerworm) stage, before the insect has wings; it simply gnaws on whatever is nearby. **Second**, the "swarming" (or actual "locust" stage) is when the insect develops wings and begins to fly, making it impossible to keep contained. **Third**, the "creeping" (or cankerworm) stage is when the insect marches forward (see 2:4–11, where the insect invasion is characterized as an army marching over the land). **Finally**, there is the "stripping" (or caterpillar) stage, where the insect reaches full growth and is extremely destructive.[35] Regardless, "Joel is not giving his hearers/readers a lesson in entomology [i.e., the study of insects—my words]; he is emphasizing in a dramatic way the fact that the land of Judah has been thoroughly desolated."[36]

Three different groups are told to "wail," "mourn," and "be ashamed" by what is about to happen (soon, it appears).

- **First**, there are the "drunkards" (1:5–10), which seems to include many of the people, and sadly is one of the worldly characteristics of God's people (see Isa. 28:1–8, for example). Drunkenness, or any penchant for wine, indicates a settled, careless, and pleasure-seeking

people rather than one that is alert, responsible, and attentive to God's laws. Thus, removing their vines (through the locust plague) serves as God's strong rebuke to this behavior.
- **Second**, there are the "farmers" (1:11–12) who depend upon what the land produces and who service the crops. In devastating their fields, vines, trees, and fruit, God implies that they have failed to give Him due honor and gratitude for what He has provided. Just as He can make a land very productive (Lev. 26:3–6), so He can lay it waste.
- **Third**, there are the priests, the "ministers of the altar" (1:13), who depend upon the produce of the land to offer what the Law of Moses prescribes. (This also affects the portions they receive from the people in the form of tithes.) By abruptly interrupting the sacrificial system, God calls for its renewal—i.e., they have taken Him for granted, and their heart is not wholly dedicated to what they are doing, and this needs to change. It is not clear whether the priests themselves have directly contributed to the problem of Israel/Judah. However, they do have the highest responsibility both to reprimand the people for their indolence *and* intercede for them through prayers and sacrifices.

Joel 1:14–20 The locust plague—really, a divine judgment against the land of Judah—will affect all strata of nature (vegetative, animal, and human). Not only is the food supply destroyed for the people, but also for the sheep, cattle, and "beasts" in general. By referring to this as a "day of the LORD" event (1:15), the prophet reveals that God is behind it, and has appropriately timed it; thus, it is not to be mistaken as a coincidental or natural phenomenon. Joel's strong admonition, then, is to petition God with demonstrations of humility (as in the wearing of "sackcloth"[37]), laments, collective prayers, and fasting (1:14). God is obviously disciplining His people to produce repentance and sobriety, since these are what is lacking among them. "The affliction is [ultimately] not removed by mourning and lamentation, but only through repentance and supplication to the Lord, who can turn away all evil."[38]

Joel 2:1–11 In this passage are further and more detailed descriptions (in poetic, figurative language) of the locust invasion. "The prophet now makes the reader feel he is actually there, beholding the scene and experiencing the numbing sensation of helplessness, as in vivid and flashing language he describes the army of locusts."[39] This section begins and ends with the "day of the Lord" expression, so that there can be no doubt of direct association between God's judgment and the plague itself (2:1, 11). In front of the locust swarm, the land is green, productive, and beautiful; in its wake, the land is left brown, desolated, and devastated (2:3). The locust's march across the land is figuratively described as that of an invading army: it is organized, systematic in its objective, and pervasive. Yet, this is an army that cannot be fought or defeated by human means. Clearly, God is the Captain of this army, and thus it will not be deterred or halted unless or until He says so. The purposely exaggerated phrases of cosmic upheaval ("the earth quakes, the heavens tremble, the sun and the moon grow dark"—2:10) are typical of apocalyptic style writing. Such hyperbole implies that this is not a natural phenomenon but is the result of a judgment God has leveled against His spiritually careless people.

Joel 2:12–17 Now we see another (but stronger) call for the people to respond to what is about to come upon them—a call that is sent out *before* the devastation appears. God speaks directly through the prophet: "Return to Me with all your heart ..." (2:12–13a; compare Jer. 24:7, Zech. 1:3, and Luke 1:17). Only when sin has been committed and remains unaddressed does God ever call for repentance. (Think of Jesus' admonitions to several of the churches in Rev. 2—3 to "repent": they were not just mistaken in one thing or another but were *in sin*.) The prophet Joel reasons with the people—in essence, "Since God is a merciful God, perhaps He might relent from unleashing a *complete* destruction upon the land" (see 2:13b–14). The prophet also requires that *all* the people be involved in this supplication to God, since all of them are going to be adversely affected by it (2:15–17). This is a time for mourning over their sins, not carrying out their mundane practices of everyday life. He especially calls upon the priests to intercede in a manner like what Moses did for Israel (in Exod. 32:11–14).

Joel 2:18–27 Anticipating the people's change of heart, and their humble petition to God to have the plague removed, the prophet Joel foresees what will happen. **First**, God will remove the locust invasion and cast it into the sea (2:20): as He has brought it about, so He can remove it.[40] **Second**, He will heal the land of its desolation and restore its prosperity and abundance, so that the produce of the land will be even better than before the locusts came (2:23–27; see 2 Chron. 7:12–14). **Third**, the people will have reason to "rejoice and be glad" (2:21)—not just because their land has been restored, their food supply replenished, and things have returned to a sense of normalcy, but more so because of God's mercy, kindness, and providential care. The lesson is summed up in 2:27: "Thus you will know that I am in the midst of Israel, and that I am the LORD your God, and there is no other." This is what the people had forgotten in the first place—the very problem that brought about God's stern warning in the form of this prophecy.

Joel 2:28–32 "After this" (2:28) indicates a long but indeterminate time after all that has just been described has passed. God is already planning *another* "day of the LORD" event in the distant future that will be even further reaching and far more significant than an unprecedented insect invasion. This future "day" will not be a locust swarm that covers that land, but "My Spirit"—i.e., not a "day" of (only) judgment and upheaval, but one in which "all the families of the earth shall be blessed" (Acts 3:22–26).[41] The same figurative, purposely exaggerated, and apocalyptic style language is used to describe *that* "day" as it was used to describe the "day" of the locust invasion. Just as apocalyptic language was not to be taken literally in dealing with the locust invasion, so it is not to be taken literally in Peter's sermon to the Jews (Acts 2:15–21). While Joel calls upon the people to repent and pray for God to relent His disaster upon the people (2:32), the future "day" will be a call for the people to repent and pray for the *salvation of their souls* (Acts 2:21, 38).

Joel 3:1–15 While God will promise salvation to those who call upon His name (Acts 2:21), judgment is still promised to those nations that have contributed to His people's moral decline and spiritual downfall. In other words, while promising grace and mercy to the penitent, God does not cease to pursue justice and retribution upon the wicked. He will pay them back for all the injustices they have committed against others. As they have stolen His people's wealth—particularly, "treasures" from His temple—and sold their children into slavery, so God will plunder their wealth and sell their people to distant lands (3:5–8).

God even taunts the foreign nations—Phoenicia and Philistia in particular, but also to Egypt and Edom (see 3:19)—to enter a court of judgment with Him.[42] He says, in essence, "You act strong and mighty when plundering My people; let's see how strong you are when you come against their God!" (3:9–11). The "valley of Jehoshaphat" (3:2, 12)—lit., "the valley where Jehovah judges"—indicates a figurative meeting place since it is not a real location in the ancient world.

The message here is that God is the Judge not only of His people (as indicated by the locust plague) but also of foreign nations.[43] This future judgment against the "multitudes, multitudes" of Gentile people (more fully expounded upon in the major prophets; see Isa. 13—23, Jer. 46—51, and Ezek. 25—32) will be, for *those* people, yet another "day of the LORD" in which their world will be shaken, turned upside-down, and (in some cases) completely obliterated (3:14). The "valley of decision" is another phrase equal to "valley of Jehoshaphat": where God judges, He also renders verdicts (or decisions; decrees) against those who stand guilty before Him. "The repetition of 'valley of decision' heightens the effect and pronounces the awful certainty of their doom."[44]

Joel 3:16–21 Meanwhile, despite all that happens against the earth, foreign nations, and even God's own people, "Jerusalem will be holy" (3:17). This passage cannot be limited to any secular historical period but has a definite messianic element to it. In this case, it speaks not only of the literal city of Jerusalem, but looks ahead to the spiritual "Jerusalem," the city of God which is Christ's church (see Gal. 4:26, Heb. 12:22, and Rev. 21:1–2). Those who choose to afflict God's people will be destroyed; those who drink the water, so to speak, that flows "from the house of the LORD" will be blessed (3:18; see John 4:13–14 and 7:37–39). "Egypt will become a waste" (3:19)—while Egypt plundered

Jerusalem under Pharaoh Shishak during the reign of King Rehoboam (2 Chron. 12:9), a future Seleucid king (Antiochus) will severely plunder Egypt (Dan. 11:40–43). "Edom" has long been an enemy of Israel and was nearly wiped out under King David's reign. Later, Edom revolted during the reign of King Jehoram of Judah, and Jehoram destroyed many of Edom's commanders and soldiers (2 Chron. 21:8–10). In other words, the "violence" these nations have brought upon Israel and Judah will come back upon their own heads—God will see to it (Obad. 1:15). In sharp contrast, Jerusalem—in essence, God's *people*, not the literal city—will be blessed "forever" and for "all generations" (3:20).

Questions on *Joel*

1.) How does a cataclysmic locust plague (of which Joel prophesied) serve as an ideal form of punishment and a wake-up call to God's people?

    a. Can we learn anything from times of crises and devastation?

    b. Might such times be regarded as God's discipline (see Heb. 12:5–13)?

    c. In any case, can natural calamities be opportunities for soul-searching and repentance?

2.) What does God mean when He says to "rend your heart and not your garments" (2:13a)? How might He say the same thing to Christians who need to repent? (Consider Mat. 23:25–26 and James 4:8–9, for example.)

3.) What is so remarkable about God promising to "pour out My Spirit on all mankind" (2:28), especially given the context in which Peter quotes this passage in Acts 2:17–21? (There are several answers.)

4.) God makes a distinction between those who will be *preserved* by Him and those who will be *judged* (or *destroyed*) by Him (3:1–21). Does He still do this today? If so, how can we know which group we belong to? (Consider Rom. 2:4–11, Rev. 7:1–3, 14:1–4, and 14:9–10 in your answer.)

Introduction to *Jonah*

Authorship: Jonah ("dove") is identified as "the son of Amittai," of whom we know nothing. Jonah himself, however, is specifically mentioned in 2 Kings 14:25, where we learn that he is from Gath-hepher, a city in the tribal territory of Zebulun in northern Israel, just a few miles from the city of Nazareth. Stuart calls him one of the "best remembered biblical characters": "People otherwise largely ignorant of the scripture's content have heard about Jonah and the 'whale.'"[45] He is one of the very few prophets mentioned by name by Jesus (Mat. 12:39–40), adding considerable weight of credibility to the prophet's account. In fact, the comparisons between Jonah and Jesus are remarkable:[46]

- Both grew up in the region of Galilee (see John 7:52).
- Both were asleep on a ship during a storm.
- Both were awakened—Jonah by the ship's captain, Jesus by His apostles.
- Both affected the ship's security—Jonah for danger, Jesus for safety.
- Both sacrificed themselves to save others—Jonah for the sailors, Jesus for all people.
- Both produced a great calm of the storm—Jonah by being thrown overboard, Jesus by His own command.
- Both were "alive" after a three days and three nights' experience—Jonah in the depth of the sea, Jesus in His tomb.
- Both converted Gentiles—Jonah, at Nineveh; Jesus, throughout the earth.

Modern liberal theologians have reduced Jonah's account to a mere allegory or parable rather than a factual and historical event. Their intention is to get rid of the miracle but keep the story. The idea of a man being swallowed by a "great fish," surviving for three days and nights in its belly, and then being vomited onto the shore, seems unbelievable. Yet, this miracle is no different than Jesus' being raised from the dead: both require supernatural intervention in an earthly, natural context. Jesus accepted the account as fact; and so have the Jews for some 2,700 years (as Jonah's account is read every year during their Day of Atonement).

We cannot only accept miracles that meet our expectations; otherwise, the authority of the entire Bible must be rejected. "The only possible reason for Jonah's being in the Jewish canon of scripture lies in their certainty that the prophet Jonah was actually the author of this book. If it had been a myth, it would have been rejected, as nothing mythological was ever accepted by them."[47] Furthermore, it is unthinkable that an Israelite would have invented a story that showed God's mercy toward a heathen nation at the expense of His own prophet.[48]

Date and Place of Writing: Because of 2 Kings 14:25, we know that Jonah prophesied during the reign of Jeroboam II (Israel), in the early 8th century BC. This corresponds to the time when Assyria began its expansionist campaign into foreign countries: no longer did Assyria invade only for mere plunder but to enforce sustained domination (and the ongoing tribute this would produce for them). Thus, Jonah's ministry seems to be near the end of Elisha's ministry. This was also a time of great economic prosperity for Israel. Little attention was being paid to God, or to the poor and underprivileged, but the message of Jonah only speaks of Israel by implication, not directly. In other words, if God is telling a heathen and polytheistic nation like Assyria to repent or be destroyed, then most certainly He expects the same response from Israel.

We do not know from what location Jonah's prophecies came, although it is plausible to think that he remained close to his homeland in northern Israel. This is also geographically the closest proximity to Assyria, given the route that all eastern armies came into Palestine (i.e., from the north, following the so-called Fertile Crescent through Mesopotamia).

Purpose and Character of Writing: One of the unique characteristics of the *Jonah* is that it is written entirely in the third person, giving it more of a story narrative than a personal one. The great message in *Jonah* is that God has concern for the moral and spiritual well-being of foreign nations as He does for Israel; in this regard, "What the book of Acts is to the New Testament, the prophecy of Jonah is to the Old Testament. It shows that God has always had concern for the heathen who are without hope apart from Him."⁴⁹ Jonah the prophet no doubt knew of Assyria's ruthless warfare against other nations; "It would seem that instead of sparing the nation God should make this an opportune time to destroy it."⁵⁰

> It is true, the great prophets had often taught the future reception of the heathen into the kingdom of God [see Isa. 49:5–6, for example]: but their predominant theme had been the denunciation of judgment; and the Israelites themselves had suffered so much at the hands of foreign oppressors that they came to look upon the heathen as their natural foes, and were impatient when they saw the judgments uttered against them unfulfilled. Jonah appears as the representative of the popular Israelitish creed. ... [Yet, in] the rebuke with which the book closes, the exclusive spirit of the author's own contemporaries stands condemned.⁵¹

Indeed, because of Jonah's preaching, Nineveh repented and God's judgment against Assyria was delayed for about 130 years. Implied is the connection to Israel, since Jonah was a prophet *from* Israel, and thus it was Israel's God that could either save or destroy Nineveh. Yet, while the Israelites often took their relationship for granted and lost sight of the great privilege they enjoyed as His people, the Ninevites took God seriously (at least initially) and responded to the words of a single prophet. "The [reading] audience of the book is thus invited implicitly to revise their understanding of what God is like, if they have indeed shared Jonah's selfish views."⁵²

Ironically, *Jonah* is the only OT book that does not mention Israel, and its only subject matter is a heathen city (Nineveh) in heathen nation (Assyria). Even so, some see in *Jonah* an allusion to the nation of Israel as well. Just as Jonah was cast into the sea, so Israel seemed to be cast into an irretrievable death (in exile). And just as Jonah was divinely preserved in the sea and then returned to "life," so Israel was called out of death and returned to life—no longer as the political theocracy that it once was, but as a spiritual people, the "New Jerusalem."⁵³ Thus, resurrection from the dead is more than hinted at, and touches on Jesus' own resurrection, and even the believer's resurrection from his being "dead" to God but "made alive together with Christ" (Eph. 2:5).

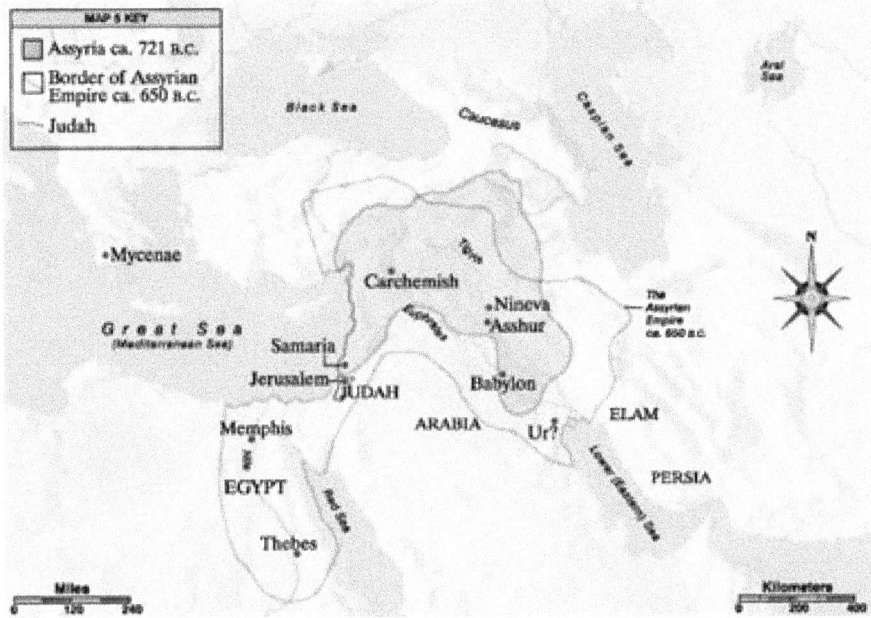

Overview of *Jonah*

Jonah 1:1–3 Nineveh, the principal city of Assyria (a rising world empire in Jonah's day), is a "great city"—not in virtue, but in physical size (see notes on 3:3), age (see Gen. 10:8–12), population (estimated between 600,000 and 1,000,000 people), and influence upon the ancient world.[54] It is also great in its cruelty and wickedness, prompting God to send one of His prophets to warn it against committing any future crimes against humanity. Jonah is a fierce defender of Israel's preeminence among the nations, and does not want God to show any mercy toward a heathen nation that defies everything the prophet believes in. God *does* want Jonah to warn of His divine judgment, but more importantly He wants the Ninevites to repent. Yet Jonah simply refuses to offer any hope to a nation that he believes deserves to be destroyed.

To say that the book of *Jonah* is unique and unusual is an understatement. It relates the only time God sends one of His prophets to a heathen nation, and the only time one of His prophets refuses to fulfill His commission. "Tarshish" is at the extreme westward end of the known world (in modern Spain). "Joppa" is a Palestinian seaport on the Mediterranean coast. Ironically, it is the place where, 800 years later, Peter will stay while being summoned by a vision to go to meet another non–Israelite named Cornelius (see Acts 9:36—10:23).

Jonah 1:4–9 God gives Jonah a specific mission to carry out, and he refuses (on the basis of his principles). Ironically, "Of all the people and things mentioned in the book—the storm, the lots, the sailors, the fish, the Ninevites, the plant, the worm, and the east wind—only the prophet himself fails to obey God."[55] Even though Jonah tries to run from his ministry, God knows exactly where he is at all times. "The LORD hurled a great wind on the sea" (1:4) which threatened to destroy the ship he is on and everyone on board. Jonah sleeps in the ship's lower compartment (suggesting a ship of considerable size for that time) while the other men struggle to maintain control of the vessel. The pagan sailors pray to their pagan gods, but to no avail. Finally, the ship's captain summons Jonah and demands him to pray to *his* God. "What a travesty on the religion of the true Jehovah this was: a heathen shipmaster rebuking a prophet of the Lord, a pagan calling to a prophet of God to awake and pray that they might not perish! But such was the situation."[56] Then all the men determine (through the casting of lots) whose fault it is that has brought such peril upon them.

> Lots were probably dice, their sides alternately light or dark in color ... The casting of lots was interpreted as follows. Two dark sides up meant "No." Two light sides up meant "Yes." A light and a dark meant "Throw again." Using this system, the sailors eliminated others on ship until Jonah was left.[57]

Both physical efforts and prayers to various gods had failed; someone, they assumed, had offended the gods. No doubt God Himself intervened to reveal Jonah as the offender, and Jonah finally identifies himself as that person (1:9).

Jonah 1:10–16 First the sailors feared the storm; then they feared their gods; now they fear *the* God of heaven and earth. They are also incredulous that a man would openly defy such a powerful God ("How could you do this?").[58] Wanting to save their own lives, they ask what can be done to stop the storm—an amazing idea, left to itself—and Jonah tells them: cast me into the sea (1:12). The men are at first unwilling to do this, not wanting to be guilty of sending a man to his death, and they try to row to shore instead. But this fails, and their situation worsens. Finally, *they* pray to God, asking Him to absolve them of any crime against His prophet (1:14). This prayer means: they believed in what Jonah said about himself *and* his God; and they believed in the sovereign authority and power of Jonah's God. Finally, they cast Jonah overboard, and the sea becomes calm. This makes such an impression upon these men that they "feared the Lord greatly," offered a sacrifice to Him, and made vows (1:16). It is possible, too, that they sought atonement from God for having thrown one of His people to his death. No doubt these men spread the story of Jonah to many other people—including the Assyrians.

Jonah 1:17[59]**—2:10** "And the LORD appointed a great fish to swallow Jonah" (1:17), but we should remember that the prophet had no idea of this but thought he would simply drown in the sea. In his mind, then, drowning was still preferable to helping Nineveh. What *kind* of fish swallowed the prophet is not important; the fact that God sent this fish to Jonah for this purpose *is* important.[60]

Jonah remained in the fish's belly "three days and three nights" (1:17). (Jesus cited this as being a "type" prophecy of His own experience: He also would be "three days and three nights" in the grave before resurrecting from the dead; see Mat. 12:40.) Our wondering about how a man can survive in the belly of a fish for any length of time is irrelevant; the God that can cause storms, *end* storms, identify runaway prophets through a seemingly random means of selection (lots), and appoint a "great fish" to swallow a man is most certainly capable of keeping that man alive in the belly of that fish. (Likewise, the God that led Jesus to His death on a cross is certainly capable of raising Him from that death.) At the same time, being trapped in a fish's belly, in complete darkness, void of all air or comfort, and likely coming into contact with whatever else the fish had already swallowed, is an awful thing to contemplate.

While in the fish's belly, Jonah has considerable time to rethink his decision to run away from what God had called him to do. "If it can be said that Jonah ran away from God in chapter one, it can easily be said that he ran toward God in chapter two."[61] Thus, he humbly and respectfully prays to God (2:1–9). In that prayer, Jonah vividly details his having been cast into the sea and sinking to the bottom, believing that he was going to die. Yet, while nearing his death, "I remembered the LORD, and my prayer came to You, into your holy temple" (2:7)—i.e., he knows that God hears him, even from the depths of the sea, and will answer him. While many men give high esteem to "vain idols" [lit., worthless vanities], Jonah chooses to give his allegiance to God, because "salvation is from the LORD" (2:9; see Psalm 3:8). In response, God commands the fish to expel Jonah from its belly onto "dry land"—that is, on a beach, likely on the Mediterranean coast from where Jonah first tried to run from what he was told to do.

Jonah 3:1–10 God again commissions Jonah, and this time the prophet offers no argument or hesitation. The journey to Nineveh itself is substantial, as it is over 700 miles from Jerusalem. Again, Nineveh is referred to as "an exceedingly great city," requiring three days' journey simply to walk around it. (Some scholars believe that this encompassed not only the actual city itself, but its surrounding suburban areas as well.[62]) Jonah's message is simple: "Yet forty days and Nineveh will be overthrown" (3:4). There is no doubt that much more was said, but this remains the core of his prophecy.[63] It is possible that the news of Jonah's attempt to flee God, including the sailors' report of what happened on the ship, had already reached this city, making them believe that the prophecy was real; as such, he became a "sign" of God to them (see Luke 11:29–30).

The Ninevites' response is amazing: from the king on down to the lowliest servant, every person is to outwardly demonstrate their belief in the prophet's message by fasting, wearing sackcloth, and praying for mercy from God. These people are ripe for this message; the timing of Jonah's appearance there is optimal.

As Israel's prosperity rose, Assyria battled with internal strife, including the Armenians who lived near the Caspian Sea. During this time, the power of the king was greatly diminished and the provincial governors wielded great influence over government. There were no large campaigns against foreign nations during this time. During the 760s BC, Assyria found itself in the middle of a great famine, and in 765 BC and again in 759 BC, great plagues spread throughout the nation. On January 15, 763 BC, there was a total eclipse of the sun, which always gave the ancients great cause for alarm. As far back as the 790s, there had been a push for monotheism within Assyria. All or some of these factors could explain the readiness of the people to repent when Jonah came calling ...[64]

In response to the Assyrians' repentance, God relented from what He had planned to do. Coffman sums this up:
- They repented with no [specific] invitation to repent.
- They repented without promise that it would do any good if they did repent.
- They repented without any wish or hope on the part of the preacher that they would repent.
- They repented even in the face of Jonah's anger at their doing so.
- They repented *en masse*, from the greatest of them to the least of them.
- They backed up their repentance by turning away from their violence and wickedness.
- Such repentance was rewarded by the blessing of God![65]

We have no idea *what* God would have done to destroy Nineveh had the city not repented; we only know that He *can* destroy it and *would have* done so. (In fact, many years later, God again predicted the fall of Nineveh. This time the arrogant city showed no humility or repentance, and as a result God wiped it from the face of the earth.[66]) Remember, this is the same God who overthrew Sodom, Gomorrah, and the other cities of the valley by raining fire from heaven down upon them (Gen. 19:24–25); He could have easily done this to Nineveh.

Jonah 4:1–11 Jonah, resuming his passionate zeal for Israel—and thus his passionate contempt for any other nation—is "greatly displeased" over God's decision (4:1).

> Jonah hated what God had done. It made him furious. If this is shocking, it is supposed to be so. The narrator carefully tells the story according to his inspired purpose, which is to arouse the

audience to disassociate itself from Jonah's narrow nationalism. Though Jonah hardly comes across as a hero anywhere in the book, he appears especially selfish, petty, temperamental, and even downright foolish in chap. 4.[67]

His prayer to God says, "I just *knew* You would not destroy these people if they repented—this is what I feared, and this is why I refused at first to preach to them!" His view is decidedly different toward the Ninevites than God's. Jonah is so distraught that he prefers death over life. Yet, God asks, "Do you have good reason to be angry?" (4:4)—a mild rebuke, but a rebuke all the same. The truth is, Jonah has no *moral* right to be angry, except that God did not meet his *personal* expectations.

Hopeful that God might still yet destroy Nineveh anyway, Jonah sets up a tent outside of the city (with a full view of it) and waits for something bad to happen to it. Meanwhile, God appoints a "plant"—some speculate a gourd or a castor oil plant—to grow suddenly and unexpectedly large to provide shade for Jonah, and he very much enjoyed that comfort (4:6). Coffman observes:

> If there was ever an example of man's being "exceedingly glad" for the wrong reasons, here it is in these two verses. There are millions of Jonahs everywhere in our society today, people who are glad, exceedingly so, for the comforts and luxuries they enjoy, rather than for the great hope of the soul's eternal redemption in Jesus Christ our Lord. They are more thankful for sports contests, outings on the beach, air-conditioning, soft drinks, plenty of beer, etc., than they are for the right to worship God without molestation. Yes, there are a lot of Jonahs who are still exceedingly glad for gourds![68]

Then God appointed a worm to destroy the plant, to the prophet's great dismay. In fact, he "became faint and begged with all his soul to die, saying, 'Death is better to me than life'" (4:8). God rhetorically asks, "Do you have reason to be angry about the plant?"—another mild rebuke. Jonah thinks he does have good reason to be angry, but this is not true. Jonah did nothing to provide *for* the plant, so he had no reason to complain when it was taken away. In contrast, the Ninevites have been created *by* God in His image, and, though they are wicked, He has every desire to entreat them to repent.

Jonah is angry that the plant was destroyed; he is also angry that Nineveh was *not* destroyed. He is miserable over his own personal circumstances but shows no concern for (what he hoped would be) the divine destruction of many human lives; he is more concerned with the loss of a plant than the loss of many souls. Thus, his perspective is entirely backward from what it should have been. This calls to mind what the landowner said to the disgruntled laborers in Jesus' parable: "Is your eye envious because I am generous?" (Mat. 20:15). Certainly, Jonah was put out by God's great mercy and grace toward people who did not deserve it—as if the Israelites *did* deserve it! Bible scholars have long thought that the "120,000 persons who do not know {the difference} between their right and left hand" refers to young children in the city and its suburbs, and there is no good reason to dispute this. It is "an idiomatic expression for a lack of knowledge, and/or innocence."[69] God cannot be saying that *all* the people are this way, but only a group within the full population are. Not only this, but God shows concern even for the many animals that would die or be killed in the case of divine judgment against the city.

Questions on *Jonah*

1.) What major lessons can we glean from the book of *Jonah*?

2.) We tend to be critical of Jonah for running from what God called him to do. But what was Jonah's *reason* for running? Was it to escape responsibility, or something else?

3.) How was Jonah's being "cast into the sea" for the sailors' sake parallel to Jesus' being crucified for our sake? How was it different? Why did the men have to *cast* Jonah into the sea—why didn't he just jump into the sea on his own volition?

4.) "The men of Nineveh will stand up with this generation at the judgment, and will condemn it because they repented at the preaching of Jonah; and behold, something greater than Jonah is here" (Mat. 12:41). What did Jesus mean by this? Could Nineveh stand up against our *present* generation and condemn it? Please explain.

5.) Notice how many "appointments" God made in the book of Jonah (both stated and implied). He appointed:

   a. Jonah to go and preach to Nineveh.
   b. a great storm to be "hurled" against the ship.

c. the lot to fall to Jonah.
d. a great fish to swallow Jonah.
e. the great fish to vomit Jonah upon a certain seashore.
f. Jonah to go and preach to Nineveh a second time.
g. a specific destruction to come against Nineveh unless they repented.
h. a reprieve against Nineveh's destruction, due to their repentance.
i. a shade plant to grow up beside Jonah's shelter.
j. a worm to devour the plant.
k. a scorching east wind to afflict Jonah.

What does all of this tell us about God Himself? About His ability—when He deems necessary—to intervene in human affairs?

Introduction to *Amos*

Authorship: Amos ("burden" or "burden–bearer") is a sheepherder and grower ("nipper") of sycamore figs (1:1, 7:14–15).[70] He is not of the school of the prophets that dated back to the time of Samuel and flourished in the time of Elijah and Elisha. Rather, he is called by God to prophesy against the northern tribes of Israel because of their unfaithfulness to their covenant with God. In other words, he is a man of relatively low status, yet bears a message—in effect, a *burden*—for God's people. He is of "Tekoa," an uninviting and impoverished area that overlooks the Judean wilderness, about sixteen miles south of Jerusalem and nearly the same distance west of the Dead Sea. Since Amos is contemporary with Hosea, and possibly Isaiah and Micah, it is possible that he knew these prophets, or at least knew of their prophecies (and/or they knew of his).

Date and Place of Writing: Amos personally provides a narrow window of time in which he preached. Uzziah [a.k.a. Amaziah] was the king of Judah for over fifty years (2 Chron. 26:3); Jeroboam II became king in the fifteenth year of Uzziah's reign (2 Kings 14:23). So, Amos received his prophetic visions in the time (approx. twenty-six years) in which both Uzziah and Jeroboam reigned concurrently, thus the middle of the 8th century BC. The "earthquake" (1:1) must have been a pretty significant event, since earthquakes are common in Palestine; it is mentioned again some two hundred years later in Zech. 14:4–5. While there is no record of this event in *2 Kings* or *2 Chronicles*, it does serve as a harbinger of divine judgment about to befall Israel.

We have no way of knowing for certain where Amos delivered his oracles, except to say that it was in Israel, their primary recipient. In 7:10–13, it does indicate that Amos spoke in Bethel (about twelve miles north of Jerusalem), but this does not mean he remained there. It is possible that the prophet moved throughout the land of Israel while he preached.

Purpose and Character of Writing: Israel has become a decidedly sinful nation, and thus God has sent His prophets to warn against continuing in this manner. Amos levels a strong condemnation against the nations surrounding Israel as well (chapters 2—3), but it is Israel that remains the prime offender. Israel has been the recipient of God's laws, His grace, His priesthood, and His prophetic oracles; these other nations have not. God's message to Israel is, "If you are going to act like the heathen nations around you, then you will share in the divine judgment that is pronounced against them." Amos does not address God as "the Lord of Israel," but characterizes Him repeatedly as the Lord over all Creation and the Sovereign over all Gentile nations. This indicates (to those listening to him) that God does not limit His dealings with men to only the nation of Israel (nor does Israel alone answer to God), but He stands above all the earth in majesty, authority, and power. All nations—all *people*—answer to Him.

It is significant to note that both Israel and Judah, under Jeroboam and Uzziah, respectively, enjoyed great prosperity and relative peace during the time of Amos' prophecies. Thus, the priest's rebuke of Amos (in 7:10–13) conveys the attitude of many of the people—in essence, "Stop depressing everyone with your negative words! Everyone knows that things are going *just fine* here in Israel." "In the existing state of things, the idea of the approaching fall or destruction of the kingdom of Israel [by Assyria, in 722/721 BC, barely 30 years from the time of Amos] was, according to human judgment, a very improbable one indeed."[71]

The Israelites rested in their might, trusted in their military resources, thought only of financial profit, and reveled in their wealth and creature comforts. "Nevertheless, it was the exploitation of the poor and defenseless by the rich and powerful that God particularly exposed through Amos' oracles and which constitutes a remarkably frequent theme in the book."[72] Thus, from God's point of view, Israel was in an advanced state of decay—a decay which was not going to reverse and from which it was not going to recover. "Unbounded prosperity, throughout history, has almost always resulted in turning away from God; and it was especially true of Israel at this time."[73] Chronologically speaking, Amos is the first prophet to predict the actual overthrow of Samaria and the deportation of Israel (5:27, 6:1–8).

Amos' character reminds us of Elijah and John the Baptist. While Isaiah's prophecies, for example, are smooth, poetic, and often formal, Amos' prophecies are blunt, forceful, and yet eloquent in their own way. He does not have the polish of a well-trained orator, yet his message is clear, exacting, and potent. "There was not in Amos the sympathy, warm love, and feeling of the statesman or citizen, but … he was the stern prophet of justice and righteousness."[74] It is hard to read *Amos* without feeling the strong passion—as well as the pained disappointment—in the prophet's voice as he point-by-point dismantles every justification for his people's behavior and pronounces God's judgment against them. Most of the prophecy (chapters 1—8) is negative, listing Israel's sins and promising judgment and destruction. It is not until the very end of the book (9:11–15) that he prophesies great promises of restoration, rebuilding, and prosperity. While these promises do have limited historical fulfillment, they do not reach full realization until the time of spiritual Israel—the church age. *Amos* is quoted twice in the NT: Amos 5:25–26 is quoted by Stephen in Acts 7:42–43, and Amos 9:11 is quoted by James in Acts 15:16–17.

Overview of *Amos*

Amos 1:1 This is an introduction to the prophecy, with a brief description of Amos and the time in which he preached (see "Introduction to Amos").

First group of prophecies or oracles (1:2—6:14)

Amos 1:2—2:16 God pronounces judgment on all the nations surrounding Israel (including Judah), but particularly the northern tribes of Israel (simply "Israel"). God does not merely speak to all these nations; He "roars" from Jerusalem (1:2), the location of His temple and the center of Jehovah worship. This indicates the deep indignation He has toward all of them for their multitude of sins and the advanced degradation of justice, righteousness, and human decency.

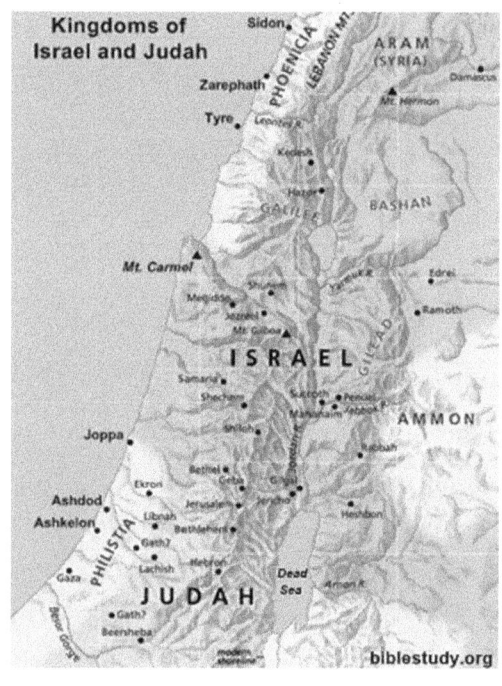

The "for three transgressions … and for four" formula "is a rhetorical way of saying that the offender has been guilty of an incalculable number of offenses, and his cup of iniquity is filled to overflowing—judgment must fall."[75] While three transgressions fill the cup, so to speak, the fourth causes it to overflow, indicating that there is no more room for patience or mercy. The nations and their crimes are as follows:

- **Damascus** (1:3–5) is also more generally known as Syria or Aram. Damascus is the city-state and capital; Syria/Aram is its land. The "threshing" of Gilead with sharp instruments refers to the inhumane and unnecessary torture of the tribes of Israel (Gad, Reuben, and the half–tribe of Manasseh) in the Trans-Jordan region, adjacent to Syria. By implication, this happened during the reigns of Hazael and Ben-hadad, two rulers of Damascus during the reigns of Jehu and Jehoahaz (2 Kings 10:32–33, 13:3–7). A "citadel" is any kind of armed military fortification, often a permanent one, that is erected along a city wall or in strategic areas of defense. The term is used frequently in this section. The "valley of Aven" is a serene area between Damascus and Lebanon where people practice sun worship and other forms of idolatry; "Beth-Eden" [lit., house of Eden] is a beautiful city near Haran. "Kir" is likely an area near Assyria (by the River Kur) where the Syrians would be taken into permanent exile in due time.

- **Gaza** (1:6–8) is one of the five (and likely the most dominant) principal city–states of Philistia, on the Mediterranean coast. The mention of some of the other city–states (Ashdod, Ashkelon, and Ekron) seems to indicate that the prophecy is leveled against all of Philistia. Their crime of selling "an entire population" probably occurred during the reign of Jehoram of Judah (2 Chron. 21:16; see also Joel 3:3–8, which speaks of the same practice, if not the same event). In that case, they sold Jews as slaves to the Edomites and Phoenicians. God promises that, as they destroyed a population of His people, so He will destroy them. However, while Judah will survive the ordeal, Philistia will not ("the remnant of the Philistines will perish"—1:8).

- **Tyre** (1:9–10), along with Sidon, is one of the principal city–states of Phoenicia, another nation on the Mediterranean coast north of Philistia. Their crime is the same as that of Gaza and alludes to the same event described above. The "covenant of brotherhood" likely refers to the long–standing friendship that David and Solomon established with King Hiram when they were gathering choice cedars for building the temple of God (2 Sam. 5:11, 1 Kings 5:2–6, 15–18, and 9:11–14). As a result of this treaty, Judah never declared war on Phoenicia; yet Phoenicia violated the agreement for its own financial gain. Amos' prophecy would not be completely fulfilled until the distant future. Nebuchadnezzar, king of Babylon, besieged the city for thirteen years (585–573 BC), but did not destroy it (Ezek. 29:18–20); later, Alexander the Great again besieged the city (4th century), which by then had been built just off the coastland on an island, and utterly destroyed it (likely, Zech. 9:1–4 refers to this).[76]

- **Edom** (1:11–12) is the nation descended from Esau, thus blood-brothers with Israel and Judah, descendants of Esau's brother, Jacob. (See "Overview of *Obadiah*" in this study guide for more extensive comments.) Edom's "anger" and "fury" are likely over the fact that their forefather, Esau, forfeited his sacred inheritance for a bowl of stew (Gen. 25:27–34), and the inheritance went to Jacob instead. Their bitter jealousy and contempt for Israel and Judah led to terrible abuses against their brethren, either by outright war or aiding and abetting their enemies. "Teman" (also spelled Tenan) is the capital of Edom; Bozrah is one of its principal cities.
- **Ammon** (1:13–15) is another nation blood-related to Israel. Their ancestor, Ammon, and his brother, Moab, were the bastard sons of Lot through the incestuous seduction of his two daughters (Gen. 19:30–38). Lot is the nephew of Abraham, who is the father of Isaac, who is the father of Jacob. Ammon has had a long-standing grudge against Israel, accusing it of stealing land from it when Israelites conquered and settled in the land of Gilead in the Trans-Jordan region (north of Ammon)—a charge that Jephthah clearly refuted (Judg. 11:12–28). The ripping open of pregnant women indicates the brutal savagery the Ammonites exercised against Israel; pregnant women are among the most helpless to defend themselves. All this, "to enlarge their borders"—i.e., to take land that did not belong to them, despite their claims. "Rabbah" is the capital of Ammon, and is a strong and fortified city; nonetheless, God promises to destroy it.
- **Moab** (2:1–3) is the nation just south of Ammon and is also blood-related to both Ammon and Israel (see notes above). To burn the bones of a king is to show utter contempt and an unstoppable hatred—one that goes beyond even the death of the one hated. While the specific event here is not known elsewhere (outside of Jewish tradition), it does serve to illustrate the Moabites' sacrilege

and inhumane character. God promises to destroy not only the "judge"—possibly in the absence of a formal king—but also his princes (or, associated rulers) in response.

- **Judah** (2:4–5) is the southern nation of God's people by covenant. (The combined nation of Israel and Judah divided during the reign of King Rehoboam; see 1 Kings 12.) While God cites moral crimes—both general and specific—against the heathen nations, He cites *covenant violations* against Judah. This is because God did not have covenants with these other nations, but He did with Judah and Israel. Thus, their crime is their rejection (through ignorance, carelessness, or apathy) of His divine law which He gave to them through His servant Moses. Their "lies" refer to their idols—all the lifeless, false, and pagan deities that they chose to serve and follow rather than heed the words of the Living God of heaven. The "fire" to come upon Jerusalem would not be fulfilled until the time of Nebuchadnezzar (586 BC), when that king leveled Jerusalem and its temple to the ground and carried the Jews into Babylonian captivity.
- **Israel** (2:6–16) refers to the northern tribes of Israel, the capital of which is Samaria. While Israel also has chronically violated its covenant with God, the prophecy focuses specifically on the abuses of power, justice, and whatever is holy to God as their crimes. The "selling" of the righteous and needy refers to the judges who are bribed to rule against these people for personal gain, even for a pair of sandals (2:6). Also, they will not give help to the helpless or humble but think nothing of a father and son both having sex with the same woman (possibly a prostitute; see Hos. 4:14). Garments that are taken from the poor for pledges are supposed to be returned by sundown (Exod. 22:25–27, Deut. 24:12–13), but the wealthy keep them instead; likewise, they drink wine purchased with those who are unjustly fined (2:7–8).

God then pointedly reminds them that it was He who subjugated the Amorites (Canaanites) who lived in the land that they (Israel) now possess, having also single-handedly led them out of Egyptian captivity (2:9–10). He also raised up prophets and Nazirites (Num. 6:2–3)—covenant-bound men devoted to God's ministry—but the Israelites have not listened to the prophets and forced the Nazirites to violate their vows (2:11–12). In other words, nothing is sacred to the Israelite nation; they have lost all sense of propriety, justice, and human decency. Thus, they have made themselves a burden to God—a crime that brings stiff consequences (2:13–16).

Amos 3:1–15 By rescuing Israel from Egypt *and* giving them a land of their own, God chose Israel over all the other nations (3:1–2; see Exod. 19:5–6, Deut. 4:32–37, and 7:6). But with privilege comes responsibility—and accountability. Israel's failure to honor God's special covenant incurs divine judgment. Not only this, but God's covenantal accountability *required* Him to punish Israel to maintain His justice and holiness.

> This was a concept which the average Israelite of Amos' time apparently found hard to understand (cf. 5:18–20). A God should protect and benefit his nation at all times, should he not? Why would a God want to harm his own people who worshiped him regularly (5:21–23)? Much of Amos' ministry was devoted to dispelling this folly.[78]

God illustrates this with cause–and–effect relationships in natural circumstances (3:3–8). Things do not happen by accident; likewise, no one can explain His judgment against Samaria (Israel) as accidental, circumstantial, or coincidental. God even calls "Ashdod" (Philistia) and Egypt to bear witness against His people—pagan, polytheistic nations who know better than do His own people (3:9–10). While Israel is at ease and morally inattentive to its own pathetic situation, "an enemy, even one surrounding the land" will come against them (3:11). The destruction will be so devastating that few will escape it.[79] The "altars of Bethel" (3:14) refers to places of refuge, first instituted by King Jeroboam of Israel (1 Kings 12:32). King Josiah of Judah will later destroy and defile these places (2 Kings 23:15–16), but the prophet here may refer to the sheer uselessness of these altars in offering any protection for the people against God's wrath. The "winter house," "summer house," and "houses of ivory" (3:15) are the residences and palaces of the wealthy—those who made themselves rich by extorting, cheating, and imposing upon the people, especially the poor and helpless. Shalmaneser, the king of Assyria will carry out the full and brutal destruction of Samaria in 722/721 BC (2 Kings 17:5–6).

Amos 4:1–5 "Bashan" is in the Trans–Jordan region, due east of the Sea of Galilee, and is well–known for its fattened livestock. Here, Amos himself calls the wealthy Israelites who control the nation of Israel (in and around Samaria) the "cows of Bashan"—fat, pampered, and prepared for slaughter (4:1; see James 5:5–6). Specifically, since the Hebrew text uses feminine forms, this refers to the wealthy women; instead of being refined and noble–minded, they are gluttons and perverters of justice. "Wine" may refer to the drunken orgies associated with idolatrous worship.[80] God promises that all this will end. Some of the women will be led away into exile; "meat hooks" alludes to the actual hooks (on a rope) which the Assyrians put into their captives' noses in order to lead them away in a line, just like a fisherman pulls upon the hook in a fish's mouth.[81] Others will try to escape through the breaches in the city walls broken down by the enemy, but they will be captured.

"Harmon" [lit., palace or high place] is used only here in the OT, and (in the context) may refer to: an intended but useless place of refuge; an alleged place of refuge that turns out to be a place of captivity instead; the enemy's own stronghold (which seems the best interpretation); or, something unknown to us. "Enter Bethel … and Gilgal" (4:4–5)—two of the religious centers in Israel. The implication is that the people are oblivious to their moral crimes against God, but still derive gratification from the religious services and offerings. "For so you love to do" indicates that this is something they did for themselves, not for God. "There was an abundance of 'religion' in the land, but no true piety and devotion to God."[82]

Amos 4:6–13 God graphically describes how He has been trying to get Israel's attention to their spiritual decay for a long time, but they have not been listening—or simply did not care. God sent them famine ("cleanness of teeth" means there is no food to chew), drought, scorching or blasting hot wind, mildew (on crops), locust invasions ("caterpillar" likely refers to a stage of the locust lifespan), plague, military defeat, the stench of death, and overthrow of their cities by foreign invasions. "Yet you have not returned to Me" is purposely repeated to show how obstinate and hard-hearted His people have become toward His word and His discipline. These people have not refused Him just once or twice, but time after time. Therefore, all that remains is full-scale destruction—God coming against them without mercy. "Prepare to meet your God" (4:12) is a summons for Israel to appear before God's tribunal for a final judgment and sentencing—and *they will not survive this.* The God of heaven is omnipotent (all-powerful) and omnipresent (everywhere), so there is no escaping His judgment and nowhere to hide from Him (4:13).

Amos 5:1–9 A "dirge" is a lament, like the sorrowful words spoken at a funeral. Amos offers a dirge for Israel, since their own funeral is coming soon, and there is no one to rescue them; only a small remnant of individuals from the entire nation will survive (5:1–3). "The virgin Israel" (5:2) may refer to the fact that Israel has not yet been conquered, but soon she will fall, and "there is none to raise her up."[83] Even so, God still implores the people to come to their senses: "Seek Me that you may live" (5:4, 6; see Isa. 55:6–7). God does not *want* to destroy His people, but He *will do so* to defend His holy name and punish their wanton injustice. However, He warns against offering hollow religious gestures (at Bethel or Gilgal, places of religious worship), for He will destroy these (5:5–7). He deserves instead sincere and genuine repentance, not mere formalities in the context of their condemned pagan religion. The God who made the constellations ("Pleiades and Orion") is certainly capable of wiping a nation from the face of the earth; God can both create *and* destroy (5:8–9).

Amos 5:10–20 Meanwhile, the prophet Amos briefly recounts the peoples' advanced state of decay to inspire a sense of urgency toward repentance (5:10–13):

- they will not listen to reproof; they hate honesty.
- they heavily tax and impose upon the poor while they themselves

- live in luxurious dwellings.
- their sins are "many" and "great."
- they mistreat the righteous.
- they take bribes to pervert justice.
- they will not defend the poor in courts of law ("at the gate").
- and they silence the "prudent" or wise counselors.

Amos also offers the solution (5:14–15): "Seek good and not evil"; "Hate evil, love good, and establish justice in the gate." In doing so, the Lord may withhold His judgment—just as He did with Nineveh (recall Jonah 3:1–10). God also contributes to this plea but implies that the people will not respond; thus, there will be mourning, weeping, and wailing throughout the land (5:16–17). Amos again intercedes, implying that Israel will not escape judgment unless they genuinely repent (5:18–20). There will be nowhere to hide from God; any attempt to escape will be useless. The "day of the LORD" will not be a "day" of deliverance for them, as they hope, but a day of darkness and desolation.

Amos 5:21-27 God returns to the discussion, showing His great contempt for religious activity that is devoid of all meaning, sincerity, or humility (5:21–24). In light of the peoples' arrogance and impenitence, God rejects their offerings of worship—they are useless, offensive, and "noise" to Him.

> Intermittent, occasional righteousness is really no righteousness at all. Partial, limited righteousness (keeping sacrifices while keeping idols) is no true righteousness either. True covenant keeping goes beyond special, discrete acts of devotion to steadfast loyalty (Mat. 7:21–23). It does not tolerate an admixture of devotions.[85]

Instead, God calls for a complete *spiritual* revival: "But let justice roll down like waters and righteousness like an ever-flowing stream" (5:24). Humility, moral purity, and justice are far more important to Him than mere offerings of animals or the trappings of religion (Mic. 6:8). He also reminds them that, even while He was preparing to bring them into the Promised Land, and even while they offered grain offerings to Him, the people of Israel kept for themselves (and some privately worshiped) the false gods of foreign lands (5:25–26; see Acts 7:42–43). "Sikkuth" is the name of Saturn, but likely refers to a god or "king" of the celestial world.[86] (In some translations, "king" is rendered "Molech," which means "king.") "Kiyyun" refers to the planet Saturn itself.[87] "Your star" reads in Hebrew, "your star gods"—i.e., the people worshiped the planets, stars, and constellations rather than the God who made them. Thus, they kept with them household idols, images, and other relics that they used in this worship. As a result, God will send them "beyond Damascus"—i.e., much farther north, which is the direction Assyria will take its captives (5:27).

Amos 6:1–14 Amos warns both Judah ("Zion") and Israel ("Samaria") of complacency, indifference to God's laws, and self-sufficiency (6:1–3; compare Rev. 3:14–19). He points to other great cities (and their nations) as evidence of Judah's and Israel's great privilege: "Calneh" is an ancient city on the Tigris River (Gen. 10:10) and may be a reference to Babylon; "Hamath" is a principal city of Syria; and "Gath" is one of the five city-states of Philistia. Judah and Israel are greater than these, and therefore bear greater responsibility to God; yet they did not live accordingly, thus bringing "calamity" on their head.

Amos cites the luxurious lifestyle of those who recline, sprawl, and fatten themselves through their wealth as evidence of their moral indifference (6:4–6). They take care of themselves, yet "have not grieved over the ruin of Joseph" (6:6b). For this, God promises to put an end to their careless and self-serving lifestyle (6:7–11). His judgment will affect every "house" (i.e., family) directly and adversely. Previously, the people boasted in the name of Jehovah; when calamity strikes, no one will dare mention His name for fear of further judgment.

Israel has long thought it could tweak justice and righteousness to accommodate its sinful lifestyle (just as people do today), but this is impossible (6:12–14). "There is a spiritual and moral order in the universe that is just as impossible to ignore as the natural order. It is as senseless to pervert justice as it is to expect horses to run on the rocks, or for oxen to plow on rock."[88] They rejoice in "a thing of nothing" (the meaning of "Lodebar"), and boast in their own accomplishments, yet do not rejoice in God or praise what He has done for them. Thus, He promises to afflict them from Hamath (i.e., Syria, to the north) to the Arabah (to the south)—i.e., from one end of the nation to the other.

Several visions, with explanations or accompanying narrative (7:1—8:3)

Amos 7:1–9 God then shows Amos a vision of a locust-swarm (i.e., creeping locusts, in the caterpillar stage) coming upon the land "after the king's mowing"—that is, after the first harvest of grass, which the king requires of the people for his use. Amos pleads with God to stop the invasion, and (in the vision), God does so. (Amos' plea may represent the collective intervention of all the prophets and righteous people who have begged God not to destroy Israel until now.)

Then God promises to burn the entire land with an enormous fire, but Amos pleads again for Him to relent, and He does so. In other words, God has been sparing Israel from being destroyed, and, while the prophets are aware of this and are those who have interceded, the people remain oblivious to this.

Then God shows Amos a plumb line—i.e., often, a heavy weight on the end of a string, to determine the plumbness (or, vertical exactness) of a wall. In this case, the plumb line shows how far *from* being vertical (or, morally upright) Israel really is, and that it (like a leaning or compromised wall) needs to be torn down. Thus, God says, "I will spare them no longer" (7:8). Even the "high places of Isaac and the sanctuaries of Israel"—venerated places of worship from ancient times—will not be spared, as nothing is worth saving. This third vision indicates to the prophet that God will not change His mind about what He has planned against Israel, so he (Amos) does not implore Him this time to stop but remains silent.

Amos 7:10—8:3 Amos' message is not only unpopular but deeply disturbing to the people's delusional sense of well-being. "Imagine how this message must have sounded to a materialistic, arrogant, and prosperous society. No doubt Amos' message fell on many deaf ears who could not possibly imagine their land being destroyed."[89] Thus, Amaziah, the priest of Bethel (the place of Baal worship, as instituted by Jeroboam; see 1 Kings 12:31–32), charges the prophet with criminal and seditious activity before King Jeroboam II of Israel. He claims that Amos said that Jeroboam II will die by the sword—which is not true—and that Israel will go into exile—which *is* true. (God pronounced a "sword" against the *house* of Jeroboam II, which will be fulfilled in the assassination of his son and successor, Zechariah; see 2 Kings 15:8–10.) Amaziah tells Amos to go back to Judah and do his prophesying there, and to leave the king of Israel alone.

Amos responds that he is not formally a prophet (i.e., is not of the school of prophets), but is simply a lowly farmer and shepherd. Even so, God called him to prophesy against Israel, and thus he did. Then Amos predicts what will happen to Amaziah personally for attempting to silence the mouth of one of God's prophets—essentially, trying to silence God Himself: Amaziah's wife will become a prostitute; his children will be executed by a foreign invader (Assyria); his land will be divided up and given away; and he himself will die in a foreign land (in exile) (7:16–17a). Any one of these is a great horror to any Israelite; the fourfold compounding of these indicates a severe divine condemnation. "Moreover, Israel will certainly go from its land into exile" (7:17b)—i.e., no number of threats, intimidation, or criminal charges against Amos is going to change what God has planned.

In another vision (8:1–2), God shows Amos a basket of summer fruit—the final harvest of fruit for the year. The implication is, again, that Israel is ripe for judgment, just as when summer fruit is ripe for picking; the earlier seasons (of mercy or the sparing of Israel) are all ended, and there will be no more seasons to come. As a result of this impending judgment, the people's songs (indicating a carefree, frivolous lifestyle) will turn to mourning (8:3); instead of scenes of pampered living, Israelite corpses will fill the land.

Second group of prophecies or oracles (8:4—9:15)

Amos 8:4–14 While Amos' prophecies are against Israel's manifold sins, God's anger is particularly directed against Israel's total disregard for—and exploitation of—"the needy" and "humble of the land" (8:4–7). The people also have little regard for the holy days (i.e., Sabbath, new moon, etc.) that are to be honored according to the Law of Moses. Instead, they cannot wait until these are over so they can continue selling and making a profit—all through illegal and deceptive means. Consequently, God promises not to forget Israel's many sins. The metaphorical references to floods, earthquakes, and the disappearing of the sun during the middle of the day all indicate the heavy devastation He will bring upon the land and its people (8:8–9). This will produce a time of great difficulty and mourning (8:10), and a famine not only for literal food and water, but for the words of the prophets (8:11). Since the people do not want to hear the word of God *now*, He will not reveal Himself *then*—through His wrath. Those who make oaths according to the false and impotent gods in Samaria and Dan "will fall and not rise again" (8:14).

Amos 9:1–10 The Lord makes clear, through the prophet Amos, that no Israelite will escape the divine judgment He is about to bring upon them. No matter where the people flee to escape, God will find them; even in the exile, God will continue to bring against them "evil and not good" (9:4). God reminds Israel just how powerful He is: He has full authority over the land and sea (9:5–6). Not only this, but He moves nations from one place to the next, as He sees fit. In fact, He has already done this by moving Israel from Egypt to the Promised Land, the Philistines from Caphtor (the island of Crete) to the mainland, and Syria from Kir (ancient Babylonia) to Damascus. God's full authority over the nations gives Him the right to *destroy* those that repeatedly ignore His words and His warnings. "[N]ot a kernel will fall to the ground" (9:9) may mean, "No sinner will escape," or, "No righteous man will be forgotten." In fact, both statements are true: no sinner *can* escape God's judgment, but in His judgment, God does not fail to preserve those who honor Him (Rev. 7:1–3, in principle). "All the sinners of My people will die by the sword" (9:10) indicates that judgment is inevitable; war is coming; there will be much bloodshed; and the people of Israel will be decimated.

Amos 9:11–15 Despite the awful things to come, God still offers hope for the distant future. "In that day" is often OT code language for "during the reign of the Messiah," which is the church age. The "booth" [lit., house, shelter, or tabernacle] of David will be revived and forever established through the reign of an Eternal King (Christ). While the prophecy here uses language that seems to refer to a literal or physical restoration, it is really a spiritual restoration of which the prophet speaks (see Acts 3:19–26). The idea of the plowman overtaking the reaper, etc., indicates a time of "unparalleled activity and abundance"[90]—not regressing nor declining, but moving ahead faster than all natural expectations. The restoration of the "captivity" [lit., fortunes] of Israel (9:14; see Jer. 30:3) does not refer merely to the people's removal *from* captivity, but also the restoration of what they had *before* it. Again, this is not to be taken literally here, especially since we never see Israel gain the wealth, power, and greatness that it once had, but spiritually—in the church, under the leadership of Christ.

Questions on *Amos*

1.) Amos prophesied during a prosperous and calm period in Israel's history. Because of this, his predictions of doom and gloom were not only very unwelcome, but the Israelites regarded them as unbelievable.

   a. Why do peace and economic prosperity cause people not to listen to warnings about future troubles?

   b. Does this still happen today—i.e., through the study of the OT prophets, is God warning *us* (our nation, or the world in general) about *our* future?

2.) In chapter 1 and 2, God condemns foreign nations for their crimes against humanity; He condemns Israel and Judah for crimes against His covenant with them. How does this compare with Christ's judgment against the ungodly world versus His judgment against the unfaithful members of His church?

3.) Since God reveals His plans through His prophets (3:7), what do we know factually about God or His plans *apart* from them? What has Jesus, as *the* Prophet of God (Luke 24:19, Acts 3:22, and 7:37), revealed about God that no *other* prophet has said?

4.) Amos lays particular condemnation upon the rich women of Samaria, the capital city of Israel (4:1–3). What does the moral indifference of a nation's women reveal about the spiritual state of being of the entire nation—and why? Is this still true today?

5.) God gave Israel numerous opportunities to repent through various forms of discipline (4:6–11), yet Israel would not listen (compare with Rev. 9:20–21 and 16:9–11). Why did Israel so chronically resist Him? What did God promise would happen because of their stubborn refusal to obey Him?

6.) In 5:21–27, it appears on the surface that God "hates" the very things that He commanded of Israel—festivals, solemn assemblies, burnt offerings, etc. But what is the real issue that He addresses here (see also 5:14 and Isa. 1:10–18)? Are things different today regarding our "spiritual sacrifices" (1 Peter 2:5)? Please explain.

7.) During the time that Amos prophesied, the word of God was readily available to the people (through the written Law of Moses, the written word of the prophets, and the spoken word of their contemporary prophets). Yet, God promised that "days are coming" when the people will be desperate to hear His word (8:11–12).

   a. Does this suggest that there has always been a limited window of opportunity to hear what God has said (see Isa. 55:6 and Mat. 25:1–13, for example)?

   b. Is this still true today—will the gospel always be readily available? Or will there be a time when people will be desperate to hear God's word?

Introduction to *Hosea*

Authorship: Hosea ("salvation") was the son of Beeri, and probably a contemporary of Amos who prophesied in Israel, and of Isaiah and Micah who prophesied in Judah (Isa. 1:1, Mic. 1:1). Except for what is written in the book of *Hosea*, nothing else is known of this prophet. However, his prophecies—including the object lessons in which he personally participated—have made him a celebrated prophet and his book an intriguing study of God's relationship with Israel. "Because of the tragic details of his personal life, Hosea has been known as the brokenhearted prophet and provides a good illustration of the brokenhearted Lord in His relationship with sinful mankind."[91]

While Amos was thundering and severe in his prophecies, Hosea is more tender and compassionate. While both prophets focus on the same sins, they tend to do so from different perspectives: Amos reveals stern contempt, Hosea reveals strong disappointment. Both, however, speak of God's wrath against and condemnation of Israel. Hosea especially emphasizes Israel's unfaithfulness to God as symbolized in his troubled marriage to Gomer, who became a prostitute. Just as Gomer was "a wife of harlotry" to Hosea, so Israel—as one betrothed to God through covenant—prostituted herself to all the surrounding nations and their idolatries (1:2). (This is graphically detailed in Ezek. 16:15–34. However, Hosea's ministry pre–dated Ezekiel's by about 150 years.)

Date and Place of Writing: Hosea prophesied "during the days [or, reigns] of Uzziah, Jotham, Ahaz, and Hezekiah"—all kings of Judah, and "the days of Jeroboam [II]," the king of Israel. This means that his prophecies covered anywhere from 25 to 50 years, depending on what time during Uzziah and Jeroboam's reigns he began and ended his prophetic career. (Both kings had unusually long reigns: Uzziah, 52 years [2 Kings 15:2], and Jeroboam, 41 years [2 Kings 14:23].) In any case, Hosea's prophecies seem to have ended only a few years before Assyria invaded Israel and began deporting Israelites into foreign exile. It seems, from the nature of the prophecies themselves, that Hosea was a native of Israel, but we do not know to which tribe he belonged. "His keen insight into the religious, social, and political conditions of his day indicates that he knew in an intimate way the things of which he spoke. His tender love for Israel argues for his being a citizen of the nation of whom he spoke."[92] Also, it is uncertain as to whether he delivered his prophecies verbally or only wrote them down for the people to read.

> [It seems clear] that Hosea himself wrote out the quintessence of his prophecies, as a witness of the Lord against the degenerate nation, at the close of his prophetic career, and in the book which bears his name. The preservation of the book, on the destruction of the kingdom of the ten tribes, may be explained very simply from the fact that, on account of the intercourse carried on between the prophets of the Lord in the two kingdoms, it found its way to Judah soon after the time of its composition, and was there spread abroad in the circle of the prophets, and so preserved.[93]

Purpose and Character of Writing: Hosea's sad marriage to Gomer parallels God's sad marriage to Israel (i.e., through covenant). "Hosea's personal tragedy is an intense illustration of Israel's national tragedy. It is a story of one-sided love and faithfulness that represents the relationship between God and Israel."[94] The subject matter is often emotional, therefore, and bounces from one topic to another often abruptly, making this a difficult book to outline. While God clearly expresses His love and affection for His people, He also just as clearly expresses His anger and disappointment with them. It is difficult, sometimes, to determine whether Hosea is expressing his personal love for Gomer or if he is relating God's love for Israel; in a sense, the interwoven characteristics of both relationships are intentional.

Israel's sustained spiritual infidelity is a most serious matter, however. God's love for His people does not mean He will spare them from the consequences of their poor decisions. The situation is not just bad, it is irreparable. What Hosea—the prophet *and* the book—expresses is not just a nation in trouble, but the *end* of a nation. "It was the sad duty of Hosea to prophesy the inevitable end of such a nation, which so long had enjoyed the special privileges of being 'God's chosen people,' but who had forsaken everything in the pursuit of their own lustful desires."[95]

Several passages in *Hosea* provide a general theological underpinning to NT doctrine. Jesus, for example, cites 6:6 in Mat. 9:13 regarding God's compassion for sinners. Also, Paul cites 1:10 and 2:23 in Rom. 9:25–26 with reference to the inclusion of Gentiles into God's plan of salvation, and so does Peter (1 Peter 2:10). And Paul again cites from *Hosea* (13:14) regarding the Christian's release from God's condemnation of sin through the victory of Christ (1 Cor. 15:54–55).

Overview of *Hosea*

Hosea 1:1 This verse is the only introduction to the prophet Hosea, and gives the general timeframe in which he prophesies (see "Introduction" on the kings mentioned here). "The word of the LORD" is a formulaic expression which supports the authority of both the message and the prophet. It is as when Paul introduces himself as "an apostle of Jesus Christ, by the will of God" (1 Cor. 1:1).

God's Relationship with Israel, as Symbolized by Hosea's Marriage (chps. 1—3)

Hosea 1:2-11 God instructs Hosea to "take to yourself a wife of harlotry" (1:2), specifically, a woman named Gomer.[96] This instruction can mean: marry a known prostitute; marry a woman who will be sure to engage in prostitution thereafter; or marry a woman who is wholly caught up in the "harlotry" of idolatry in Israel.[97] The last two meanings are most fitting to the book. Since Gomer represents Israel, she likely began as a morally pure woman, but then descended into harlotry after her marriage. If this is the case, then God tells Hosea ahead of time that this is what he can expect to happen, making his marriage to her particularly grievous. Just as Gomer will sin with other men, so Israel *has* sinned with foreign nations; just as Hosea loves Gomer and takes her back, so God desires to take Israel back—if she would quit her harlotry/prostitution with these nations. It is clear, however, that this latter scenario will not happen, and so God will send her away as an unfaithful wife (see Jer. 3:8).

The three children's names have symbolic reference to God's relationship with Israel:

- The firstborn son is named **Jezreel** ("God sows"; "God scatters [seed]") (1:3-5). In this case, the idea is that God will not sow peace and prosperity for Israel, but disaster. Just as Jehu, king of Israel, destroyed Ahab and Jezebel in the literal valley of Jezreel (2 Kings 9 and 10), so God will destroy Jehu's dynasty, to which

Jeroboam II belongs.[98] Even though Jehu carried out the will of God by destroying Ahab's dynasty, he showed no lasting loyalty to God (2 Kings 10:31); his successors showed even less. The prophecy, however, extends beyond merely the end of a royal dynasty; it also spells the end of the nation of Israel (1:4–5).

- The second child, a daughter, is named **Lo–ruhamah** ("she has not obtained compassion") (1:6–7). God has shown great patience, mercy, and forbearance to Israel so far; but the time for patience and compassion has ended; now it is time for judgment and punishment. However, God still maintains compassion for Judah and will continue to defend that nation, but not by helping them fight their battles as before. He will only act through His own supernatural intervention, as when He destroys 185,000 of Sennacherib's army overnight (2 Kings 19:35).
- The third child, a son, is named **Lo–ammi** ("not my people") (1:8–9). The theme of the entire Bible, regarding God's relationship with those faithful to Him, is: "I will be their God and they will be My people" (Exod. 6:7, Lev. 26:12, Jer. 24:7, 2 Cor. 6:16, etc.). But this covenantal promise is contingent upon continued faithfulness; in the absence of this, the relationship is no longer functional, and fellowship—but not the covenant—will end. Thus, "you are not My people and I am not Your God"—a chilling thing to hear from a people who has long enjoyed God's presence and providence.

On the heels of such depressing information, Hosea (or God?) erupts in a very positive view of Israel's future (1:10–11).[99] This is clearly messianic in nature, which means it will not be fulfilled until the time when Messiah (Christ) is reigning over God's kingdom and, with that kingdom authority, has established His church. This is because, based upon the passage:

- the fellowship between Israel and God is restored—but this demands a *new* covenant to be made, since the *old* covenant is fulfilled in the Messiah.
- Israel (or, simply, God's people) is numberless, but not limited to the physical lineage of Abraham, Isaac, and Jacob (see Gal. 3:28–29 and Rev. 7:9, for example).

- God's objective ("I will be…they will be…") is fulfilled (see Rev. 21:7).
- Israel and Judah will be regathered—a reference to the restoration of Israel that did not happen until Messiah came (see Mat. 19:28, Acts 1:6, 3:19–21, etc.).
- Israel and Judah are united under "one leader"—that is, Messiah (prophetically known as "David" or "the Branch" in the OT; see Isa. 11:1–5, Ezek. 34:23–24, etc.).
- "they will go up from the land" alludes to the departure of Israel from Egypt (Exod. 1:10), and thus—in Hosea's future—Israel's departure (so to speak) from the sin and shame that led to their exile in the first place.
- "for great will be the day of Jezreel"—i.e., this will be "day of the Lord" *not* for judgment (as was just promised in 1:4–5), but salvation, as depicted in Acts 2:16–21.

Hosea 2:1–13 Before God executes judgment against Israel, however, there is still opportunity for them to repent and come back to Him. Thus, God calls upon the "brothers" and "sisters" of Israel—likely, the faithful remnant—to plead (or "contend") with the disobedient while they are still "Ammi" ("my people") and "Ruhamah" ("obtained compassion"). As for the collective people of Israel, "she" is not acting like a faithful wife to God but is practicing harlotry with foreign nations. (It appears that whatever is being described here between God and Israel has already happened between Hosea and Gomer, especially in light of 3:1.[100]) God has done nothing but good for Israel; when she was "born" (i.e., when He rescued the children of Israel from Egypt and made them a nation), He saved her from destitution, shame, and hopelessness. But He can return her to this state unless she repents ("[puts] away her harlotry…") (2:2–3).[101] Furthermore, He will not show compassion to the present generation's posterity, since they are corrupted with cultic idolatry (2:4). Israel thought that they would profit by embracing the idolatrous practices of the surrounding nations; yet they forgot that it was God who has always been the source of their success and prosperity. (Again, Ezek. 16:15–34 presents this entire picture in far more graphic detail.)

In response to Israel's harlotry, God will no longer be the supportive husband, but will become an enemy to Israel, impeding her success and forcing her—ultimately, through the indignation of exile—to return to Him (2:6–7). Whatever He had given to Israel for her prosperity, He will reclaim (2:8–9); whatever joy, benefits, feasting, and agricultural abundance with which she had been blessed, He will remove (2:10–12). Instead of honoring the God who gave Israel life, made her rich by plundering others, and provided for her national security, Israel gave her heart instead to idols ("the Baals") and sacrificed to gods that could not hear, speak, save, or destroy (2:13). She chose adulterous "lovers"—the false gods of foreign nations—over the "living and true God" (1 Thess. 1:9).

Hosea 2:14–23 This section has a dual meaning: first, it states what God wants Israel to do *now* (but, historically, remains unfinished); second, it states what *will* happen "in that day"—a prophetic reference, again, to the messianic period (recall 1:10–11). After roaring from heaven with judgment (recall Amos 1:2), God will "speak kindly" to Israel to win His people back (2:14) and will restore His blessings as before. "Achor" (2:15) is the name of the valley where Achan and his family were executed in the days of Joshua (Josh. 7:26); while there was no hope for Achan, God promises hope for Israel. God wants to be a gentle and benevolent Husband ("Ishi") to Israel, not a "Baali," a Canaanite term for "lord" or "master" (2:16–17).[102] (Incidentally, Israel's exile would forever remove any inclination for the Jews to serve Baal or any other Canaanite idol.)

"In that day"—that is, in the messianic dispensation—God will protect His people from the ravages of the natural world and from warfare (2:18). Since this refers to an era of the spiritual people of God, rather than a people defined by ethnicity or geography, the natural world and human warfare will not be able to destroy them (Rom. 8:33–39). "In that day" God will establish an entirely new relationship with His people that is based upon righteousness, justice, mercy, compassion, and fidelity (2:19–20). A new betrothal can only be possible through a new covenant; in fact, it will not be God who will be the Husband to spiritual Israel, but His Son. "In that day," God will bless His people richly, and will "sow" within them spiritual blessings (Eph. 1:3). This new relationship will not only include literal Israelites, but also those who previously had no connection to Israel—i.e., those who were "not My people." We know for certain that this has reference to the inclusion of the Gentiles into God's salvation because Paul quotes this passage (2:23) regarding this (see Rom. 9:25–26), as does Peter (1 Peter 2:10).

Hosea 3:1–5 While God has been speaking with direct reference to Israel (2:1–23), it is the relationship between Hosea and Gomer that He references as well. While Hosea cannot do what God has said that *He* will do, nonetheless he is suffering from a wife who has abandoned him to prostitute herself to other men, just as Israel has left God to prostitute themselves to idolatry. The prophet speaks in the first person ("to me"; "I bought"; "I said"; etc.) rather than in the third person as before (recall 1:2).

God tells Hosea to "Go again, love a woman [Gomer]," even though she is clearly "an adulteress" (3:1), just as God loves Israel even though she has committed spiritual adultery against His covenant with her (see Jer. 3:6–13). Hosea, though heartbroken and shamed over what his wife has done, nonetheless—because of his great devotion to God—does what is asked of him. The price he pays for her to be restored to him is equivalent to what a slave is worth by Law (Exod. 21:32); barley is a food eaten only by animals and the poorest people. This low redemption price indicates just how low she had sunk in her moral degradation, devaluing herself in the process. He makes this payment to a man who has become a "companion" to Gomer, but not a true husband (recall 2:7); she may have become his slave-concubine.[103]

Hosea also tells Gomer that she is to remain with him from now on. The implication in chapters 1 and 2 is that God divorced Israel for all her infidelities, but He will still care for her. This seems to be the case between Hosea and Gomer: he will take her back and care for her. However, clearly their relationship has changed; "there is certainly no new marriage, nor any resumption of the old one."[104] She will remain in his house "for many days," but neither one will have conjugal relations with the other. Furthermore, Hosea does not allow her to leave his house to "play the harlot," but she must submit to his oversight.

> Mention of the bride price makes clear one of the points of the passage: the wife is Hosea's property. She is paid for, and under Israelite law, he owns her and can do with her as he wishes. He can now *enforce* chastity, keeping her at home, allowing her to be intimate with no one, not even himself.[105]

The connection to God and His relationship with Israel is clear (3:4–5). Even so, He will redeem Israel from their shame and hopelessness—i.e., He will once again identify Himself as their God—but they will remain without the full rights and privileges they once had—i.e., they will not (yet) be known as "His people." "God will restrain Israel's promiscuity in a drastic way—by dissolving it as a nation, leaving it fatally deprived of basic national institutions of government, worship, divination, etc."[106] This is evident in the historical record between Israel's exile into Assyria and the New Testament era: they had no king; they were bereft of the sacrificial system; they had no ark of the covenant (see Jer. 3:16) or high priestly intercession (represented by the ephod). Furthermore, they no longer had anything to do with idols, nor did they erect sacred pillars in honor of false gods.[107] They would live under God's providential care, but would not enjoy the privileges of marriage until the time when God will provide a new husband for His people under a new covenant (Jer. 31:31–34).[108] This new husband will be a King ("David"), making the reunified nation of Israel *and* Judah a royal people. All this will happen "in the last days," i.e., in the messianic dispensation, which refers to the time in which Christ reigns over the kingdom of God and becomes the head of His church (Acts 2:33, Col. 1:18).

God's Rebuke of His People (4:1—6:3)

<u>Hosea 4:1–19</u> In this chapter, the prophet Hosea speaks to Israel on behalf of God. His message is: God has a case against Israel, and it is one that they cannot rebut or annul (4:1a). In other words, God has been

faithful to His covenant, yet His people have been grossly unfaithful; His case against them, then, is just; He substantiates it through manifold charges of sin, specific violations of covenant, and idolatry. Therefore, "let no one find fault [or, contend, as in a court of law]" with *God*, since He is not the one who is guilty or on trial (4:4a).

Hosea (speaking for God) charges his people with acting as if they had no knowledge of God at all, and for having no desire to learn of or obey Him (4:1b–6). He lists specific charges: swearing (either vulgar language or the making of false vows), deception, murder, stealing, adultery, violence, and much bloodshed. These lawless and godless sins are the gutter behaviors of unspiritual heathens; yet the Israelites regularly engage in them. They live as though they had no spiritual direction, despite being recipients of the finest theocratic law the world had ever known (i.e., the Law of Moses) to govern them. As a result, "the land mourns" (4:3)—i.e., the moral degradation of the people warrants divine judgments, punishments, and curses that negatively affect the natural world (e.g., drought, famine, pestilence, blight, etc.).

The Israelites, in their blinding pride and open defiance, nonetheless deny any wrongdoing; as they contend with the righteous priests, so they contend with God (4:4). As a result, they continue to "stumble" (sin) instead of taking responsibility for their actions (4:5). God says, through Hosea, "My people are destroyed for lack of knowledge" (4:6)—not because of a shortage of truth or relevant information, but because of their careless disregard for anything God has revealed from heaven.

As a result of such irreverence and moral carelessness, God promises to reject Israel as His priest—characterizing the entire nation as a holy priesthood (Exod. 19:5–6)—because a priest who has forgotten the law of the God to whom he is to minister is worthless. "I also will forget your children"—the immediate descendants of Hosea's wicked generation will not know or enjoy the manifold blessings that God has been lavishing upon Israel for centuries. Instead, they will only know exile, separation from the Promised Land, and the hardship of living amidst heathens.

The many sins of the people have only increased their punishment; regardless of *who* has sinned—whether priests or laymen—God will see to it that they will not profit *from* their sin but will face shame and retribution (4:7–10).

The rest of the chapter (4:11–19) focuses specifically on the ignorant, foolish, and hopeless trust Israel has put in its idolatry. "Harlotry" has a two-fold meaning here: **first**, it refers to the people's violation of God's covenant (i.e., spiritual adultery) (as in 4:11–13a); **second**, it implies sexual immorality, which was rampant in the cultic worship and festivities of idolatry (as in 4:13b–14). Thus, promiscuity, sexual indulgence, and orgiastic rites—all fueled by the spirit of false religion and the intoxication of alcohol—have rendered the people insensitive to their own depravity and lacking in moral judgment; "so the people without understanding are ruined" (4:14b). Even so, God holds the men—the husbands, fathers, and rulers—more responsible than the women ("daughters," "brides"), since the men are the ones who have set a wicked example for them.[109]

God also warns Israel not to infect Judah with their penchant for idolatry; likewise, He warns Judah not to follow Israel's stumbling (4:15–19). "Gilgal" used to be the place where the school of the prophets (under Elisha) was located (2 Kings 2:1, 4:38); now it has become a place of idol worship. "Beth-aven" [lit., a house of nothing] is a region near the ancient site of Ai, on the northern boundary of the tribe of Benjamin (Josh. 18:12). In the present text, however, it may be a symbolic name for Bethel, the southern city in which Jeroboam I set up calf worship (1 Kings 12:26–33). In other words, it is, in God's eyes, a place of nothing. Judah has been warned, but Israel pays no attention to any of this; they are "joined to idols" (4:17) and "play the harlot [i.e., worship idols—MY WORDS] continually" (4:18) and do so without shame. ("Ephraim," one of the most prominent tribes, represents the entire nation of northern Israel.)

Hosea 5:1–7 From Mizpah (on the southern border of Israel, and to the west of the Jordan) to Tabor (on the northern border, to the east of the Jordan)—in other words, from one end to the other, and from side to side—the people have revolted against God (5:1–7). God reminds them that He knows all that they have done—nothing is hidden from His sight (compare Heb. 4:13)—and that "they do not know the LORD" (5:4). Furthermore, "their deeds will not allow them to return to their God" (5:4). This can mean: their pursuit of idolatry destroys any *desire* to return to God; they are too spiritually and morally vacant to know *how* to return to God; there is no more *opportunity* to return to God; or all of these. Judah, while warned not to follow suit, has already "stumbled with them" (5:5); later, Judah will become even worse than Israel (Ezek. 16:46–52). "[T]he new moon" (5:7) refers to a month's time (i.e., from one new moon to the next); this vague reference seems to mean that in a brief time, their land will be devoured or destroyed.[110]

Hosea 5:8–17 God calls to the people to *pay strong attention* to what He is saying (5:8–9). This warning not only goes out to Israel, but also to Judah. (Benjamin is part of what is known as "Judah.") This is because Judah is already showing signs of moral failure; "those who move a boundary" refers to those who are dishonest, deceitful, and unlawful (Deut. 19:14, 27:17). As for Ephraim (Israel), God will be like a destroying enemy to them—a moth, a rottenness, a sickness, an ulcer (or wound), and a lion (5:12–14).[111] In other words, not just in one way but in many ways He will bring upon them many pains, sorrows, and losses for having turned away from Him. (These warnings were predicted in Deut. 28:15–68 and Lev. 26:14–43.) "King Jareb" [lit., king of contention; the avenging king] is likely a nickname or epithet for the king of Assyria (5:13; see also 10:6). This refers to the time when Menahem and Hoshea, kings of Israel, paid tribute to Assyria (2 Kings 15:19, 17:3), but nothing good came of this. It may also be a prophecy for when Ahaz, king of Judah, sends for Tiglath-pileser, king of Assyria, to help him fight against Israel and Syria's collusion against him (Ahaz). That appeal will not help Ahaz but will only hasten Judah's own destruction (see 2 Chron. 28:16–21 and Isa. 7:1–25). In any case, God will send Israel into exile "until they acknowledge their guilt and … will earnestly seek Me" (5:15)—i.e., long enough for them to come to their senses and take responsibility for what they have done (compare Luke 15:14–19).

Hosea 6:1–3 This section appears to be a plea from Hosea himself, offering a hopeful petition to his countrymen to wake up from their delusional state of mind and "return to the Lord." He seems to look beyond the time when God has already unleashed His wrath against them (6:1); there would no need to talk about healing, bandaging, and reviving unless there had already been tearing, wounding, and striking down (in death). (The "raise us up on the third day" conspicuously foreshadows the resurrection of Christ from His death as a symbolic raising up of Israel from their own death.) Instead of God being a moth, rottenness, sickness, etc. (recall 5:12–14), He will be like the dawn of a new day (or era), like a welcome "spring rain," implying healthy and abundant crops. The prophet pleads with his people to come to their senses, but God's response in the verses that follow reveal that this is a hopeless entreaty. Israel simply does not *want* to repent of its sins or "know the Lord."

Israel's Crimes and God's Promise of Judgment (6:4—13:16)

Hosea 6:4—13:16 The rest of the book of *Hosea* is a series of pronouncements of judgment against "Ephraim" (Israel). In this section we see:

- **Repeated descriptions of Israel's moral crimes against God, including:** false or superficial loyalty (6:4); violations against God's covenant with Israel (6:7, 8:1); murder (6:9); rebellion (7:13); idolatry (8:4, 13:1–2); seeking help from foreign nations rather than God (8:9–10, 12:1); and all sorts of wickedness, injustices, and lying (7:2, 10:13, 11:12, 12:7).
- **Repeated promises of punishment** (7:12, 9:7, 13:16), including exile to Assyrian lands (9:17, 10:6).
  - The repeated mention of "Egypt" (8:13) is meant figuratively. It recalls the time when Israel was still enslaved to the "iron furnace" of Egyptian bondage (Deut. 4:20). God is telling them that they will return to a form of enslavement, as a people under the bondage of the Assyrian Empire (9:3, 11:5). "Egypt stands for their captivity and Memphis, a chief city of Egypt, represents

a burying ground for their [Israel's] luxuries."¹¹²
- Israel has made for itself idols of wood, designed by craftsmen, indicating that the nation would rather bow to a man-made god than to the living and true God (8:6). Thus, "they sow the wind and they reap the whirlwind" (8:7)—i.e., they will be thoroughly disappointed in that in which they have placed their trust. Their harvests will either not produce a crop, or it will be eaten by "strangers" (i.e., foreign invaders; an invading army).
- Hosea speaks here: "My God will cast them away because they have not listened to Him; and they will be wanderers among the nations" (9:17). This succinctly sums up not only Israel's awful future, but also the cause of it. The more God called His people (through the prophets) to return to Him, they more Israel turned to idolatry and pagan sacrifices (11:2). Thus, "the sword will whirl against their cities" (11:6) and will slaughter the people.
- Even though God had been Israel's Savior from Egypt, the people became proud and arrogant once they settled in the land of Canaan (13:4–6; see Deut. 8:11–20). Therefore, God will be like a lion, leopard, and bear to them—an animal that will tear them to pieces and show them no mercy (13:7–8). This is even more graphic in 13:16: "They [the Israelites—MY WORDS] will fall by the sword, their little ones will be dashed in pieces, and their pregnant women will be ripped open." In other words, the brutality of a foreign invasion will bring various atrocities to Israel, but they brought this upon their own head.
- **Repeated recollections of Israel's ancient past:**
  - The sin of Israel at Baal-peor, in the land of Moab (9:9–10; see Num. 25:1–5). As God did not spare those people (but killed 24,000 of them with a plague), so He will not spare Israel for their own fornication with idols.
  - The sin of Gibeah, when certain men of that city (of Benjamin) raped and killed a Levite's concubine, erupting in civil war when the tribe of Benjamin refused to condemn them (10:9; see Judg. 19—20). Likewise, God will virtually decimate Israel just as Benjamin nearly became extinct through civil war.

- God "called" His "son" (Israel, represented by Ephraim, one of its most prominent tribes) out of Egypt, referring to Israel's exodus out of their imprisonment with Egypt (11:1, 3–4). As God's "son," the Israelite tribes should have respected Him as their Father.
- References to the cities of the valley (Admah and Zeboiim) which God destroyed, along with Sodom and Gomorrah (11:8; see Gen. 14:8 and 19:1–29). Israel has proven to be no better than these cities, and therefore will share in their destruction.[113]
- The birth of Jacob and Esau, and Jacob's wrestling with an angel (12:3; see Gen. 25:24–26, 28:13–19, and 35:10–15). God promised that the older son would serve the younger, overriding all natural expectations, to bring Jacob (Israel) to glory, but Israel showed little gratitude for this. And Jacob, for all his personal faults, was a man who sought out God; yet his descendants have little desire for Him.
- Jacob's (a.k.a. Israel's) working for a total of fourteen years to acquire Rachel as his wife (12:12; see Gen. 28:5 and 29:chapter). In other words, Jacob knew the meaning of perseverance and endurance to obtain a desired outcome; Israel, however, was unwilling to deny themselves immediate gratification (through idolatry).
- God's providential care for Israel in their sojourning through the wilderness (13:5; see Deut. 8:2–4). As God took care of Israel then, so He could do so now—*if* Israel would submit to Him.
- God's having given Israel a king (i.e., Saul) and having torn his kingdom from him (13:10–11; see 1 Sam. 8:4–20, 15:26). Human kings are of no match for God, cannot rival Him, and certainly will never replace Him. Israel should have known this but were blinded in their pursuit to be like all the other nations.
- **Repeated appeals of tender compassion from God to "Ephraim" (Israel), and the pain of their having rejected Him:**
  - "I would redeem them, but …" (7:13).
  - "And they do not cry to Me from their heart …" (7:14).
  - "Yet they devise evil against Me" (7:15).
  - "Yet it is I who taught Ephraim to walk, I took them in My arms,

but they did not know that I healed them. I led them with … bonds of love" (11:3–4).
- "So My people are bent on turning from Me … None at all exalts Him." (11:7).
- "How can I give you up, O Ephraim?" (11:8).
- "Ephraim surrounds Me with lies … even against the Holy One who is faithful" (11:12).
- "It is your destruction, O Israel, that you are against Me, against your help" (13:9).

This section (6:1—13:16) also produces several prophecies that are quoted in the NT:

- "For I delight in loyalty [Heb., *chesed*; lit., piety, in the form of mercy or compassion][114] rather than sacrifice" (6:6)—quoted by Jesus (Mat. 9:13) in response to the Jews who were indignant toward Him for spending time with "sinners."
- "Then they will say to the mountains, 'Cover us!' And to the hills, 'Fall on us!'" (10:8)—quoted in Luke 23:30 and Rev. 6:16, regarding those facing God's judgment.
- "When Israel was a youth I loved him, and out of Egypt I called my son" (11:1)—attributed to Jesus, whose family fled to Egypt when He was very young to escape Herod's wrath, but then returned to Nazareth (Mat. 2:15).
- Israel's smug statement of "Surely I have become rich, I have found wealth for myself" (12:8) is virtually quoted in Jesus' letter to the church in Laodicea (Rev. 3:17).
- "O death, where are your thorns? O Sheol [lit., the grave; the realm of the dead—MY WORDS], where is your sting?" (13:14) is quoted by Paul (1 Cor. 15:55) with reference to Christ's victory over the grave and our victory *through* Him, anticipating our own resurrection from the dead.

Future Blessings Promised (14:1–9)

14:1–9 As is typical with the minor prophets, after all the talk of judgment, doom, and destruction, God offers hope for the future. In virtually every case, this refers to the far distant future—i.e., the messianic age, which is another 700+ years after the fall of Israel—but it is promised, nonetheless. The redemption/restoration of Israel is one of the great promises of the OT and cannot be fulfilled historically except through God's invitation for Israel (first) and then the Gentiles to enter the kingdom of God. This kingdom, ruled by God's own Son (Messiah/Christ) will also unify the two kingdoms of Israel and Judah as one people, and *all* believers—Jews and Gentiles alike—will be united as "one new man" in Christ (Eph 2:13–18).

In this future state of being, God will heal the nation of Israel, His anger having already been spent upon them through their exile into Assyria (14:4). Instead of being sick, wounded, and greatly harmed by divine punishment, Israel will be like a healthy, luxurious plant, filled with life, beauty, and fruit (14:5–7). God will finally break Israel of their fixation on idolatry and will prove Himself once again to be the source of their health and prosperity (14:8).

The book ends with an invitation to the reader to take all its words to heart: "Whoever is wise, let him understand these things …" (14:9). This is reminiscent of Jesus' own words at the end of His sermon on the mount (Mat. 7:24–27). The message is: God's ways are *always* right, and those who are truly righteous will *always* "walk in them"; but those who resist His ways and sin against Him will *always* fail and ultimately be destroyed. "The words [of the book of Hosea] are not simply directed to his contemporaries, thus being of no more than arcane [deep; mysterious] interest to us. Rather, the 'ways of Yahweh [Jehovah]' are a guide to the righteous, and a source of understanding to the intelligent of all successive periods."[115]

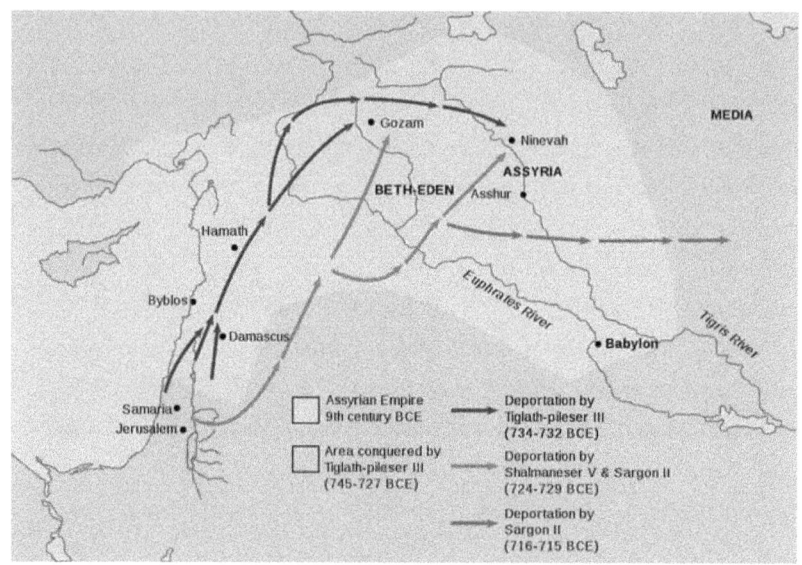

Questions on *Hosea*

1.) What most captures your attention as you read *Hosea*?

2.) Why did God put the prophet Hosea through a heartbreaking marriage just to make a point with the nation of Israel? (There are several answers.)

3.) The idolatry described in *Hosea* involves far more than merely bowing down to a carved or graven image. What are these other characteristics? Do we see similar characteristics in worldly people today?

4.) What exactly is meant by "the spirit of harlotry" (4:12, 5:4)? Can a person have a sinful *heart* without committing visible sinful *actions*? Please explain.

5.) In 4:6, God said, "My people are destroyed for lack of knowledge." It was not that God *withheld* "knowledge" from them, but that they *rejected* it. Can *Christians* be "destroyed" by lack of knowledge? What is the *nature* of this destruction?

6.) The Israelites in Hosea's day lived in a kind of alternate reality: what they *claimed* was "true" was not, and what God *said* was true they ignored. How might people do this today regarding their moral responsibility to God?

7.) God's voice in *Hosea* is one of the most emotionally charged of all the prophetic books. Why do you suppose He chose to reveal Himself in this way? How does this benefit us? What if we never saw God's "emotional side," so to speak?

Introduction to *Micah*

Authorship: "Micah" ("who is like Jehovah?") was a native of Moresheth, a city in the tribe of Judah, about twenty miles southwest of Jerusalem (1:1). His full name is Micaiah, though he is not to be confused with the prophet Micaiah in 1 Kings 22:8ff.[116] Micah, along with Hosea and Amos, was a contemporary of Isaiah who had already been engaged in his ministry several years before Micah began his own; "In some ways, Micah is an Isaiah in miniature."[117] Unlike Isaiah, who lived in the city and was a counselor to the king, Micah was apparently a man of humble means; Isaiah spoke to the leaders of the land, Micah spoke on behalf of the poorer people; Isaiah spoke predominantly about Jerusalem, while Micah spoke of Judah and Samaria. Yet, "Each [prophet] recognized the divine sovereignty and holiness of God, and each pointed out that to violate that would bring inevitable doom. Jehovah's favor could be obtained only by the faithfulness and righteousness of the people as they leaned on God for help, and not from the strength of men."[118]

Apart from what appears in the opening of the book of *Micah*, nothing else is known about the prophet himself. "Nothing is known of Micah's occupation. From his book one can surmise that Micah lived close to both the people and the soil and possessed a keen sympathy for both."[119] He is mentioned later in Jer. 26:18–19, but no new information is provided, other than that no harm came to him as a result of his preaching, and King Hezekiah actually listened to him and changed his own heart as a result of his messages. "A man of dauntless courage and conviction, Micah must have been a man of extraordinary personality."[120]

Date and Place of Writing: Micah himself provides the dating for his book: "… in the days of Jotham, Ahaz, and Hezekiah, kings of Judah" (1:1). These kings reigned from the mid-8th century to the very early 7th century. This is about a fifty–year span, although this does not mean that Micah's prophetic career spanned this entire period. A conservative timeframe for this career is ca. 735–700 BC, with the majority of his prophecies closer to the earlier date (735). This would put these prophecies in the few years or decades ahead of the destruction of Samaria (Israel) by Assyria (722/721 BC). "The reign of King Ahaz, one of the most wicked kings of all Judah's history, is in the background of much of Micah's prophecy. It is possible that the dark picture presented by Micah's prophecy reflects the reign of Ahaz, while the brighter aspects of Micah's prophecy reflect the godly rule under King Hezekiah."[121]

It is not known where Micah wrote down his prophecies. Likely, it was over a course of time, and possibly in various locations. Based upon Jer. 26:18–19, he seems to have given his prophecies first vocally, possibly in Jerusalem, and then wrote them down afterward.

Purpose and Character of Writing: The book of *Micah* has three main sections (chps. 1–2, 3–5, and 6–7), each of which has three basic elements: the indictment of the people's sin; God's judgment because of that sin; and God's ultimate restoration of His people. "The most prominent theme in Micah is judgment. … The judgment motif is so strong in this book that several scholars have claimed that Micah only preached judgment."[122] While this is an extreme view, it is fair to say that Micah's prophecies to Israel are indeed a voice of doom, since their "wound is incurable" (1:9) and therefore must be subjected to the very worst punishment of all—destruction and exile. Israel, the capital city of which is Samaria (and the prophets often identified the northern tribes of Israel as "Samaria"), has exhausted all the patience, mercy, and opportunities for repentance that God had extended to them over the last several hundred years. There is nothing left to do, nothing left to say, and nothing left to save (as a nation); the people of Israel will either be destroyed by Assyria in a brutal invasion—the Assyrians were unmerciful and barbaric in war—or will be carted off to foreign lands, forever removed from the land God had gifted them as an inheritance.

The final decades of Israel reveal a nation that has lost its moral compass, its leaders being unable or unwilling to stand in the gap and instigate social or political reform. To Judah, Micah's prophecies are intended as a voice of reason—and stern warning—not to follow in the footsteps of Israel, otherwise Jerusalem itself "will become a heap of ruins"

(3:12). Given Hezekiah's reforms (2 Chron. 29), his reinstitution of the Passover (2 Chron. 30), and his destruction of many of the idols in the land of Judah (2 Chron. 31:1–2), the Judean king took Micah's and his fellow prophets' words seriously.

While Hosea dealt heavily with Israel's idolatry, Micah focuses (like Amos) more upon the social injustices from the men in power to those who are powerless and treated as expendable. Much of Micah's writing is severe in tone; such passages remind us of Amos' blunt and fiery thundering. However, it also contains some poetic beauty like what is found in *Isaiah*.[123] It seems that when Micah is being severe, his language is sharp, his sentences short and brittle, and his transitions (of subject matter) sudden and without warning.[124] While he is speaking of better things, however (as in chapter 4, for example), his language settles down, is fluid and flowing, and is much easier to read. There are several lengthy passages in which the prophet speaks of much better things to come—a glorified and (by implication) unified Israel and Judah—after the Israel's punishment has run its course. This looks forward to "the last days" (4:1), a messianic timestamp that looks far ahead to the time of Christ and His church. Indeed, Micah calls upon God to "Shepherd Your people with Your scepter, the flock of Your possession" (7:14) during a time when He will "have compassion on us" and will cast "all their sins into the depths of the sea" (7:19).

One of the more notable prophecies in *Micah* is the prediction of the city (Bethlehem) from which the Messiah (the "ruler in Israel") will come (5:2). This passage was so well-known by the Jews that when Herod the Great sought information about Jesus, the chief priests and scribes quoted it to him (Mat. 2:1–6). Another well-known passage (7:6) is quoted by Jesus, with reference to his gospel being a message that will divide families and entire households (Mat. 10:34–35). Probably the most familiar passage to modern Bible students, however, is in 6:6–8: "He has told you, O man, what is good …" These powerful words sum up the entire message of all the prophets, and serve as the moral platform for the gospel of Christ.

Overview of *Micah*

Micah 1:1 Micah introduces himself as a prophet of God—one to whom "the word of the Lord came"—who prophesies in the pre-Assyrian captivity of Israel (late 8th century BC). His prophetic career spans the reigns of three Judean kings—Jotham, Ahaz, and Hezekiah—but his prophecies deal predominantly with the decadent nation of Israel ("Samaria").

Micah 1:2–16 The book opens with an immediate pronouncement of divine judgment against Israel ("Samaria"). Micah portrays God as a warrior-king who comes to execute a much-deserved punishment against His rebellious people. The language is purposely exaggerated and poetic (1:2–3), but the meaning is serious and very real. The "Lord God [Yahweh]" (1:2) has been watching "from His holy temple" all that Israel has been doing for many, many years; He cannot simply watch any longer, but must act in order to preserve His holy name *and* put an end to His people's multiplied transgressions. Their idolatry has not only corrupted Israel, but also Jerusalem (Judah), where His temple is located (1:5, 9). Thus, He promises to turn Samaria, the capital of Israel, into "a heap of ruins" and "pour stones into her valley" (1:6)—i.e., the stones of their city and cultic shrines will be cast into the valley to make way for vineyards. The idea is that the *city* will be turned into a place of *agriculture*, to remove a centralized power from northern Israel forever. The idols that Israel took so much delight in worshiping and frolicking over will be destroyed (1:7). God typically likens idolatry to a spiritual harlotry (prostitution), in which the Israelites prostituted themselves to idols, but it was *they* who had to pay the price (see Ezek. 16:30–37).

The prophet Micah then personally involves himself in the prophetic oracle (1:8). The prophet's grief and lament are due to the "incurable" wound of Israel—a reference to the unavoidable assault of Assyria that will come against them due to their persistent idolatry. The effects of this "wound" will be felt in Jerusalem as well as Gath (Philistia) (1:9). God tells Micah, however, to "tell it not in Gath" (1:10)—i.e., do not give Israel's enemies an opportunity to rejoice over Israel's affliction.

Assyria will also assault several ancient cities of Judah (Beth–le–aphrah, Shaphir, Zaanan, Beth–ezel, and Maroth) (1:10–12), likely because they have all participated in Israel's idolatry. But God speaks against Lachish in particular, apparently because it was the first city to bring Israel's idolatry into Judah ("the beginning of sin") (1:13). "Moresheth–gath" is the Micah's birthplace (1:14; recall 1:1), the suffix "–gath" indicating its proximity to the Philistine city of Gath (and possibly because it was once under Philistine control). "Achzib" and "Adullam" are cities between Jerusalem and Moresheth (1:14–15). God is promising to destroy all these cities for whatever part they played in promoting idolatry in Judah: "they [i.e., your children, or descendants—MY WORDS] will go from you into exile." The Assyrian invasion is simply a foreshadow of an even greater calamity to come upon Judah; the Babylonian captivity will give reason for serious mourning (i.e., shaved heads).

Micah 2:1–13 Chapter 2 of *Micah* provides a strong indictment against those in Israel who oppress the weak and helpless, especially those who are princes and rulers. The aristocracy has become powerful and arrogant, having no remorse for imposing upon those who cannot resist them (compare James 5:4–6). A "woe" is tantamount to a curse (2:1) since the oppressors have violated the basic human rights of their own countrymen. They covet another man's field, house, and possessions, and then steal them (2:2; think of Ahab's theft of Naboth's vineyard, 1 Kings 21:1–16). They walk haughtily, as if they could get away with all of this (2:3), yet their own land and possessions will be given over to "the apostate" (Assyria) as a bitter calamity for their sins (2:4–5). They exploit the people by stripping them of their clothes and possessions (2:8–9), bringing upon themselves "a painful destruction" (2:10). God mocks the people by saying, in effect, "If a lying and drunken man were to claim to speak the oracles of God, you would give him your full attention" (paraphrase of 2:11). This is similar to Paul's charge against the Corinthians, who gave full attention to false teachers, but resisted the instruction of a genuine apostle of Christ (2 Cor. 11:4–21).

Micah's prophesying is undoubtedly unpopular, because the truth is *always* unpopular to those who live in defiance of it. The people tell

Micah not to speak out, but if he and other prophets (the "they" in 2:6) remain silent, then God cannot hold the people accountable for their crimes (this is comparable to Ezekiel's role as "the watchman"—Ezek. 33:1–9). His message will be good to those who listen to the "Spirit of the Lord," but those who want to silence God's prophets will reject it (2:7).

The "assembling" of Israel (and Judah) into one "fold" (2:12–13) indicates a re-gathering of His people long after His punishments and their exiles have run their course. The shepherds of Israel have failed the people, and have dishonored God (see Ezek. 34:1–10), but God will raise up a new Shepherd ("the breaker")—an obscure reference to the Messiah—who will "break out" His people from darkness, shame, and captivity, and will lead them forth as a heavenly king to a glorious future.

Micah 3:1–12 Meanwhile, Micah continues his denouncement of the rulers of Israel (3:1). They hate justice but love evil; they devour people as though cannibalizing them, as though the people were but animals to cut up and consume (3:2–3). But when they themselves cry out to God for help (against the Assyrian invasion), He will refuse to help them because of their penchant for "evil deeds" (3:4).

The false prophets of Israel only prophesy "Peace" to those who have something to give to them (as a bribe or extortion); otherwise, they will "declare holy war" upon them (3:5). They offer nothing better for Israel than do its wicked rulers. But God is about to silence their alleged visions: He will give them darkness instead of light; He will give them shame instead of (self-serving) glory; they will "cover their mouths" in humiliation because they will have no message for the people (3:6–7). Micah, on the other hand, is "filled with power—with the Spirit of the Lord" (3:8) because he is a genuine prophet of God and declares nothing but what is right and true. And in this role, he levels a strong judgment against the wicked rulers who abuse the people, and against the false prophets who preach "Peace" when God promises calamity (3:10–11). These men and their ungodly influence have infected Judah, and Jerusalem in particular, so that "on account of [them]" God will bring disaster upon His people in Jerusalem just as He is about to do in Samaria (3:12).

> What a bombshell this oracle [3:9–12] must have been in Jerusalem. The city of Jerusalem and the temple were sacred. How could any disaster fall on the city? It was unbelievable. The [false] prophets, priests, judges, and government leaders "leaned on" Yahweh. They believed in the Davidic covenant. They "trusted" Yahweh. They did not consider it relevant to the covenant that they constantly hated justice and always perverted the way of righteousness. ... These leaders sought to increase the power of Jerusalem, but only so their power could grow with it. Because of their personal motives, the rulers killed and cheated anyone who stood between them and greater authority. Nevertheless they could justify their greed by claiming that Yahweh supported them in their efforts.[125]

When men decide only to do evil, they become blind to the truth and the reality of their own depraved situation (2 Thess. 2:10–12). Even though Judah's destruction still lay over one hundred years in Micah's future, God pronounces here the surety of that destruction, and Judah will not be able to rescind it.

Micah 4:1–13 After such dark and strong language, Micah now sees the future of Jerusalem long after these disasters have passed (4:1ff). (This section [4:1–5] is comparable to Isa. 2:2–5.) "[I]n the last days" indicates the final age or dispensation of God's people—one that will not be followed by yet another age or dispensation. This passage cannot refer to anything other than the church age in which Messiah (Christ) reigns as the Redeemer. The "mountain of the house of the Lord" refers prophetically to Zion, upon which Christ will build the spiritual city of God; figuratively, this refers to Christ's church, the New Jerusalem (Gal. 4:25–26, Heb. 12:22, and Rev. 21:1ff). God will raise this mountain/city above all others since it will be the sanctuary of God's people. Many people from every nation will stream to it since it is from there that God's word will "go forth" (4:2) as a light for all those who seek Him.

In this spiritual/messianic context, people will need implements for agriculture (plowshares) rather than implements of war (swords), since their focus will then be upon bringing in a great harvest (4:3). God is all that His people will need for protection (compare Zech. 2:1–5), and they will no longer need to engage in physical warfare. All the "wars" at that time will be spiritual in nature (2 Cor. 10:3–5, Eph. 6:12). Instead of the threat of a foreign invader, or oppression from a foreign power, God's people "will sit under his vine and under his fig tree" (4:4)—i.e., will live in peace, security, and prosperity. While Micah's contemporaries "walk" in the name of a false god, in the reign of the Messiah "we will walk in the name of the LORD our God forever and ever" (4:5).

"In that day" (4:6) further indicates the "last days" (recall 4:1)—a time in which the present conditions, expectations, and limitations will all be changed. This is not a prediction of a future Paradise on earth, as Premillennialism assumes, but a spiritual life unencumbered by human weakness, physical circumstances, or the debilitation of sin. The "lame" and "outcasts"—for example, think of lepers (Lev. 13:45–46) or eunuchs (Deut. 23:1)—will no longer be excluded due to any physical deformity, imperfection, or disease. All such human or earthly problems will not keep them from serving God as their King (4:6–7). "Mount Zion" is, in messianic prophecies, the code phrase associated with Christ's church. The "tower of the flock" (4:8) alludes to a raised wooden tower that the shepherd of a large flock might use to oversee his sheep. Some commentators see the Hebrew words here (*Migdal–eder*, "tower of Eder"; *Ophel*, "high place") as proper names for a city near Bethlehem (David's birthplace) and Jerusalem (where David reigned), respectively. Thus, this signals a (spiritual) restoration of what Israel once enjoyed under their greatest king.

Having looked away from their future glory, Micah now returns to the pathetic condition of contemporary Israel—a nation on the verge of being subdued by "Babylon," going into shameful exile, and then being "rescued" (4:9–13).[126] While God is the cause all these actions, it is the people's sins that have made them necessary. The Messiah will come, but not until Israel undergoes this due process, which the prophet likens to the painful birthing of a child. The foreign nations want to destroy Israel (or God's people in general), but no one can alter or sabotage God's purpose for His people. Thus, while Israel (and later, Judah) will have to endure their shameful punishment, in the end, God will restore them to greatness (4:13). The "pulverizing" of "many peoples" is not meant literally but carries the idea of a great spiritual battle in which God overwhelms all His enemies with divine truth and finally destroys them (compare Rev. 19:11–21).

Micah 5:1–9 In Micah's call for the "mustering" of soldiers in preparation for battle, it is difficult to determine which battle and "siege" he refers to: Assyria's three-year siege against Samaria (2 Kings 17:1–6) or Babylon's two-year siege against Jerusalem (2 Kings 25:1–2). In a real sense, both may be meant, but the mention of the "judge of Israel" (i.e., Israel's king) indicates that he speaks specifically of Assyria's siege against Samaria (5:1–2).

Embedded in this pathetic scene is a most important prophecy about the physical birthplace of the future Messiah (5:2–5a). We know this because this passage the chief priests and scribes quote it to Herod the Great when we questioned them about Him (Mat. 2:1–6). There were two towns in Israel named "Bethlehem" ("city of bread"): one in northern Israel, in the tribal land of Zebulun near Mount Carmel; and Bethlehem "Ephrathah" ("fruitful"), about six miles southwest of Jerusalem.[127] Given the NT reference, the city near Jerusalem is meant. While the "judge [i.e., king] of Israel" will be smote on the cheek—i.e., deposed and taken into captivity—One will arise from Bethlehem to become Israel's King. "His goings forth are from…the days of eternity" (5:2) indicates not just an ancient ancestry (i.e., David's lineage), but One who comes from God Himself. This is a rare implication of the Messiah's divine nature in the OT prophecies (compare with John 8:58). "[S]he who is in labor" is not Mary, Jesus' mother, but instead refers to the faithful remnant of Israel that would have to bear the pain of captivity (and then centuries of hardship) before giving birth, so to speak, to the world's Savior (see Isa. 66:4–8; compare Rev. 12:1–6).[128] The Messiah's role as a new, powerful, and majestic "shepherd" is consistent with other prophecies concerning Him (Ezek. 34:23–31, where "David" is Messiah/Christ; see also John 10:1–16).

Micah's reference to "the Assyrian" (5:5b) goes well beyond the literal nation of Assyria and seems to represent all of Israel's enemies. "Then we will raise against him seven shepherds and eight leaders of men"—symbolic of a perfect number of men (seven), and a *new beginning* of power (eight). These "men" will all serve under the one Shepherd mentioned earlier (5:6), but the text does not refer to a physical war or historical uprising; just as the reign of the Messiah is spiritual in nature, so are the battles against His enemies (Eph. 6:12). The indication here (5:5–9) is that of a new King fighting for a spiritual "Israel"—and a spiritual "remnant"—with a power and authority that is unprecedented and undefeatable. The faithful remnant—in the ultimate sense, *Christians*—will overcome their enemies not through war and bloodshed, but in a manner that is not dependent upon human strength.

Micah 5:10–15 As we have seen many times before, "in that day" puts a timestamp on when all these things will take place, and the nature of what is being described: it is the reign of the Messiah. Israel's dependency upon military might (horses and chariots), its reliance on sorceries and fortune-tellers to predict the future, and its fond penchant for idolatry (carved images, sacred pillars, "the work of your hands," and goddesses of the Canaanites) will all be destroyed.[129] The new Israel—the spiritual remnant over whom the Messiah reigns—will be purged of all these worldly and cultic practices. The physical nation of Israel will not be a part of this new world order: it will be destroyed, as will many other godless nations (5:14b–15). There will be no place or any tolerance for any pagan worship in the Messiah's kingdom.

Micah 6:1–5 Again, God summons Israel to give an account—any evidence at all—that would incriminate His unfaithfulness to His people. He even calls the mountains and hills to witness His innocence, indicating that the case is so clear, even inanimate witnesses will testify on His behalf (compare Isa. 1:2). "The case against the people has been presented. Let the people now present their case before Jehovah. Like Hosea, his senior contemporary, Micah calls the nation to come before Jehovah in a court of law."[130] This is not a mere rhetorical dispute; God demands a legitimate response: "Answer Me" (6:3).

But before Israel can say anything, God reminds them of how He delivered them from Egyptian slavery, provided leaders for them, thwarted Balak's intended curses against them (and turned them into blessings instead—Num. 22—24), and took care of them on their journey into the Promised Land. "Shittim" [pronounced sheh-*teem'*] in Moab was Israel's first encampment after the Balak/Balaam incident; "Gilgal" was their first encampment in the Promised Land after crossing the Jordan River, just prior to the destruction of Jericho (Josh. 4:19). In all Israel's history, God never once had failed to honor His covenant, keep His promises, or take care of His people (Josh. 21:43–45, 1 Kings 8:56). Thus, they have *no good reason* to betray Him with their idolatry and flagrantly violate His covenant with them.

Micah 6:6–8 In this passage, either Micah answers on behalf of the people, or the prophet answers (rhetorically) on his own. The essential message is Israel's sin will not be removed by a few animal sacrifices or burnt offerings; even "thousands of rams" and "ten thousand rivers of oil" will not suffice. In fact, not even (hypothetically) a *human* sacrifice of one's firstborn will be enough. Instead, "He [Jehovah] has told you, O man, what is good" (6:8): God desires humble, genuine, and lasting repentance. This cannot be something that is merely uttered with empty promises but must manifest itself in the form of uncorrupted justice, honorable dealings with one's fellow man, and reverent humility of the heart. The "O man" address indicates that this is not limited to Israel but universally applies to *all* people or *every* nation; it is a boundless, timeless, and monumental expectation of *all* people toward their Creator (compare Isa. 1:10–17). "This verse [6:8] is considered by many to be one of the most comprehensive and all-embracing statements in the Old Testament."[131]

Micah 6:9–16 The "city" (6:9) being summoned here is likely Samaria, capital of Israel; references to Omri and Ahab (6:16)—wicked kings of Israel who once reigned from Samaria—underscores this. While it is "wisdom to fear Your [Jehovah's] name" (6:9), the people are immersed in all kinds of wicked and deceptive practices. The "short measure" (6:10) refers to a purposely diminished ephah measurement designed to mislead a buyer of wheat into thinking he is getting a full amount when he really is not. Likewise, "wicked scales" and "deceptive weights" indicate further instances of cheating (see Lev. 19:35–36, Deut. 25:13, and Prov. 20:23). Meanwhile, there is violence, lies, and deception among all the people, from the rich on down. It is a depressing, pathetic, and completely unjustifiable situation, and God will not tolerate it any longer.

For all of Israel's crimes, God will bring sickness, the sword, and desolation upon His people (6:13). He will take away all their profits; whatever they worked to enjoy will be taken away from them. It is likely that the prophet here speaks (indirectly) of the devastation of an invading army (the Assyrians). Invaders in ancient times could not bring with them enough food to feed their entire army. They relied also upon the produce of the land that they invaded, taking whatever they wanted, and stripping the people and their land of all its food and provisions. Since the people have chosen to walk in the sins of their wicked kings, God will "give you up for destruction," "derision," and "reproach" (6:16).

Micah 7:1–6 The prophet Micah answers God's pronouncement against His people, as though speaking on behalf of the believing remnant of Israel. He likens himself to a harvester of grapes or figs but cannot find any fruit (compare Isa. 5:1–7 and Mark 11:12–14). He admits there is no one left who is godly and upright. (This must be taken figuratively, since obviously there *are* godly men and women in Israel, just as there were in the days of Elijah; see 1 Kings 19:18 and Rom. 11:2–5. However, they are very few in proportion.) The picture Micah paints—everyone lying in wait to shed blood, both hands committed to doing evil, rampant bribery, no one can be trusted, and widespread disrespect within the family—is dark and disturbing, and calls to mind the moral condition of the world in the days of Noah (Gen. 6:5, 11–12).

Micah 7:7–13 Again, as if speaking on behalf of the righteous remnant, Micah expresses his confidence in "the God of my salvation" (7:7). "Salvation" here is not what we think of today (i.e., an eternal heaven with God); instead, it speaks of God's providential care for those who are faithful to Him—His safety, protection, and deliverance. Thus, even though the nation sinks beneath divine judgment, God will not forget those who believe in Him and will preserve them (as a group).

Micah also expresses his confession of sin—again, on behalf of all the righteous remnant—and looks forward prophetically to the restoration of his people (7:9).[132] Once God does deliver His people, this will take away the reproach that the remnant has had to bear—those who taunt them with accusations that God has deserted them. Those people will be "trampled down like mire on the streets" (7:10b), but the righteous will enjoy the rebuilding of Israel in a context that extends far beyond its natural boundaries (7:11–12). Meanwhile, the rest of "the earth" will suffer under God's judgment (7:13).

Micah 7:14–20 Micah pleads with God to shepherd His people "with Your scepter" (7:14)—an indication that God will again rule over (spiritual) Israel, but through the reign of His Messiah (Christ). "Bashan" and "Gilead" refer to the lush, well–watered, and fertile pasture lands that became the possession of Gad, Reuben, and the half-tribe of Manasseh in the Trans-Jordan region (Num. 32:1–4, 33). Prophetically, this refers to a time of spiritual prosperity (Jer. 50:19). God responds (7:15) and promises to show His people "miracles" on the level of those that Israel saw when He delivered them from Egypt. No doubt that the numerous and varied miracles that Christ performed is a fulfillment of this prophecy. Instead of flagrant defiance, constant rebellion, and contempt for God and His laws, "nations"—an OT word for Gentiles (non-Jews)—will fear God and be ashamed of their sins (7:16–17). When they come before Him in reverence and humility, God will forgive them because "He delights in unchanging love" (7:18)—i.e., He is a God of mercy, compassion, and pardon to those who seek Him. Their sins will be as if "cast…into the depths of the sea" (7:19). This is similarly expressed in the NT: "I will be merciful to their iniquities, and I will remember their sins no more" (Heb. 8:12; see Psalm 103:12).

Questions on *Micah*

1.) What striking impressions has the book of *Micah* left upon you?

2.) Why do you suppose people think they can sin against God and yet escape punishment (1:2–7, 2:1–13)? What line(s) of reasoning leads them to think this way? Do people (including Christians) *today* reason this way?

3.) Please read again Smith's quote on 3:9–12. The ruling class of Jerusalem thought that because they were in the right city and had within their midst the right temple, they were invincible to foreign enemies. Instead of living in compliance with God's covenant, they believed that it gave them immunity from destruction.

    a. Might Christians reason similarly today? (Consider Rom. 6:1–2 in your answer.)

b. How are God's people *supposed* to regard their covenant with Him?

4.) Micah 4:1–5 is one of the greatest passages in the book, even the entire OT. While the "last days" is depicted in figurative language, what are the several *truths* that this passage communicates regarding life in the New Jerusalem?

a. Do Christians always *see* things this way? If not, why not?

b. While the fulfillment of this passage is spiritual and not literal, is it still not true that God takes care of His people *literally* as well as *spiritually*? Please explain.

5.) Given a passage like 6:8, do you think that God has sufficiently told the entire *world* "what is good" and (thus) how to live rightly before Him? Can any person in modern America, for example, claim ignorance as to what He expects of him or her?

6.) Some have said that 7:18 provides one of the finest summaries of God's character in all the OT, on par with John 3:16 in the NT. Do you agree?

Introduction to *Zephaniah*

Authorship: Beyond the superscription in 1:1, nothing is known about Zephaniah the prophet. His name means "defended (or, protected, hidden, or treasured) by Jehovah," and he reveals himself to be the great-great-grandson of King Hezekiah. This makes Zephaniah of royal lineage, which makes his condemnation of the "princes, the king's sons" (1:8) even more striking.

Date and Place of Writing: Zephaniah's prophecy is "in the days of Josiah," king of Judah (ruled 640–609 BC). Josiah was quite young when he became king (2 Kings 22:1), and we know that he instituted major reforms later in his reign, at least 18 years later (2 Kings 22:3ff), after someone discovered the "book of the law" of the Lord in the temple during its repairs. The prophetess Huldah's strong words against the land of Judah (in 2 Kings 22:14–20) are consistent with the strong words of Zephaniah's prophecy. Thus, it may well be that Zephaniah's prophecy was given prior to Josiah's reforms—and possibly even helped to spur them.[133] This gives us a rough idea as to the date of Zephaniah's prophecy—sometime between 640 and 622 BC.

As to where Zephaniah lived, or where he was when he wrote this prophecy, nothing is known for certain. The northern tribes of Israel had already been taken into Assyrian captivity; because of his royal lineage, it is likely that the prophet not only lived in Jerusalem but may have resided somewhere in the palace complex.[134]

Purpose and Character of Writing: One cannot help but notice the great contrast in Zephaniah's prophecy: his depiction of God's judgment is dark and heavy; yet his depiction of Israel's future restoration is glorious and filled with great hope. He speaks with the skill of a great orator, no doubt the result of a good education. He does not limit his declarations of God's judgment to Judah but includes all of Judah's enemies as well. At the same time, "Zephaniah goes further than any other of the minor prophets in emphasizing the future conversion of the Gentiles to the worship of the true God."[135]

George Adam Smith has well summarized its spirit when he writes, "No hotter book lies in all the Old Testament. Neither dew nor grass nor tree nor any blossom lives in it, but it is everywhere fire, smoke and darkness, drifting chaff, ruins, nettles, salt pits, and owls and ravens looking from the windows of desolate places." However, out of this grim picture of destruction would come redemption, which must not be overlooked nor minimized.[136]

Zephaniah speaks candidly and boldly about "the day of the Lord" (1:7, 14), and specifically "the day of the Lord's wrath/anger" (1:18, 2:2). This short prophetic book communicates a profound sense of judgment and finality. God has been putting up with the sins of Judah for centuries yet has not seen any meaningful improvement. Even Josiah's reforms will not change the moral rottenness of the nation of Judah as a whole (see 2 Kings 23:25–27). Likewise, God has had enough of the worldliness of all the neighboring nations around Judah that have infected His people with idolatry and other moral crimes. Because of His holiness, and for the sake of His people (the source of the future Messiah), God must punish their sin. The "day of the Lord" will not just be a "day" of punishment, but it will be a "day" of cleansing, purification, and renewal.

It is true that in Zephaniah's day, the Babylonian invasion of Judah was still years in the future. "Nevertheless, the dark and ominous clouds of world-revolution were gathering when Zephaniah wrote."[137] Not only was Babylon gaining great strength and would soon crush everything in its path, that nation, too, would face divine judgment. "God sent many messengers during the period [prior to the invasion] in the person of His servants the prophets to warn and correct the people; but for the most part they refused any correction."[138] A nation's heart can become so hardened that not even God's mercy and patience can pierce it; over time, it loses all sensation of moral responsibility or desire for spiritual enlightenment.

Overview of *Zephaniah*

Zeph. 1:1 The prophet Zephaniah provides a timestamp of his ministry, as well as an indication (albeit extremely limited) of his personal identity, through the lineage of King Hezekiah. Hezekiah's reforms (2 Chron. 29:3–19) foreshadow those of King Josiah, after hearing Zephaniah's prophecy.

Zeph. 1:2–6 The "word of the Lord" (recall 1:1) begins, appropriately, with the Lord Himself speaking. His discourse is immediately bold, shocking, and fearful. This is the message of a powerful and angry God. The language is purposely exaggerated to heighten this sense of shock and fear: "I will completely remove all things from the face of the earth, etc." (1:2ff). This is not to be taken literally but *is* to be taken seriously. "The day of Yahweh will reach every dark corner of the earth and the hidden recesses of men's minds and hearts."[139] God is plainly expressing His sovereign authority and supremacy over *all things* upon the earth, including the earth itself. "This all–embracing declaration is not to be explained away simply as hyperbole [i.e., purposely exaggerated language]"[140]; at the same time, God is filled with wrath over Judah's persistent sin. He reminds them that it is well within His power to destroy them, their land, and everything *in* their land. The "ruins [lit., stumbling blocks]" (1:3) refers to the idols that the Jews have so endeared.[141]

While God's prophecy begins in a very general sense, He quickly identifies the primary offenders who have angered Him: His own people (1:4). There are four groups mentioned (1:4–6): the priests of Baal, the god of the Canaanites; those who bow to the "host of heaven" (i.e., worship of the sun, stars, and planets) from the rooftops; those who give allegiance to Milcom, the national god of the Ammonites; and those who simply refuse to follow the Lord. The fact that Baal and Milcom have their own priesthoods, as well as many loyal followers who "bow down" to them every day, shows how widespread and deeply penetrative this idolatry has become. The fact that people "swear to the Lord and yet swear by Milcom" indicates a syncretism (or, blending) of religions:

they have united the worship of Jehovah with that of pagan idolatry. But then, other people have simply abandoned Jehovah worship altogether (1:6). These latter people "are utterly indifferent to Jehovah; they have turned back; they have not sought nor inquired after Him. They could not care less for His favor or disfavor."[142]

Zeph. 1:7–13 In leveling His judgment against His people, "the Lord God [lit., the Lord Jehovah]" calls for a great hush over the land, as He prepares for a great sacrifice (1:7). Indeed, it is His own rebellious people that will be slain, and His "guests" will be the Chaldeans (Babylonians) whom He will invite to partake of that feast. As for Judah, this will be a day of great (and well-deserved) punishment in which every stratum of society—from the king to the priests to all who commit sacrilege against God and His "house" (temple)—will be directly affected (1:8–9). Rampant "violence and deceit" indicates a lawless society in which justice, virtue, and care for one's fellow man have all but evaporated.

This "day of the Lord" (from 1:7) is a day of divine vengeance, national destruction, social upheaval, and purging of sinful elements from the land. All of Jerusalem will be affected, from the Fish Gate to the Second Quarter to the Mortar district—referring to different parts of the city—as well as the merchants ("the people of Canaan") who have adopted the business culture of the Canaanites and Phoenicians.[143] No one will escape: God portrays Himself as one who searches the city with lamps (1:12), looking for anyone who will try to hide or abandon the city. He characterizes the inhabitants of Jerusalem as "stagnant in spirit," apathetic to the moral concerns of their nation, and who think that He will not bring either good or harm to them.[144] However, instead of profiting from their business transactions and comfortable lifestyles, all that they own will become plunder to the invading army (the Babylonians) (1:13).

Zeph. 1:14–18 This section heightens the intensity of "the day of the Lord" with frightening and graphic descriptions. **First**, *it is coming*—the time of patience, mercy, and waiting for Judah to repent is over. **Second**, it is coming *quickly*—not just in nearness of time (historically-speaking, it is about twenty years away), but also when the people are not prepared for it. **Third**, it is a "day" of *wrath*—Babylon's siege against Jerusalem will not be explained away as an accident, a coincidence, or an unwarranted persecution of God's people. Instead, it will be clearly and irrefutably the outpouring of divine wrath upon the city, much in the same way as Jesus later predicted of Jerusalem in His own generation (Luke 19:41–44, 21:21–24).[145] **Fourth**, it is a "day" of great *trouble, calamity, pain,* and *loss* ("trouble and distress," "destruction and desolation," "darkness and gloom," and "clouds and thick darkness"). The people will be completely humiliated, dispirited, and destroyed through the ravages of invasion and war. **Fifth**, it is a "day" in which *nothing* and *no one* will be able to deliver them. "[T]he fire of His jealousy" (1:18) refers to "His righteous resentment and indignation at being supplanted in the affection of His people by empty idols and having His righteousness exchanged for pagan wickedness."[146]

Zeph. 2:1–3 Once the "decree" of God's judgment has been issued, there will be no turning back; yet a portal of hope still remains for the humble (or, meek) who have kept God's law and have sought Him rather than the folly of idolatry. It is difficult to know in this passage whether this final offer is for these people alone, or for the entire nation. If Zephaniah's prophecy coincides with Josiah's reforms (see "Introduction to Zephaniah"), then this is a prophetic call for Josiah and men with a heart *like* Josiah's to do their best to turn the tide of the people away from idolatry and back to the Lord. On the other hand, "Perhaps you will be hidden in the day of the Lord's anger" (2:3) may indicate that the judgment is coming no matter what, but that God will spare those who genuinely repent or keep themselves free from what brought about the decree in the first place.

Zeph. 2:4–15 This section is like a very condensed version of the pronouncements of judgment in the major prophets against foreign nations that surround Judah (Isa. 13—23, Jer. 46—51, and Ezek. 25—32). Some of these nations have infected and corrupted Judah with their idolatry, pagan religions, and godless lifestyles. Others (like Assyria) have been enemies of Judah and have inflicted great harm upon God's people.

> Oracles against foreign nations seem to be an important element in OT prophecy. These oracles were not [always] spoken or written for the benefit or response of the nations. The message was directed primarily to Israel or Judah. They emphasize Yahweh's sovereignty over the nations and the nation's responsibility and accountability to Yahweh.[147]

In any case, God presents Himself as the Judge not only of people called by His name, but *all* people in *any* country. God's power and authority are by no means limited; He has the right to dispense justice and judgment over one nation as He does over another. His judgment concerns nations to the west, east, south, and north of Judah. "Then he focuses on Jerusalem, the center of God's dealings (3:1–7). Jerusalem is characterized by spiritual rebellion and moral treachery."[148]

Specifically, God pronounces judgment against Philistia, the warring nation on the Mediterranean coast (2:4–7). This nation has long been a thorn in Judah's side, long before the time of David, and yet their idolatry and godless ways have permeated Judah's borders. Philistia is comprised of five city-states—Gaza, Ashkelon, Ashdod, Ekron, and Gath—and these are all mentioned in this passage except for Gath. The "Cherethites" may refer to the Cretans (inhabitants of the nearby island of Crete), since the Philistines are a seafaring people and may be responsible for settling the island of Crete and other coastal locations in the Mediterranean theater as well. God has had enough of this stubborn, warmongering, and barbaric people. He will make their prized seacoasts uninhabited and turn them into a place for shepherds from "the remnant of the house of Judah" (2:7), after God's wrath has been poured out upon Judah. We should remember, too, that the Philistines were among the Canaanite nations that Israel was supposed to destroy upon taking possession of the Promised Land (Josh. 13:1–3).

Also, Moab and Ammon—two fraternal nations east of the Jordan River—have long "taunted" Israel and Judah and thus warrant divine punishment (2:8–11). Moab and Ammon originally were the sons of Lot by the incestuous relationship that he (Lot) had with his daughters, soon after the destruction of Sodom and Gomorrah (Gen. 19:30–38). This means that the Moabites and Ammonites are blood relatives of the Israelites, though they seldom honored this relationship. Instead, they have been a thorn in the side of the Israelites since the time of Moses (Deut. 23:3–6), the days of the judges (Judg. 3:12–30, 10:6—11:33), and the reign of David (2 Sam. 8:2, 10:1–14). God calls these two nations arrogant, proud, and reviling. He promises to turn their territories and cities into a deserted wasteland, "a place possessed by nettles and salt pits, and a perpetual desolation" (2:9). The destruction of Moab and Ammon will strike terror in other nations as well, as God "starves" their false gods from the lack of power, honor, and worship (2:10–11).

God also makes a very brief but potent denunciation of Ethiopia (also known as Cush, or Nubia) in Africa, south of Egypt (2:12). This oracle may include Egypt as well, since Ethiopia ruled over Egypt from 720 to 654 BC, shortly before Zephaniah's prophecy.[149] The Ethiopians have a strong, impressive, and ancient history, but none of this will matter when God's judgment comes upon them.

Finally, God turns His attention to Assyria, the capital of which is Nineveh (2:13–15). When the prophet Jonah preached to the Ninevites many years before, the city—really, a cluster of city-states—was one of the largest and most powerful in the ancient world, "an exceedingly great city" (Jonah 3:3). Assyria invaded the northern ten tribes of Israel and carried many of them away into foreign exile.

> Brutality was justified from the Assyrian viewpoint on religious grounds. The [Assyrian] god Assur had willed that his country and his king should achieve world domination; and all other gods, kings, and peoples had to be subservient to Assur's will. Any resistance meant rebellion against the great god and was put down with condign [i.e, fitting or deserved, especially regarding punishment] severity.[150]

Assyria's cruelty, disregard for human life, and supreme arrogance made it a target for divine judgment, as God promised through the prophet Isaiah (Isa. 10:1–19). He will bring down the Assyrian Empire and will bury Nineveh in obscurity; instead of a dwelling place for 600,000 people (as it had in its prime), the city will be the home of birds, small creatures, and herds of wild animals. "The utter destruction of the Assyrian capital [in 612 BC] is a fact of history. It was so completely destroyed that its very location was lost to the memory of man until the nineteenth century when it was discovered by archeologists."[151]

Zeph. 3:1–13 While these other nations certainly warranted God's judgments, none of them had the privilege of knowing Him like Jerusalem (Judah) did. The strongest—and most vocal—blasts of judgment, then, are against the "tyrannical city" of Jerusalem that defied its own God in search of foreign gods. (Not even the pagan cities of foreign nations did this!) "She" (Jerusalem) did not listen, rejected all instruction, and failed to trust in God's promises; "she" was a rebel, a prostitute (Ezek. 16), and an apostate (i.e., one who turns from the truth). All the ruling classes—the princes (kings), judges, prophets, and priests—are like wild animals, unholy creatures, and unafraid to profane God's sanctuary (temple) (3:3–4). God has proven His ability to destroy Judah's enemies in the past, and thus deserved Judah's gratitude and respect; He revealed His law to them to guide and deliver them. However, the Jews "[know] no shame," and are "eager to corrupt all their deeds" (3:5–7).

As bad as the situation is—and as awful as His judgment against Judah/Jerusalem will be—God still tells His righteous people to "wait for [or, continue to put your hope in] Me" (3:8, bracketed words added). He will indeed "pour out [His] indignation" and "burning anger" upon His people, but it will not be to remove them from the face of the earth (as He will do with other nations). Rather, it will be a means of purification for a much better future, when His people will once again "call on the name of the LORD" (3:9, a foreshadow of Acts 2:21). In *that* day—a "day" well beyond the "day" of indignation and destruction that must come first—His "dispersed" people will no longer feel the shame and despair of a punished people. Those who are "proud" (in themselves) will not be allowed "on My holy mountain" (3:11; see Isa. 66:19–23).

All of this speaks of a *new world order*, the old order having become obsolete. Prophetically speaking, it looks forward to the reign of the Messiah and the establishment of His church. The "remnant" (3:12–13) refers to the (comparatively) small number of believers in Jehovah who have not succumbed to idolatry and have remained pure in heart. These are people who, despite the wicked disposition of the rest of Jerusalem and Judah, are honest, good, and virtuous (compare Rev. 14:4–5). God has a special place in *His* heart for such people; He will keep them specially protected; He will honor them with safety and provision.

Zeph. 3:14–20 As dark and foreboding as the promise of the "day of the LORD" has been, so the promise of future glory radiates with exuberant joy and anticipation. Zephaniah now speaks (in 3:14–17), and he does so as if the judgment has already passed, and now *new* and *better* times have already come. Now it is time for shouting—not a battle cry, as before (recall 1:16), but a shout of immense joy and celebration! The prophet tells his people to "Rejoice and exult with all your heart" (3:14) because God has removed the time of indignation brought about by faithlessness and idolatry. God's wrath has been spent; His anger has subsided; the time of punishment is over; "you will fear disaster no more" (3:15). Instead of God fighting *against* His people, now He will be fighting *for* them as a "victorious warrior" (3:17). Instead of His fierce anger for their sins, now He will show them His joy, love, and fellowship.

At this point, God Himself speaks through the prophet to His faithful remnant with comforting words (3:18–20). While it is necessary for His people to be dispersed to foreign nations during their exiles (Israel's and Judah's), He speaks of a time when they will be regathered as one people (3:20). Those who once had been regarded as outcasts and worthless to society (such as lepers and the lame) will share in the honor and glory of this jubilant regathering. Those who once oppressed His people will be removed; their "fortunes"—likely, referring to captives—will be restored to them. Instead of woes and punishment, God promises fellowship and healing. "I will give you renown and praise"—i.e., instead of shame, humiliation, and derision (see Isa. 60:18, 62:7, and Jer. 13:11).

God scattered His people when they (as a nation) did not listen to Him; He will also regather them once their punishment has run its course (Mic. 2:12). No pagan god has ever scattered *or* delivered its people, but Jehovah God can do both, despite whatever human interference or physical circumstance stands in His way (Isa. 60:1–5). There is no question that this regathering refers prophetically to the context of the Messiah and His church in the "regeneration" (Mat. 19:28) or "restoration" (Acts 1:6, 3:21) of Israel. While Zephaniah speaks to the physical nation of Judah, it is the *spiritual* nation of Israel that will be the recipient of these promises. The Jews will be the first to share in them, but not the only ones (John 10:16, Rom. 1:16).

Questions on *Zephaniah*

1.) *Zephaniah* opens with a terrifying blast of divine judgment against all who have blatantly defied Him, bowed down to idols, or were simply indifferent to Him and His holy law (1:2–6).

   a. How does this compare with the "God so loved the world" sentiment expressed in John 3:16? Has God softened His approach to sin and sinners?

   b. On the other hand, the NT does speak of God's "wrath" toward "all ungodliness and unrighteousness" (Rom. 1:18). Is God (in the NT) merely exaggerating His disappointment with people, or will this really happen?

2.) The prophet Zephaniah describes the "day of the LORD" with frightening and graphic language (1:14–18). Despite passages like this (in the OT *and* NT), most people today remain unconvinced of or indifferent toward God's promises of judgment (see 2 Peter 3:3–12). Why is this? Is there something more that God could do to convince them?

3.) God "hears" the bragging, taunting, and arrogance of the ancient nations, and promises to bring them to justice for this (2:8–11). Is this also true about individual *people* who boast in themselves, taunt God's people, and show great arrogance against God Himself? Please explain.

4.) Zephaniah 3:1–4 speaks of the godless character of Jerusalem: even though these people had every reason to succeed, they failed miserably. What happened? Is it possible that a *Christian* can begin well, have every reason to succeed, and still fail? If so, will the cause of that failure be the same as what caused Jerusalem to fail?

5.) Even after a scathing pronouncement of judgment, *Zephaniah* ends with beautiful and inspiring words of hope and restoration (3:14–20). What does this tell you about God and the intention He has in punishing His people?

Introduction to *Nahum*

Authorship: Nothing is known about the prophet Nahum ("comfort" or "consolation") except that he was an "Elkoshite" (1:1), hailing from the city of Elkosh, which may have been in the region of Galilee.¹⁵² The city of Capernaum, the headquarters of Jesus' ministry (Mat. 4:13, Mark 2:1) was also in Galilee (Luke 4:31); "Capernaum" literally means "village of Nahum," and some believe that this is the ancient city of Elkosh, renamed in honor of the prophet.¹⁵³ Some think, however, that Elkosh was in the land of Judah (citing 1:15), and that Nahum prophesied in or near Jerusalem against Nineveh.¹⁵⁴

Date and Place of Writing: The only historical reference in the book of Nahum is in 3:8–10, where No-Amon (a.k.a. the city of Thebes in Egypt) is said to have already been destroyed by Assyria. We know this destruction occurred in 663 BC by the Assyrian king Ashurbanipal.¹⁵⁵ Nahum predicts the fall of Nineveh, which occurred in 612 BC. The prophet likely wrote between these two dates, thus placing his prophecy somewhere in the mid-7th century BC (ca. 650 BC), and possibly closer to 612 than 663. Nahum cites the Assyrian conquest of Thebes to say something to the effect of, "If *that* great city can fall, then certainly *you* [Nineveh] can fall, for you are no better than they."

As to the place of writing, nothing is known for certain. The reference to the feasts (and, by implication, the temple) in Jerusalem (1:15) makes it appear that Nahum is not only speaking on behalf of Jerusalem but is very possibly in that city.

Purpose and Character of Writing: The writing style of the book of Nahum is unlike anything else in the OT. (For comparison, it is similar to the animated, fast–moving, and graphic language of *Jude* in the NT.) "[Nahum's] language is strong and brilliant; his rhythm rumbles and rolls, leaps and flashes, like the horsemen and chariots he describes," says one commentator.¹⁵⁶ "As one reads it, he feels himself carried from thought to thought at a rapid and highly excited pace. The style is forceful, brilliant, and life–like. One feels he is sharing with the prophet the excitement of the moment."[157] In describing the doom of Nineveh, "Nahum writes lyric poetry of the highest quality. It has been called the most poetical of all the prophetic writings and certainly is the most severe in tone of any of the minor prophets."[158] Nothing is mentioned of Judah's sin, the captivity of the northern ten tribes, or any other subjects; the prophet's sole focus is on the destruction of Nineveh *and*, by association, the comfort of God's righteous people in Judah who will be spared Assyria's iron-fisted rule any longer.

Nineveh was the capital city of the Assyrian Empire (which, at its peak, ruled from ca. 900—612 BC), and one of the largest and greatest cities of the ancient world. Assyria went from being a rogue nation, attacking cities and nations only for plunder, to an expansionist empire, establishing itself as a world power. In 722/721 BC, Assyria invaded Palestine, overwhelmed the ten northern tribes of Israel, and took much of the entire population into foreign captivity. Assyria also  seeded the invaded land with foreigners from other conquered nations, creating the "Samaritans" of the NT (see 2 Kings 17). Jonah once prophesied against Nineveh and predicted its fall ("Yet forty days and Nineveh will be overthrown"—Jonah 3:4) unless it repented, which it did. But Nineveh's arrogance returned, greater than before, and it exalted itself as an indestructible nation (Isa. 10:1–15).

When Nahum prophesied against Nineveh, the Assyrian Empire was still enormously powerful, and seemed impossible to defeat. It was also excessively brutal in its invasions and conquests of foreign nations. In their chronicles, the Assyrians boasted about how they:

- ran out of space for the corpses of all their victims.
- flung away the bodies of soldiers like clay.
- made pyramids of human heads of those whom they executed.
- impaled "heaps of men" on stakes.

- cut off heads of kings and nailed them on walls, leaving their bodies to rot on the entrance gates of conquered cities.
- covered pillars with the flayed skins of rival monarchs.[159]

Not only this, but Nineveh itself seemed an impregnable fortress. It was surrounded by an impressive wall, with huge towers along the wall that served as military outposts. Outside of the wall was a moat 150 feet wide and 60 feet deep. It was believed that Nineveh could withstand a 20-year siege.[160] However, Assyria also had many enemies, and these enemies were slowly chipping away at Assyria's territories and power. Historically, Assyria was attacked through at least three different military campaigns in the late 7th century, one of which was led by Nabopolassar, the father of the future Babylonian king Nebuchadnezzar. Having repelled these attacks, the Assyrian king, Sardanapalus, presumptuously declared a great (and drunken) feast in Nineveh. At this time, the Tigris River, which flowed alongside the city of Nineveh, flooded, destroying part of the city's walls and fortifications (1:8). The combined army of the Medes and Babylonians (a.k.a. the Medo-Babylonians), which was laying siege of Nineveh at that time, seized the opportunity to invade through this breach, and took the city by surprise. The Assyrian king, seeing all hope was lost, burned his palaces down upon his wives, his servants, his concubines, and himself,[161] and this ignoble event marked the end of the Assyrian Empire.

Nahum's prophecy, however, is not only against Assyria. It is a parable–like prediction of God's supreme power over *all* human arrogance. Just as nations think they are undefeatable, so people think themselves to be invincible; just as God can easily bring down entire nations or empires, so He can just as easily bring down the most powerful of rulers. Assyria's pompous, arrogant, and boastful attitude is no different than that of many nations before and after it. Even today, nations, governments, rulers, and individual people think that they are in full control and do not have to answer to anyone. Yet, God has already demonstrated that He has sovereign authority over all the earth.

The glee of Nineveh's victims over her fall is easily understood when one remembers the scourge of such rulers as Adolph Hitler [ruled over Germany from 1933 to 1945] and Idi Amin [ruled over Uganda, Africa, from 1971 to 1979]. Assyrian kings boasted on tablets that have survived the years of the way they were able to drag women and children away from their dead husbands and fathers as the spoils of conquest to the great fortress at Nineveh. The annals reflect their pride in the complete devastation of their enemies.[162]

We should remember that, while it was men who overthrew Nineveh, it was God who made it happen, predicted it *before* it happened, and gave the details of *what* would happen. It is encouraging to know that not only will *every* evil nation (or person) fall, but also that God's divine justice will be what brings about that fall.

Overview of *Nahum*

Nahum 1:1 God communicated the "oracle [or, burden] of Nineveh" to the prophet Nahum through a revelatory vision. God is telling His people ahead of time what is going to happen to Nineveh. Why He chose Nahum, and whether He used Nahum for any other prophetic purposes, is unknown to us.

Nahum 1:2–8 This section contains a poetic description of God's power, justice, and majesty. The prophet portrays both sides of God: He is "slow to anger" (1:3; see 2 Peter 3:9), yet "avenging and wrathful" (1:2). He is "good," and "a stronghold in the day of trouble" for those who seek His protection (1:7), yet He "will by no means leave the guilty unpunished" (1:3). His presence (in the form of judgments against nations) directly affects the natural world. "Bashan" is a region in the Trans–Jordan known for its lush pastures; "Carmel" is known for its wheat fields and vineyards; "Lebanon" is known for its large and luxurious forests (1:4).[163] The poetic message is: these fertile and fruitful regions will be laid waste in the wake of God's judgment against the impenitent. Likewise, His indignant and righteous anger will severely affect mountains, hills, rocks, and the entire physical earth (1:5–6). If the physical earth withers under the great and awesome power of God, how can a mere nation of men—even one as powerful as Assyria—hope to withstand His judgment?

All this is the language of a "day of the LORD" scenario, even though Nahum does not use this phrase. The "overwhelming flood" (1:8) against Nineveh is ominous, since it will be through an unexpected flooding of the Tigris River that will compromise the city's bulwarks, allowing its enemies to take full advantage of the breach. The "flood" metaphor here can also refer to the great mass of soldiers that will pour into the city to overthrow it. "As the city is to vanish and leave no trace behind, so shall its inhabitants perish in darkness."[164]

Nahum 1:9–15 God, through the prophet Nahum, warns the Assyrians (as He has done before) not to think that they can outwit, outmaneuver, or overwhelm Him with their clever plans. They once thought they were going to defeat God when Sennacherib laid siege against Jerusalem in the days of King Hezekiah, but this failed when God struck down 185,000 Assyrian warriors overnight (see 2 Kings 18:13—19:36). "Distress will not rise up twice" (1:9): in other words, God is saying, "Do not think you will have another opportunity to come against Jerusalem, because you will not." The depiction of the Assyrians as "those who are drunk with their drink" may be a reference to their drunken partying at the time when their enemies breached the city's defenses on the day Nineveh fell (1:10).

In plotting evil against Jerusalem (in the days of Hezekiah), the Assyrians really plotted against the LORD Himself (1:11); it is a "wicked counselor" who decides to do this. Verses 12 and 13 seem to recall God's words spoken through the prophet Isaiah (Isa. 37): Assyria has come against you (Judah) at full strength—and God *allowed* them to do so because of Judah's sins—but "I will afflict you no longer" with this nation. Furthermore, God promises Judah that He will break the heavy yoke that Assyria has placed upon Judah (in the form of domination, fear of a future invasion, and tribute money). In 1:14, God addresses Nineveh itself; He issues a "command" (i.e., a pronouncement or decree of divine judgment) against the city and its nation. While Assyria expects to be around indefinitely, God promises otherwise; its name will disappear from the nations of the world. He will "cut off" its idols and gods, which is another way of saying that these have no power to stop Him. This decree of doom ends ominously with, "I will prepare your grave, for you are contemptible."

All of this is *good news* for the inhabitants of Judah, who have long feared the Assyrian threat and have seen that nation's brutality and destruction up close (1:15).[165] (While Jerusalem was spared destruction, the Assyrian army mercilessly destroyed many of the cities of Judah.) In light of this promise, the prophet Nahum tells Judah (Jerusalem) to celebrate the feasts ordained by the Law of Moses, and to fulfill their vows to the Lord (because He has been faithful to fulfill *His* vows). Once God destroys Nineveh/Assyria (the "wicked one"), His people will never have to fear them again.

Nahum 2:1–13 This passage vividly, graphically, and remarkably describes the actual invasion in which Nineveh falls to their enemies. It is "a battle account in poetry."¹⁶⁶ Its attention to detail of a future event makes this one of the most unique passages in the entire Bible. "The one who scatters" (2:1), in the prophetic and historical context of this message, likely refers to the Medo–Babylonian army which has marched up the Tigris River to lay siege against Nineveh. But, because these men are acting as God's servants in fulfilling His prophecy, "the one who scatters" is God Himself. The prophet Nahum virtually taunts the Assyrians to do their best to "man" their fortress, keep watch for the enemy, and strengthen the military forces, even though it will all be in vain. The destruction of Nineveh is, *in particular*, divine retribution for what Assyria has done to His people. They have robbed the "splendor" of Israel and Judah and have devastated their lands (2:2). Now, God promises to devastate Nineveh.

The color of the Medo-Babylonian army's uniforms is red (or, scarlet, or vermillion; see Ezek. 23:14) (2:3).¹⁶⁷ "The chariot was to the army of the prophet's day what the tank is to the modern army. It was an ominous weapon made even more terrifying by attaching sharp implements at right angles to the axels so they literally mowed down any who came against them."¹⁶⁸ The "flashing steel" (2:3) refers to the sun's reflection off of the metal chariots as they blitzed throughout the streets of Nineveh. The Medo–Babylonians drove  these chariots and raced their horses wildly through the city, cutting down anyone they could find. The prophecy depicts a battle scene in full progress, the enemy being an almost invincible force that both terrorizes and obliterates the city (2:4). "He [the Assyrian king—MY WORDS] remembers his nobles..." (2:5)—i.e., the Assyrian nobles and warriors "stumble in their march" to protect the city. (According to the ancient historian Diodorus Siculus, these were all involved in "drunken carousings" when the attack came, so they were completely unprepared to do battle.¹⁶⁹) The nobles try to escape by climbing the walls, even while the Medo–Babylonians set up their siege towers ("the mantelet") against it.¹⁷⁰

It is not known for certain what "the gates of the rivers" refers to—whether literal gates to the Tigris River, or metaphorical "gates" referring to breaches in the wall through which poured "rivers" of invaders (2:6). The "dissolving" of the palace may refer to its having been burned to the ground by the Assyrian king himself (see notes in the "Introduction to Nahum" above). It also metaphorically can refer to the dissolving of courage and hope, through a flood of dreadful anticipation of an attacking army. "It is fixed" (2:7)—i.e., the ruin of the city is divinely appointed, determined, and cannot be stopped; "she" (Nineveh) is stripped naked, so to speak, and is completely debased. (Some think that the "she" here refers to Assyria's principal goddess, Ishtar, and that "her handmaids" are the priestesses and temple prostitutes that served her. While this may well be true, there is no way to verify it.)

Describing Nineveh as (formerly) "a pool of water" (2:8) refers to a body of water filled by many streams. In other words, Nineveh's power, wealth, and luxuriousness were all fed by the many conquests, plundered treasures, and commercial trade of other nations. The "pool," then, figuratively describes Nineveh's great storehouses of treasures. Now, in the prophetic vision, the people of Nineveh flee for their lives; their city is looted by invaders (2:9); the "pool of water" is "emptied" (2:10) and left "desolate and waste." The inhabitants of Nineveh quake with fear, their morale "melting" at the sight of what is happening to their city, and their faces made pale with horror and the anticipation of their own demise. Once Nineveh (Assyria) was like a great den of lions—killing, tearing flesh, and unafraid of a foreign attack—but now all that has changed (2:11–12). God's chilling announcement at the end of this prophecy makes it clear: this attack, when it does in fact come, will be no accident, and the Medo–Babylonians will not have acted on their own. Rather, it is "the LORD of hosts [lit., Jehovah and His army]" that will bring down the Assyrian Empire (2:13). "[T]he chariots of which she [Assyria] had been so proud and on which she had relied for her conquest of the world were now to be burned and destroyed."¹⁷¹

It is the most remarkable montage ever produced, presenting with the most dramatic impact the burned palaces, the flood, the slaughter, the fleeing inhabitants, the battering rams and engines of warfare, the horses, chariots, and spears, the fevered anxiety, the drunken walk of the nobles, the looting of treasures, and the heartbreak of defeat! There were miles of walls and buildings in Nineveh covered with friezes [i.e., carved artwork] depicting captives from all the nations tortured and destroyed by Nineveh, the most cruel and heartless of all nations. There were the lines of captives, led by chains in their lips or ears; there were the brutal slaughter of whole populations, the slave–masters with their whips, and the burden–bearers with intolerable loads; there were the treasures of palaces and temples, and the arrogant king receiving tribute from humbled kings in the act of kissing his feet! The life of the city was built upon such things; but now it was happening to them![172]

Nahum 3:1–7 God makes it clear that Nineveh has brought upon its destruction upon itself. It is a city "full of lies and pillage"; it does not cease to plunder other nations (3:1). Their unceasing and shameless wickedness makes them ripe for divine judgment. All the horror of invasion with which the city once imposed upon foreign nations will now be *their* horror: horses, whips, chariots, and spears will assault the Ninevites in their own city streets. The great city will become an enormous site of death and human carnage. It will be a scene of mortally wounded citizens and soldiers alike, tremendous bloodshed, and multitudes of corpses (3:2–3).

Nineveh is a "type" of the world-city of any given age in human history. It is a city filled with sin:

- it shows no pity or compassion for the human suffering it creates.
- it mercilessly destroys others so that it itself can indulge in excess and extravagance.
- it is rampant with idolatry, and the promiscuous culture of idolatry.
- it is defiled with all sorts of sexual immorality, sexual crimes, and deviant practices.

- it is characterized by drunkenness, decadence, shameless gratification, and sickening brutality.

"Harlotries" (3:4) refers here, as it often does in the OT, to pagan idolatry and the sensual/sexual lifestyle that so often accompanies it. "Harlotry" also implies a falling away (or, apostatizing) from the truth: these people have fallen so far from God and so deep into their sinful ways that there is simply nothing left to save, and nothing left for God to do but to destroy them. "Sorceries" adds another dimension to this picture: not only has Nineveh fallen so far from God, but they seek very ungodly powers to justify themselves, make themselves rich, and (attempt to) foretell the future. To "lift up your skirts over your face" (3:5) is God's common way of shaming those entrenched in pagan idolatry (see Jer. 13:22, 26–27, Ezek. 16:36, and Hos. 2:8–9). The Assyrians literally treated female captives this way[173]; now God will figuratively do this to *them*. Nineveh will be completely exposed, looted, and humiliated. God's decree is to throw "filth" upon them, so that no one (i.e., traders, merchants, etc.) will want to have anything to do with them anymore (3:6). This symbolizes His great contempt for this arrogant and idolatrous people. No one will grieve when Nineveh falls; no one will offer laments, as one would for a truly great and honorable city, because Nineveh is repulsive and contemptible. People will, God implies, be glad to see it destroyed.

Nahum 3:8–19 "No–Amon" [lit., the city of Amon] is another name for Thebes on the Nile River, one of the capital cities of Egypt (during the 18th, 19th, and 20th dynasties of the Pharaohs). Both Jeremiah (Jer. 46:25–26) and Ezekiel (Ezek. 30:14–16) prophesied against Thebes for its wickedness and idolatry. These prophesies were about one hundred years *after* Nahum, whereas Nahum speaks of something in the past tense—namely, Assyria's particularly brutal defeat of Thebes under the Assyrian king Ashurbanipal in 663 BC.[174] The city was so devastated that it never recovered from this invasion. But at least Thebes had allies (Ethiopia, Put, and Lubim[175]), while Nineveh has no allies and no protection. And, just as Thebes fell as a drunken man, so Nineveh will fall (3:11). This indicates a disgraceful fall—one that *could* have been avoided if both cities had not been "drunk" with pride, sin, and idolatry. While Nineveh became rich from the plunder of other nations, now its wealth will be like fig trees full of fruit: "when shaken, they fall into the eater's mouth" (3:12). This is made possible because "your people are like women in your midst" (3:13)—i.e., untrained, unprepared for a full–scale attack, and (by implication) preoccupied with lesser things. Its gates will be destroyed, allowing the enemy full and easy access to the heart of the city.

God (through Nahum) chides the city of Nineveh (3:14–15)—in essence, "Go ahead and see if you can resist what is coming upon you!" All such efforts will be in vain, especially since God has decreed Nineveh's destruction. The many citizens of Nineveh—estimated to be around 600,000 at this time—are like a swarm of locusts, but the aristocrats, city officials, and noblemen are unable to give direction to this swarm. They are like locusts "on a cold day" (hiding to protect themselves), but as soon as they get a chance, they will attempt to flee instead of helping to save the city (3:16–17). "Your shepherds are sleeping…" (3:18)—i.e., the military leaders, noblemen, etc. are not taking seriously what is happening; the inhabitants of the city will soon be scattered, "and there is no one to regather them."

Nahum's prophecy ends with a sense of doom and despair (3:19). While God's prophecies to Israel and Judah nearly always end with a hope of a regathering and reestablishment of glory (albeit in a spiritual context), Assyria is given no such promise, not even a glimmer of hope. There will be no relief or respite from its fall; there will be no healing from its injury. People will "clap their hands" over Nineveh's fall—they will *rejoice* that the city that brought so much death and destruction to others will now receive divine justice for all its arrogance and crimes against humanity. As Nineveh has brought an untold amount of evil to others, so now its evil will be repaid against it (compare Rev. 18:1–8 and the fall of the mystical "Babylon" [i.e., the Roman Empire]).

Questions on *Nahum*

1.) Before addressing the main subject (the overthrow of Nineveh), the book of *Nahum* opens with an all–encompassing statement concerning God's divine wrath toward *all* His enemies (1:2).

   a. Why is it important to acknowledge God's wrath *as well as* His power to save? What if we only focused on one aspect of His divine nature but not the other?

   b. How is the subject of divine wrath in conflict with the contemporary "mainstream Christianity" view of God? What effect has this had on people?

2.) While God pours out wrath upon His enemies, "[He] is a stronghold in the day of trouble" for "those who take refuge in Him" (1:7). How does this view help us to appreciate both sides of justice: that which punishes the wicked, but also protects the righteous? What if God could only do one or the other—what would this say about His divine justice?

3.) Nahum's depiction of the destruction of Nineveh is that of great fear, much bloodshed, and utter chaos. Yet, God shows no mercy toward the Ninevites. Why not?

   a. Are there limits to God's patience and mercy?

   b. Can a nation—or even an individual person—go beyond the point of no return in receiving God's mercy? (Consider Heb. 10:26–31, for example.)

4.) The inhabitants of Nineveh are characterized as being overcome with pride, idolatry, lying, sorcery, harlotry (sexual immorality), and drunkenness. Sadly, these are the same vices we increasingly see in modern–day America. Is it possible that God will overthrow *our* nation for the same reasons—and, to some degree, in the same way—that He overthrew *theirs*?

Introduction to *Habakkuk*

Authorship: This book identifies its author only as "Habakkuk the prophet" (1:1). Habakkuk ("embrace[r]"; or, possibly, "wrestler") is otherwise unknown to us.[176] "The fact that the prophet is known to us only by name once again indicates the relative unimportance of the prophet and the major importance of the prophecy and, more importantly, the God who sends the prophecy."[177] The context of the prophecy implies that his home was in or near Jerusalem, but this is merely an educated guess. In 2 Kings 21:10–14, God "spoke through His servants the prophets" that He would bring such a calamity upon Judah "that whoever hears of it, both his ears will tingle." In other words, no one would believe such difficult news. Habakkuk is to be regarded as one of these "servants" by which God would reveal this information.[178]

Date and Place of Writing: Habakkuk's prophecy concerns God's call for the Chaldeans (i.e., Babylonians) against Judah, in response to the prophet's cry for justice in the midst of (what has become) a godless nation.[179] God's description of the Babylonians (1:5–11) portrays them as being in full power, very aggressive, and unstoppable. This characterization fits the early expansionism of Babylon under Nabopolassar and his more famous son, King Nebuchadnezzar, but before Babylon had invaded Palestine. The fact that no one would *believe* that the Babylonians could be a world power (1:5) indicates that Assyria is still in command, but its power is waning. Thus, this prophecy is most certainly in the late 7th century, possibly just a few years prior to the destruction of Nineveh (see notes on the book of *Nahum*), during the reigns of the final kings of Judah. (Hailey puts this book during the reign of Jehoiakim, who reigned for eleven years in Judah[180]; see 2 Kings 23:34–37.) Thus, a good estimate is somewhere between 650—625 BC.

We have no information on where Habakkuk was when he wrote his prophecy. His self–written psalm (3:1–19) suggests that he has access to the Levite singers in Jerusalem, but we cannot know this for certain.

Purpose and Character of Writing: As mentioned, Habakkuk's prophecy concerns God's promise to bring the Chaldeans/Babylonians against Judah for its many crimes. In a real sense, "Habakkuk ministers during the 'death throes' of the nation of Judah."[181] Ezekiel blasts Judah's penchant for idolatry and its courting of foreign nations for wealth, protection, and other advantages (Ezek. 16). Israel, to the north, also indulged in idolatry and showed contempt for God's covenant, but "you [Judah] acted more abominably than they [Israel], they are more in the right than you" (Ezek. 16:52). Judah watched Israel go into captivity for the same crimes that they (Judah) are now practicing, but with even greater intensity! It is this godless, irreverent, and wicked situation that Habakkuk—a holy prophet of God—sees all around him every day. His plea, then, is essentially: "God, what are You going to do about this? And *when*?" (1:2–4).

> In a bold and dramatic presentation of the profound theological problem involved in God's longsuffering toleration of wickedness—the execution of wrath against it through the use of agents themselves more wicked than those punished— Habakkuk confronted God himself with the problem and waited patiently for the answer! There is nothing else quite like this in all the Bible.[182]

God's answer is blunt: the solution is already in the works and will soon enough fulfill His justice. Long before Habakkuk has had to deal with the sins of his people, God has already been dealing with them. The time for mercy has passed; now it is time for judgment.

While we do not know anything about Habakkuk's life, we can know about his *heart* in the way that he writes. His dialogue with God indicates his high standing in His sight: He would not allow such dialogue with a man who was not holy and pure in heart. While it appears at first that Habakkuk is taking God to task over being negligent in dealing with the wicked people of Judah, the entire book reaches a completely different conclusion. Habakkuk is, like Jonah, very passionate for his people and his nation; his questions to God are an expression of that passion. While he wants God to bring Judah to justice, he wrestles with the idea of a nation even more wicked than them—namely, the Chaldeans—to carry this out (1:12–13). In the end, however, he shows great respect and reverence for the Lord, and submits to Him entirely. God's people, the Lord says, are to live by their own faith in Him (2:4); they need to trust that He knows what to do, when to do it, and by whom to carry it out.

Overview of *Habakkuk*

Hab. 1:1 As we have seen in other books, "oracle [or, burden]" refers to something given by God to the prophet to make known to His people. The fact that it is a "burden" indicates it is not, in this case, good news; it involves divine judgment, destruction of human lives, and retribution for sin.

Hab. 1:2–4 This passage presents the prophet's complaint to God. "How long…?" is not meant to be an accusation, but a cry of *exasperation*. Habakkuk is not doubting God's power or authority, but he is asking for a *sign* or *revealed information* that something is being done in response to Judah's many sins. "How long…?" also indicates that the prophet has been asking this question for some time, but until now has not received an answer. The crimes that Habakkuk lists—iniquity, wickedness, destruction, violence, strife, contention, lawlessness, and the perversion of justice—reveal just how deeply Judah has sunk into moral depravity after many years and decades of careless disregard for God and His law. This hardly describes a people under covenant with God; instead, it sounds like any other heathen nation—or even worse—and brings shame and reproach upon God and His holy remnant of believers.

Hab. 1:5–11 Habakkuk (and Judah, for that matter) is focusing only on Judah; God is looking at all "the nations" (1:5). "Far from being disinterested in the events now transpiring, God is at work on a universal scale in order to bring His universal power and influence to bear on the evils that Habakkuk and the righteous of Judah are experiencing."[183] This means that when the things happen that God has predicted, they will know that He is the One who has brought them about. While the Chaldeans are already a rising world power, ready to take on and displace Assyria's long reign, God promises to bring this rising power directly to Judah as a punishment for Judah's abundant sins.

God's portrayal of the Chaldeans/Babylonians is both impressive and unimpressive. It is impressive in that they are a fierce and dreaded people who are well-organized, well-prepared for battle, and extremely resourceful. It is unimpressive in that they are impetuous, greedy, violent, and—most of all—will *themselves* be held guilty by God for their *own* crimes against humanity (1:11). Their "strength is their god" says much: they did not rely upon their own gods for success, although they did pay tribute to them, but trusted in their own strength, pride, and authority. King Nebuchadnezzar later reveals this attitude: "The king reflected and said, 'Is this not Babylon the great, which I myself have built as a royal residence by the might of my power and for the glory of my majesty?'" (Dan. 4:30).

Even so, the Jews (and other Palestinian nations) will be no match for the Babylonian attack when it does bear down upon them. Babylon's horses and horsemen are trained for war; "their horde of faces" (1:9) moves forward as a massive assault against their enemies; "they collect captives like sand." The Babylonians, like the Assyrians, practiced trans–population—the act of transporting captured citizens to already–captured foreign countries, and then putting people from those foreign countries into lands that the Babylonians had just captured. "This would discourage any spirit of nationalism and revolt."[184] They show no fear of kings or rulers, but rest in the confident assurance that they are the most powerful nation on the earth—which, during the reign of Nebuchadnezzar, was unquestionably true. Babylon would soon destroy Nineveh, then Harran (the relocated capital of Assyria after the fall of Nineveh), and then an allied army of remaining Assyrians and Pharaoh Neco at the critical battle of Carchemish.[185] After this, they would move southwestward into Palestine to take Syria, Judah, and finally Egypt. "One of the amazing characteristics of the Chaldean rise to worldwide authority was the speed of its accomplishment, another facet of Habakkuk's remarkable prophecy."[186]

Hab. 1:12–17 The prophet Habakkuk now responds to God's revelation. While he has another complaint—we use this word in the formal sense—he does not lose sight of who it is that he addresses. Thus, he refers to God as "my Holy One" and "O Rock" (1:12). "We will not die" means: we (Judah) deserve to be judged, corrected, even punished, but not destroyed.[187] Habakkuk is no doubt familiar with other prophetic writings that speak of a reunification of Israel and Judah in a glorious future under the Messiah's reign. Even so, he is baffled as to how God can use one ungodly nation to punish another ungodly nation.

> [God's] answer did not completely solve the problem as it was understood by Habakkuk. The destruction of Assyria which had already been revealed through other prophets by the Lord was welcome news indeed; but the answer God gave (in 1:6–11) was a vision of another Assyria, a variation of the same old disaster. This meant that there was to be no permanent improvement of life upon earth.[188]

Furthermore, the prophet wondered, since God's eyes are "too pure to approve evil" (1:13), how can He *use* evil (i.e., an evil nation) as an arm of His divine justice? The Babylonians are "those who deal treacherously" with other nations; can God allow "the wicked [to] swallow up those more righteous than they?" Perhaps Habakkuk is saying: Judah has its problems, to be sure, but Babylon is far more wicked than Judah. Or his reference to "those more righteous" might be the faithful remnant of believers in God that have always existed in either Israel or Judah, no matter how awful either nation became.

As if to buttress his case, Habakkuk goes on to speak of the crimes of the Babylonians, indicating that he is already familiar with them to an extent (1:14–17). This nation is like a fisherman with a net: they catch *people* to satisfy their appetite for war, expansion, and power. After this, they treat the "net" itself—i.e., their pride, authority, and conquering ability—as a god and "burn incense" to it. An untold number of people suffer terribly because of them; the nations are like food to them; after they empty their "net" of one conquering victory, they immediately seek another (1:17). Habakkuk is unable to see how God, being so holy, can join in any cooperative effort with a people so brutal, wicked, and unconcerned with human life.

Hab. 2:1–5 God's reply to Habakkuk's second complaint is not immediate. Thus, the prophet waits, figuratively portraying himself as taking his station on one of the city's ramparts (i.e., walls erected to repel an enemy attack) (2:1). God's answer finally does come, and He tells Habakkuk to write it down on tablets (2:2). He also says that the vision (prophecy) will not be fulfilled immediately, but it will not be long delayed, either (2:3). This is another way of saying that it will happen at exactly the right time (compare Rom. 5:6). In fact, the fulfillment is already in motion; the seeds of this prophecy have been planted long ago; men and nations are all moving according to the direction of His word. More than anything: "it will certainly come"—whatever God has promised or decreed will not fail to happen (Isa. 55:9–10). Thus, "though it tarries [or, *appears* to tarry, from a human perspective—MY WORDS], wait for it."

> God's time is not necessarily man's time. Habakkuk wanted his answer immediately. He wanted God to punish the Babylonians and put an end to evil and oppression right then. God said that he had appointed a time for all that to happen but I might not happen immediately. Habakkuk, like all of us, was living "between the times," between the promise and the fulfillment. Habakkuk was to wait in faith for God to act. He was assured that judgment on evil would surely come. It will not be late. But Habakkuk was not to wait with folded hands and bated breath for all this to happen. He was to live a life of faithfulness.[189]

God goes on to level a judgment against "the proud one" (2:4). This undoubtedly refers to the Chaldean nation as a single person, to the Chaldean king himself, or both. The proud one's "soul [or, life]" is not right within him"—i.e., God is fully aware of the crimes and arrogance of the Chaldeans. He knows them far better than does the prophet Habakkuk. "[B]ut the righteous will live by his faith [or, faithfulness]" (2:4)—a profound and theologically significant verse. Paul cites this twice (Rom. 1:17, Gal. 3:11); the *Hebrews* writer also cites it (Heb. 10:38). Paul spends most of the book of *Romans* expounding upon this statement, since it serves as the backbone of God's system of justification of sinful men. To "live by faith" means to put one's trust, confidence, and allegiance in God's ability to perform (as exemplified in Rom. 4:18–22).

God is telling Habakkuk, in so many words, that *his* job is not to worry about what nation the Lord uses to carry out His bidding, but to *have faith* that He knows what to do, what He is doing, and why it should be done.

God then returns to the "proud one," now referring to him as "the haughty man" (2:5). His characterization of Babylon is accurate: the nation is not content to "stay at home," but has an appetite for power, conquest, and plunder that is as large as Sheol (the realm of the dead). And, like Sheol, this appetite is never satisfied; death never says, "Enough" (Prov. 30:16).

Hab. 2:6–20 God underscores what He has revealed to Habakkuk with five distinct "woes" against Babylon. "Woes" are divine curses leveled against those who refuse to listen to law, repeated warnings, or acts of discipline (see Amos 4:6–13). It is important to remember, too, that God's judgment against Babylon was determined before that nation ever came to power.

- **The first woe (2:6–8):** While Babylon enjoys a period of insatiable gluttony, God promises that the price for its arrogance and crimes will eventually come due. He portrays the heathen nation as one borrowing time, power, and success; in time, its creditors will call in the nation's debts. This figuratively indicates God's own justice—He is the ultimate "creditor," and all the nations from which Babylon has looted will turn upon their destroyer at a time when its power has run its course and is exhausted. The principle put forward here is that evil nations, just like evil people, sow the seeds of their own destruction. They may carry on as though they answer to no one for a time, but their reign will not last forever. God remains in control of *all* nations; no matter how powerful a nation thinks itself to be, it cannot escape His oversight or His judgment. Crimes against Him and His people will and *must* be brought to justice.
- **The second woe (2:9–11):** Babylon will be judged for building a "house" (i.e., empire) through human cruelty and dishonest gain. What will soon become the Babylonian Empire will be built upon the atrocities, bloodshed, and corpses of millions of people, both

soldiers and civilians. That blood will cry out for justice (as did the blood of Abel [Gen. 4:10] or the souls killed in the tribulation [Rev. 6:9–11]). Even the stones and rafters (2:11)—inanimate things—will testify to the Babylonians' crimes, they will be so obvious (compare Deut. 4:26).

- **The third woe (2:12–14):** God will hold Babylon accountable for all the crimes it committed against the men (i.e., slaves, including prisoners of war) who "toiled" under its officers. A city built with bloodshed and violence also rests upon the labor of conquered people. "It is to hold life cheap and employ it in building and beautifying one's own palace, city, and nation,"[190] with no respect for human life, dignity, or suffering. An infinitely greater kingdom is coming, however, that will not treat people as expendable but will instead fill them "with the knowledge of the glory of the LORD" throughout all the earth (2:14). This can refer to nothing other than the reign of the Messiah over the kingdom of God—i.e., the Gospel Age.

- **The fourth woe (2:15–17):** The "drink" and "drunk" metaphors here are not meant to be taken literally; the context is figurative, yet potent (2:15). The picture here is of one who gives his neighbor a stupefying drink to strip him of his possessions (or wealth) and thus see him naked. "Nakedness" implies being unprotected, made vulnerable, and thus put to shame (Ezek. 16:39, 23:29). The Babylonians will take advantage of their situation to inflict as much pain, damage, and bloodshed as possible for their own selfish ambitions (see Jer. 51:1–9, 20–24). Yet, instead of Babylon disgracing other nations, God's "woe" will thoroughly disgrace Babylon. "[E]xpose your own nakedness" (2:16) in the Hebrew text refers to one who is uncircumcised (i.e., not in a covenant relationship with God; see Gen. 17:9–14). Thus, while serving as an instrument of God's wrath against all the ungodly nations, Babylon never *belonged* to God (in the way that Israel and Judah did). Isaiah's prophecy against Babylon is appropriate here:

> Sit silently, and go into darkness, O daughter of the Chaldeans, for you will no longer be called the queen of kingdoms. I was

angry with My people, I profaned My heritage and gave them into your hand. You did not show mercy to them, on the aged you made your yoke very heavy. Yet you said, "I will be a queen forever." These things you did not consider or remember the outcome of them. Now, then, hear this, you sensual one, who dwells securely, who says in your heart, "I am, and there is no one besides me. I will not sit as a widow, nor know loss of children." But these two things will come on you suddenly in one day: loss of children and widowhood. They will come on you in full measure in spite of your many sorceries, in spite of the great power of your spells. … But evil will come on you which you will not know how to charm away; and disaster will fall on you for which you cannot atone; and destruction about which you do not know will come on you suddenly. (Isa. 47:5–11)

Babylon will pay dearly for its crimes against the land ("Lebanon"), the animals ("beasts"), and especially human beings ("the town and all its inhabitants") (2:17).[191] Because Babylon will show no respect toward any of God's creation—or toward the Creator—but only for itself, God will bring that nation to its knees in disgrace.

- **The fifth woe (2:18–20):** Finally, God lays a divine curse upon Babylon for its flagrant idolatry (Jer. 51:47). Before stating the curse, however, God humiliates the very *idea* of idolatry: bowing down to a motionless, speechless, and helpless image in which there is no intelligence or breath of life. Men carve idols out of wood, chisel them out of stone, cast them from molten metal, and overlay them with gold or silver, and then expect them to perform as intelligent and capable *gods*. The God of heaven asks mockingly and contemptuously, "And that is your teacher?" (2:19). In sharp contrast, God sits as a Living Being within His heavenly temple (Psalm 11:4), and expects—and rightly deserves—"all the earth" to pay reverent homage to Him (2:20).[192]

This ends the prophet Habakkuk's inquiry of God. He has asked questions, and God has given him answers. He has asked more questions, and God has given him more answers. But in the end, despite however many questions are asked and answers are given, the ultimate answer is always the same: God is in heaven, and humans are on earth. Nothing that happens upon earth—no crime or injustice, and no good deed or act of kindness—goes unnoticed by Him. He will reward those who live by faith in Him (recall 2:4), but He will destroy those who seek self-gratification and idolatry of any form. This is reminiscent of the end of *Ecclesiastes*: "The conclusion, when all has been heard, is: fear God and keep His commandments, because this applies to every person. For God will bring every act to judgment, everything which is hidden, whether it is good or evil" (Eccles. 12:13–14).

Hab. 3:1–19 In reverent response to God's answers to his prayer, the prophet Habakkuk offers a psalm of tribute, praise, and even trembling fear concerning what the Lord has said about what is to come upon His people (i.e., the impending Babylonian invasion). "Shigionoth" indicates an excited, emotional song; this refers either to the content of the psalm, its music, or both. The meaning of "Selah" (at punctuated intervals of the psalm) is uncertain but is thought to indicate a pause in the singing, or possibly a crescendo of music. It occurs over seventy times in *Psalms* but nowhere else in Scripture except three times in Habakkuk's psalm.[193]

Habakkuk begins with a very poetic, almost overwhelming, anticipation of God's awesome glory as He comes near to carry out His judgment (3:1–7). He imagines God's literal presence (a poetic theophany, or showing of God) coming down from the mountains of neighboring nations toward Judah, carrying with Him agents of destruction (pestilence and plague—3:5), surveying the land of men that have not given Him recognition (3:6). ("Teman" is a city of Edom, southeast of Judah; "Mount Paran" is a mountainous/wilderness area south of Judah; "Cushan" refers to Cush, an ancient name for Ethiopia in Africa; "Midian" is a nomadic people southeast of the Jordan River, with ancient associations with Moab.) The implication from all these place names seems to be this: just as God "came" to Israel in the days of their wandering in the wilderness, so He will come to the "Israel" (Judah) of Habakkuk's day in their wandering in the spiritual wilderness of their idolatry. Then, it was to save them; soon, it will be to punish them.

All physical Creation is subject to the One who created it: the rivers, seas, mountains, and even the sun and moon (3:8–15). Declaring His power *over* these things, however, does not mean God is angry *with* them. He always directs the power of His salvation, as well as His righteous indignation, at people, not inanimate objects. In Israel's past, God had overcome the natural powers of the world to save His people; He intervened in the physical realm to defend His covenant with Israel (3:12–15). Habakkuk portrays all this in highly poetic, sometimes graphic, language (in keeping with the nature of all Hebrew psalms), but the essential truths he communicates are real and significant. Even though God has often come as a rescuer of His people, He will also serve as their judge if they choose to violate His covenant flagrantly and persistently.

This last thought is a segue way into the closing section of the psalm (3:16–19). Habakkuk, after extolling and admiring the great rescuing power God has displayed in the past, now shudders at what this same power can bring against his people (Judah). The "day of distress" (3:16) is coming; God has made this clear. The "people ... who will invade us" (the Babylonians) are also coming, and they will not be unsuccessful in their campaign against Judah. This causes the prophet great consternation and fear because all he can do is sit back and wait for these things to run their course. What God has pronounced *will indeed happen*, and there is no one on earth who can stop Him. In 3:16–17, the prophet mentions all the food sources for Judah, in anticipation of the invading Babylonian army consuming all of them or simply destroying them during the invasion itself.

> This [3:17] is a vivid description of the results of the "scorched earth" policy of the Babylonian invaders. The end result of such destruction would be starvation and death to multiplied tens of

thousands of the population. Everything of value that could be transported would be carried away by the ruthless invaders, and what remained would be wantonly destroyed for the precise purpose of making the lands uninhabitable. That such a prospect was a source of great agony in the heart of Habakkuk is certain. Leaving such a pitiful lament without any further comment, Habakkuk went on to declare his joyful trust in the Lord no matter what would happen.[194]

In the end, we should not remember Habakkuk as a prophet of doom and gloom, but of great and reverent faith. Even though the judgment must come, and horrible distress will come upon the land of Judah, the prophet's faith remains firm and focused: "Yet I will exult in the LORD, I will rejoice in the God of my salvation" (3:18). Even though judgment must come against Judah for its idolatry and many other moral crimes, the prophet Habakkuk—and all those who live by faith as he does—finds strength in God to endure what lies ahead, overcome the day of distress, and carry on in service to Him (3:19). ("Hinds" refers to deer or gazelles, and to have feet like hinds' feet means to be swift and sure-footed.)

Questions on *Habakkuk*

1.) What does the manner in which Habakkuk approaches God (1:2–4, 12–17, and 2:1) tell us about how *we* are to approach Him, even when we are disappointed, frustrated, and/or bewildered by what we see happening (or, as in Habakkuk's case, *not* happening)?

2.) Why do you suppose God does not bring about *immediate* justice—either for His people (Israel or Judah) or those whom He uses to punish them (Assyria or Babylon)?

a. Why do *we* often seek immediate justice? (There are several possible answers.)

b. What does "the righteous will live by his faith" (2:4) have to do with God bringing justice for all the moral crimes of a given person or nation?

3.) What does Babylon think about itself, its sovereignty, and its survivability, as implied in the five "woes" against it (2:6–19)?

a. Is this also how a godless person today may think about himself or herself?

b. Is it possible that a *Christian* might think this way, having forgotten who he (or she) really is and what God has done for him (2 Peter 1:9, in principle)?

4.) One of the most memorable verses in *Habakkuk* is 2:20: "But the LORD is in His holy temple. Let all the earth be silent before Him."

a. What does this tell us about God's majesty? About our "place" in His world?

b. What does "be silent" imply, beyond simply being quiet? (Consider Rom. 3:18–19, 11:30–32, and Gal. 3:21–22 in your answer.)

5.) The book of *Habakkuk* ends with a psalm about God and His glory (chapter 3). What impression does this psalm leave upon you—not only regarding its content, but also why (or how) it was written?

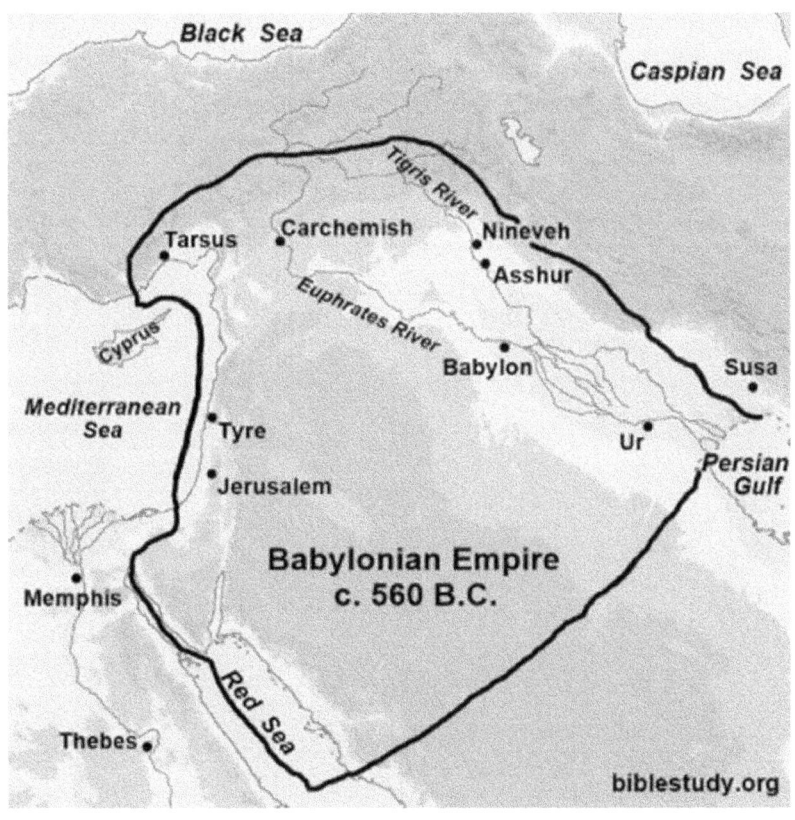

Introduction to *Haggai*

Authorship: We know nothing about Haggai except that he is several times referred to as "the prophet" (1:1, 3, 12, 2:1, etc.). His name in Hebrew means "festive," "festival," or "festal one." Some think it is a shortened form of Haggiah, "festival of Jehovah."[196] He is also mentioned in Ezra 5:1 and 6:4, where the only further information concerning him is that he is a contemporary of the prophet Zechariah. Some assume (from 2:3) that Haggai was an eyewitness to the temple in Jerusalem before King Nebuchadnezzar of Babylon razed it (586 BC). If so, this would mean that Haggai had lived through the seventy years of Babylonian exile and was an old man when he gave his prophecies concerning the rebuilding of the temple. But this conclusion is based upon the assumptions of a single passage and remains entirely unsubstantiated. In any case, "He was a man that God raised up at a specific time for a specific mission."[197]

Date and Place of Writing: There is a great span of time between the last prophet (Habakkuk) and Haggai. Habakkuk prophesied shortly before the destruction of Jerusalem and the seventy-year Babylonian captivity of the Jews. Haggai was among those Jews who returned from this captivity (see Ezra 1—2). The book of *Haggai* is dated during "the second year of Darius the king [i.e., Darius I, a Median who became the Persian emperor in 521 BC]" (1:1).[198] Darius' early kingship was filled with assassinations, revolt, and numerous wars (nineteen different battles against nine different kings). Darius' reign coincided with the release of the Judean captives from the land of Babylon; he is the same "Darius" mentioned in the book of *Ezra*. Cyrus the Persian proclaimed freedom to the Jews to return to their homeland ca. 538 BC, but they did not actually make the 800-mile trip until a few years later, under the leadership of Zerubbabel.

Purpose and Character of Writing: When the Jews did arrive back in Judea (ca. 536–535 BC), they found the situation there very disheartening. Jerusalem lay desolate: the walls of the city were broken down; the temple was destroyed. They immediately went to work laying the foundation of the temple (Ezra 3) but went no further. The reason for this was partly because of the nature of the returnees themselves. "[T]here were no doubt a considerable number of men among those who had returned, who had been actuated to return less by living faith in the Lord and His word, than by earthly hopes of prosperity and comfort in the land of their fathers. As soon as they found themselves disappointed in their expectations, they became idle and indifferent with regard to the house of the Lord."[199] Thus, they focused on building their own homes and establishing their lives.

Another reason for inactivity was because they met opposition from non-Jews who had occupied the land of Israel to the north, having been transplanted there by the Assyrian king Esarhaddon (Ezra 4:1–2; see 2 Kings 17:24). These people are known as Samaritans, whom the Jews denied participating in the rebuilding of their temple. In response (or retaliation), the Samaritans resorted to intimidating the Jewish workers. As the work on the temple increased, so did the opposition. According to the book of *Ezra*, this tension remained until a written decree came from Darius to give the Jews full permission to build their temple, along with a promise to punish anyone who interfered with this (Ezra 5:6—6:12).

The actual rebuilding of the temple did not resume for about sixteen years after the people laid its foundation. It was the prophet Haggai (and Zechariah) who prompted this rebuilding, by bringing a stern message to the people that they had had time enough to focus on their own homes. It was time now, God said, to finish *His* "house" (1:9). Furthermore, God had caused a drought to afflict the land because of His anger over their delay (1:10–11).

Hailey says, "The writing of Haggai is unlike that of his predecessors. Lacking in his work is the rhythm and rolling grandeur of Nahum, the poetry and charm of Habakkuk, or the fire of Amos. In comparison his work seems subdued and prosaic. But he was completely successful."[200] Within weeks of his prophecies, the Jews resumed work on a temple they had left alone for many years. It should be noted, too, that, "when judged by the results which followed, no prophet of the OT, with the exception of Jonah, was any more successful" than Haggai.[201] Because of his words and influence, the temple of God was rebuilt and lasted for the next several hundred years to come.

The book of *Haggai* is the shortest book in the OT after *Obadiah*. Yet, while the message is brief, it is potent; the prophet Haggai is direct and to the point; there is no need for elaborate explanation. Work needs to be done, he says, and God not only expects the Jews to do it, but He promises to be with them in the process (2:1–5). Once the work begins in earnest, God also promises to restore whatever they had lost during the imposed drought (2:18–19). "In this message he [Haggai] revived the Messianic hope, point out that the house [of the Lord] would be filled with glory, a glory that would surpass anything previously seen."[202] He also identifies Zerubbabel as a prefigure of the future Messiah (see Zech. 4).

Overview of *Haggai*

Hag. 1:1 "Haggai" is simply known to us as "the prophet." Twenty-six times in this short book, he claims that what he speaks are the words of God. (On Darius I, king of Persia, see information in "Introduction.") "Zerubbabel" [Heb., "shoot (or descendant) of Babylon"] is listed in Ezra 2:2 and Neh. 7:7 as one of the leaders of the returned captives from Babylon to Judah (ca. 536 BC). Likely, "Zerubbabel" is the name given to him in captivity, as he seems to be identified as Sheshbazzar elsewhere (Ezra 1:8, 11, 5:14, 16). "Shealtiel" is the son of Jehoiakim, one of the last kings of Judah (2 Kings 23:34—24:6), making Zerubbabel the grandson of Jehoiakim and therefore a rightful heir to the throne of David.

However, God made it clear that *no descendant* of David—especially, no descendent of Jehoiakim, or his son, Jehoiachin [a.k.a. Coniah]—will be king over His people (Jer. 22:24–30). Zerubbabel is thus referred to as the "governor of Judea" (an appointment likely made by the Persian emperor Cyrus) rather than the *king* of Judah. He does appear in the genealogy of Joseph, Jesus' alleged earthly father (Mat. 1:1–17), but Jesus' biological lineage is traced through Mary, His mother (Luke 3:23–38), since Joseph was not his literal father. While both lineages trace back to David, Jesus' lineage through Mary is His *royal* lineage. (Joseph's lineage comes through David's son Solomon; Mary's is through David's son Nathan.)

"Joshua" (a.k.a. Jeshua in Ezra 3:2) is the Jews' high priest at the time of the return from Babylon. His father was Jehozadak (a.k.a. Jozadak in Ezra 3:2), who was the high priest when the Jews went *into* Babylonian captivity (1 Chron. 6:15). "The remnant of the people" (2:2) refers to the relatively small number of returnees from captivity in comparison to the large group that was deported to Babylon seventy years previously. Remember that Haggai's prophecies are sixteen years *after* the actual return. Zerubbabel, then, was the political leader of the people; Joshua was the religious leader.

Hag. 1:2–11 God, through Haggai, addresses the Jews as "This people" (1:2)—"not because He has cast them off, but because they are disobedient and apathetic."[203] The *people*—not God—have decided that the time for the Lord's temple to be built "has not come." Having settled down in their original homeland, they have focused their attention on constructing their own houses rather than rebuilding God's temple (1:3–4). ("Paneled houses" indicates a sign of luxury, as was expected of kings; see 1 Kings 7:7 and Jer. 22:14.) This is particularly offensive to God, since it was *He* who removed them from Judah in the first place because of their irreverence toward Him, and it was *He* who brought them back so that they could honor Him. Instead of showing reverence or gratitude, however, the people show disinterest toward God and His "house." The problem was not the building of their own fine houses, but that their priorities were backward. God's house should have received *primary attention*, not left sitting half-done for sixteen years.

Because of this, God calls upon them to "Consider your ways!" (1:5)— another way of saying, "Take a good, hard look at yourselves and what you are doing, and see for yourself that it is *not right*." God's judgment on the matter has already been demonstrated in the form of small, pathetic harvests, the lack of wine, the lack of clothing, and the inability to put money aside for savings (1:6). In other words, in every area where they tried to *flourish*, they were left with only enough to barely *survive*. Not only was the harvest small, but even what they gleaned seemed to disappear before it brought any good.

God's message to the people is, "Stop focusing on your own houses, and finish Mine! *Then* I will bless you with abundant harvests, wine, clothing, and money." He does not apologize for making them *work* to finish what they started ("Go up to the mountains …") because He deserves to be glorified, and the temple is one important way in which He is to be glorified (1:7–8). He then identifies the *reason* for the drought (and the resulting poor harvests): it is not mere coincidence, but their disobedience. In other words, it is not as though God could not provide more, but He *withheld* success and abundance from them as a means of punishment (1:9–10). Divine blessings are always dependent upon the obedience of those who seek them. Disobedience negatively affects everything (1:11).

Hag. 1:12–15 Despite the people's previous indifference, God promises that "I am with you" if they would but finish His "house" (temple). To demonstrate this, He energized and emboldened both Zerubbabel and Joshua to organize the people in this matter. Actual construction began twenty-three days after Haggai proclaimed his message. This does not indicate delay, but implies the need for organization, gathering of materials, and architectural design to finish the project (see Ezra 5:1–2).

Hag. 2:3–9 Nearly a month into the work of rebuilding, God brings another message to the people through the prophet Haggai. As the temple takes form, God asks, "Who remembers the original temple built by Solomon?" There were men among the returned captives who were old enough to recall the glory of that original temple (Ezra 3:8–13). But Nebuchadnezzar fully destroyed that temple, and the new one cannot compare to it (1:3).[204] Not only this, but the ark of the covenant had disappeared, just as God promised it would (Jer. 3:16). (To this day, no one knows what happened to it, whether it was hidden and forgotten, or destroyed.)

Even so, God again inspires Zerubbabel and Joshua to lead the people in finishing the temple—not because God needs temples (see 1 Kings 8:27–29 and Acts 7:48–50), but because the *people* need a holy place for sacrifice (Deut. 12:5–6), pilgrimage (Deut. 16:16), and the ministry of the priests and Levites (Num. 3:5–10). God's encouragement ("take courage"; "I am with you") is reminiscent of what He spoke to Joshua after the death of Moses (1:4; see Josh. 1:1–9). As God was with Israel when He led them out of Egypt and into the Promised Land, so He is with them now in the rebuilding of the temple (1:5).

God also promises that "Once more" He will "shake the heavens and the earth" (i.e., the physical human domain), and that "the wealth of all nations" will "fill this house [i.e., the temple] with glory" (1:6–8). While the people had lived through a shameful past (what Isaiah called the time of "indignation"—Isa. 26:20), God promises them a glorious future. This "shaking" likely refers to the overthrow of the Persian Empire, then the Greek Empire, and ultimately culminating in the destruction of the Roman Empire—the final end of the four-empire statue of Nebuchadnezzar's dream (see Dan. 2:31–45). (See Heb. 12:26–29 in connection with these ideas.)

This has reference, then, not to a literal shaking (as in an actual earthquake), but to the end of the existing world order "by means of great political convulsions, and indeed ... by wars and revolutions, by which the might of the heathen world is broken and annihilated."[205] This "shaking" not only destroys the old world order, but also introduces a *new* order—one that is ruled by God's Messiah. In another sense, God has always had but one house. In order to build the new "house" (Christ's spiritual temple), the old "house" (the Jewish temple and its attending law, rituals, priesthood, and sacrificial system) had to be torn down.[206] "For here we do not have a lasting city [i.e., no city built of men *will* or *can* last], but we are seeking the city which is to come" (Heb. 13:14, bracketed words are mine).

The picture of all the nations bringing their "wealth" to fill God's "house" is a messianic prophecy (Isa. 60:1–22, Rev. 21:24). It is not physical or monetary wealth that God speaks of, but *human souls*. The establishment of His kingdom will supersede (in power, glory, and duration) the fourfold Gentile kingdoms of men (Babylon, Persia, Greece, and Rome). While these man-made kingdoms are located on earth, God's kingdom will not be "of this world" (John 18:36). *In this sense,* "the latter glory" of His temple (i.e., the church in prophecy) will be far greater than even Solomon's temple (2:9; see Eph. 2:19–22 and 1 Peter 2:4–5).

<u>Hag. 2:10–19</u> Two months after Haggai's second prophesy—three months after his first one—God speaks again through His prophet, asking for a "ruling" (or decision; legal interpretation) from the priests. The ruling concerns whether holiness can be transferred to something unholy (to make it clean or holy), or whether contact with something unholy corrupts what is holy.[207] ("Holy" here refers to that which is

used in service to God or represents anything that belongs to Him.) The priests answer: holy food will not make unholy food holy (if one touches the other), but the exact opposite will happen—the holy food will become unholy (or, unclean). Likewise, a man defiled by death (touching a corpse) cannot become clean by touching holy food, but the opposite is true—holy food is defiled by contact with the defiled man. Thus, the ruling is: ceremonial cleanness is not communicable to unclean things, but ceremonial *un*-cleanness is a contaminant to whatever is clean (2:10–13). "Haggai did not say to the priests, make us a law about the situation mentioned; but 'tell the people what the law is!'" as written in Num. 19:11, 22.[208]

God has a point to all this, namely, to teach a spiritual lesson to His people. "It is the priest's responsibility to interpret the Law to the nation and the prophet's responsibility to apply it."[209] While only the foundation of the temple had been laid (and the altar—see Ezra 3:1–7), the people had been making sacrifices to God, but these holy sacrifices were rendered unclean because of the failure of the people to build the temple (2:14–17). Again, God reminds the people that the drought, "blasting wind, mildew, and hail"—all natural phenomena by themselves—collectively paint a picture of divine punishment. "Though these catastrophes took their toll on the economy, they did not achieve their purpose of causing the people to repent and obey Jehovah."[210] Even so, God promises that, if the people continue in their commitment to rebuild the temple, God will bless "the seed still in the barn" so that it will produce a bountiful harvest (2:18–19).

Hag. 2:20–23 This passage repeats what God said earlier (recall 2:6–7), with added information as well. The message is directed personally to Zerubbabel, the appointed governor of the returned exiles from Babylon. God speaks highly of this man, likely because he has proven himself to be diligent to rouse the people to action in the rebuilding of the temple. He is a capable leader, and therefore God has "chosen" him. A "signet ring" is the ruler's ring that imprints the waxed seal of official documents. It symbolizes great authority and power (as in Gen. 41:38–43). God is telling Zerubbabel, in so many words, that he will represent

Him before the people in all that he did.[211] Not only this, but Zerubbabel will be included in the lineage of Joseph, the alleged father of the coming Messiah. God said these things to bolster this man's confidence as he faced the daunting challenge of rebuilding the temple as well as the difficulty of facing local enemies (Ezra 4:1–4).

This ends the short but potent prophecies of Haggai. Because of his words, the people are inspired and motivated to finish what they started (compare 2 Cor. 8:10–11). Good intentions are not enough to honor God; completing the deeds He expects of His people is also necessary (compare Rev. 3:2–3).

Questions on *Haggai*

1.) What are your overall impressions of the book of *Haggai*?

2.) God was not angry with the Jews because they built houses for themselves, but that they did so *before* and *regardless of* their work on finishing God's house (the temple). What can Christians learn from this? Might Christians sometimes put their own pursuits ahead of God's interests (see Mat. 16:23)? Please explain.

3.) Failing to finish God's work had a detrimental effect on the Jews' physical and economic prosperity (1:7–11). Will neglecting our personal ministries to God have any detrimental effect on our circumstances—both physical and spiritual?

4.) Please read Luke 9:62, 2 Cor. 8:10–11, and Rev. 3:2–3. What is the consistent message in these passages? How does this tie directly to the message Haggai brought to the Jews? What should *we* gain from this for ourselves?

5.) We learn from 2:11–14 that *unholy people* cannot conduct *holy work*, and that no one becomes holy simply by his association with holy work. What do these principles have to do with Christians, if anything? (Consider 2 Cor. 6:14—7:1 and 1 Peter 1:13–16 in your answer.)

Introduction to *Zechariah*

Authorship: The name Zechariah ("one whom Jehovah remembers") is popular in the OT, identifying at least twenty-seven men. Zechariah the prophet is of priestly descent; his grandfather, Iddo, was one of the priests who returned from Babylonian captivity (Neh. 12:4). He is not the same Zechariah to whom Jesus referred (in Mat. 23:35), since that man lived hundreds of years earlier (see 2 Chron. 24:20–22).[212] Zechariah the prophet is a "young man" (2:4), but this is likely a comparison of his age to that of other men of his profession. If he is an active priest, he entered the priestly ministry at age thirty (Num. 4:3, 23, etc.)—the same age that John the Baptist and Jesus entered their ministries (Luke 3:23)—a relatively young age for a prophet.

Date and Place of Writing: Haggai and Zechariah both began their prophetic ministries at the same time, in "the second year of Darius," the Persian emperor (see "Introduction to *Haggai*"). This is about sixteen years after the first wave of Jews returned to Judah from their Babylonian captivity (ca. 520–518 BC). While Haggai's ministry ended within a year, Zechariah's prophecies (or visions) continued at least until the "fourth year of King Darius" (7:1), and likely beyond. Modern scholars have assumed that the last part of Zechariah (chapters 9—14) was written sometime later, and possibly not even by Zechariah himself. Their reasoning for this is because of the many messianic references that are so different from the first half of the book, as well as the rest of the minor prophets. The ancient Jews, however, have always considered *Zechariah* to be one complete work of a single author. *Zechariah* is also quoted a number of times in the NT, from all parts of the book, and all quotes are attributed to the same prophet. "We have never for one moment allowed the claim that modern 'scholars' are any better qualified than the ancients to determine the date of biblical books; indeed, we believe that the ancients were far better qualified, due to their proximity in point of time and their access to much material now lost."[213] All said, there is no justifiable reason for a so-called "deutero-Zechariah" author.[214]

Jerusalem is the natural (but unstated) place of writing of *Zechariah*, since that is where the temple is, and that is where the people are who need encouragement to rebuild it. To fix on any other location is pure conjecture.

Purpose and Character of Writing: For a historical background of the book of *Zechariah*, see "Introduction to *Haggai*." Haggai and Zechariah are two prophets that God sent to admonish and encourage the returned captives to finishing building the temple in Jerusalem. (The ruined wall around Jerusalem is a separate matter; this will later be rebuilt under Nehemiah's direction; see Neh. 1—4 and 6:15) Haggai's prophecies are more practical and focus on the immediate situation; much of Zechariah's prophecies, however, look well beyond the current state of Jerusalem, and look forward to the reign of the Messiah. In fact, *Zechariah* is easily the most "messianic" of all the minor prophets. It is also the longest and one of the most difficult to interpret of all the minor prophets, due to its highly visionary, symbolic, and cryptic language (especially in chapters 9—14). "[The] future blessing is contingent upon present obedience. The people are not merely building a building [i.e., the temple]; they are building the future. With that as their motivation, they can enter into the building project with wholehearted zeal, for their Messiah is coming."[215]

Bible scholars consider *Zechariah* as one of the "apocalyptic" books of the OT (along with *Ezekiel* and *Daniel*). "Apocalyptic" refers to literature that uncovers, lays bare, or reveals that which was formerly hidden or mysterious. This "unveiling," however, is not for the casual reader, but for one who understands the symbols, signs, and veiled references used. Such literature was written during times of great anxiety, stress, persecution, or upheaval of the powers at hand—especially, powers that threaten the welfare or even survival of God's people (the Jews).[216] Apocalyptic writings go beyond mere prophecy; they deal with: the condition of the world; global forces of government, nations, and kingdoms; and major themes of the struggle between good and evil. Common characteristics of apocalyptic literature include:

- a big-picture view of the moral realm (right vs. wrong, good vs. evil, God's people vs. the world, etc.).
- great spans of time and history.
- an intense motivational call, or divine summoning, to moral purity.
- consideration of the past and present, and incorporating these into a future picture.
- references to a future glory and/or life of the individual, based on his moral goodness.
- visions, revelations, and angels (i.e., otherworldly elements).
- strong dramatic element, including deliberate overemphasis, exaggeration, hyperbole, and intentionally ridiculous proportions.
- symbols, images, and figures (i.e., tangibles) used to represent solid qualities, ideas, or principles (i.e., non–tangibles). The reader is not meant to focus on any one symbol or characteristic of it but is to view this in the context of the big–picture perspective.
- numbers (including measurements) that rarely communicate actual numerical or mathematical values, but are symbols designed to provide unstated ideas or concepts.
- a behind–the–scenes look at what is happening in the spiritual world as it affects the physical world. It is always in this sequence: spiritual warfare (think of Eph. 6:12, for example) is what drives the fight between good and evil in the world of men, not the other way around.

A major theme of *Zechariah* is the coming of Messiah (Christ) and the great upheaval to the world—including the Jewish nation—that this will bring. Zechariah focuses more on the Messiah's personal ministry more than any other minor prophet. The overall tone is one of encouragement, although there are also judgments cited against the foreign (Gentile) nations as well as implied judgments against the Jewish nation itself (see chapter 11, for example, where "I" is really the Messiah speaking). "[T]he Lord of hosts" occurs over fifty times in *Zechariah*, where "hosts" refers to an angelic army, and thus depicts God fighting on behalf of His people. "[T]hus says the Lord of hosts" is an expression that occurs sixteen times, strongly indicating a message from God, and thus not one to be ignored, doubted, or second-guessed. In short, the rebuilding of the physical temple in Jerusalem is merely a precursor to the much larger picture of the glory of the Lord (the Messiah) when He comes to visit His people and turn the world upside-down with His reign over the kingdom of God.

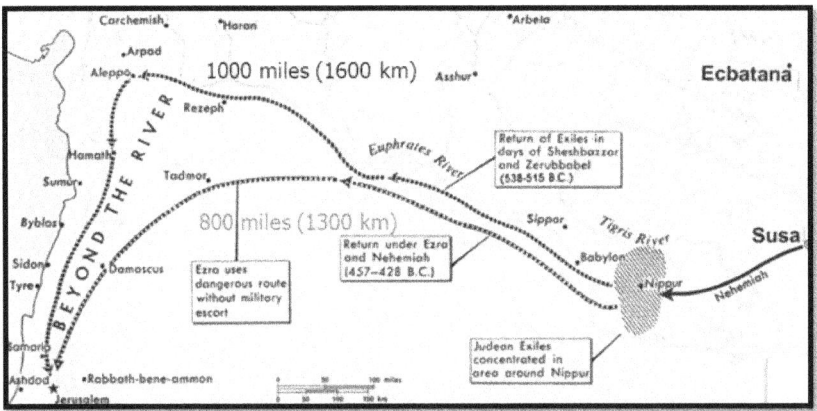

Overview of *Zechariah*

Zech. 1:1 As the book opens, God commissions Zechariah the prophet to speak "the word of the Lord" to the Jews who have returned to Judea from their seventy-year-long Babylonian captivity. "Darius" is the second ruler of Persia, having succeeded Cyrus the Persian (in whose reign the Jewish captives were set free, *and* the foundation of the temple was laid in Jerusalem; see Isa. 44:28—45:7). On "Zechariah" and "Darius," see "Introduction to *Zechariah*" and "Introduction to *Haggai*," respectively.

The first division (1:2—6:15)

Zech. 1:2–6 God begins His message to the Jews by reminding them how angry He was with "your fathers"—i.e., the generations leading up to and including the one sent into Babylonian captivity. He thus warns the present generation, "Do not be like your fathers," otherwise terrible things will happen to *them* as well (compare to Paul's warnings in 1 Cor. 10:6–12). The "fathers" did not listen and suffered dearly; the present generation, however, *is* listening (implied in 1:6). The previous generation is now dead; the present generation is alive, and has opportunity, potential, and hope. Thus, the rest of the prophecy is encouragement to continue in their faithfulness to God. This prophecy begins with a series of eight visions that Zechariah the prophet "sees" and in which he also participates. These eight visions all seem to occur in a single night. "Visions differ from dreams in that dreams appeared while the individual was asleep, whereas visions appeared to the sight during one's waking hours. The prophet sees either with his physical eye or the eyes of the Spirit as he is wrapped in ecstasy, but he sees."[217]

Zech. 1:7–17 The **first vision** occurs near the end of the eleventh month of Darius' second year of his reign, two months after Haggai's last oracle (Hag. 2:10). This vision has three parts: when it occurs (1:7); its details (1:8–12); and its promise (1:13–17). It begins with Zechariah seeing four horsemen, their horses all being of a different color; the lead horse is red.[218] These horsemen are "among the myrtle trees"—large, flowering, ornamental shrubs that are native to Palestine, indicating the geographical context of the vision: it concerns God's people in Judea. An angel accompanying Zechariah in the vision explains that these horsemen are keeping watch over the nations of the world (1:10). While Darius, in his initial ascension to the throne, dealt with numerous wars and uprisings, things have settled down and the world is (generally) at peace (1:11). Haggai promised that God would "shake the heavens and the earth," and "all the nations" (Hag. 2:6–7), but this obviously has not yet happened. "As long as the nations of the world enjoyed undisturbed peace, Judah could not expect any essential improvement in its condition, [and] the people were still under the bondage of the power of the world, without any prospect of the realization of the glory predicted by earlier prophets ..."[219]

This angel—whom some believe to be the rider of the red horse—asks God, "How long will You be angry with Your people?" (referring to the seventy-year exile) (1:12). God's answer, while not revealed to us directly, contains "gracious words, comforting words" (1:13; see Isa. 40:1–2). He has not forgotten His people; however, He remains angry with the Gentile nations that are "at ease" in their proud self-reliance. Even so, God manifests compassion for His people in His desire for them to complete His temple ("house") in Jerusalem—a sign that His presence is with them, and that they have His blessing. The "measuring line" (1:16) indicates that the people will fill Jerusalem, indicating a time of security, prosperity, and general flourishing. In apocalyptic literature, to "measure" something is to prepare for its establishment, sanction it, and *preserve* it through divine protection (compare with Ezek. 40—43, Rev. 11:1–2, and 21:10–17). It rarely has anything to do with literal lengths, quantities, or distances.

Zech. 1:18–21 In the **second vision**, Zechariah sees four "horns" and four "craftsmen." "Horns" symbolize power or strength, usually of a human source or government. "Four" denotes a world power: four corners of the earth (Isa. 11:12); four winds (Jer. 49:36, Dan. 11:4, Rev. 7:1); four beasts of the four Gentile kingdoms, represented by four metals in Nebuchadnezzar's statue (Dan. 2:30–35, 7:3, 17); etc. The explanation of the vision (1:21) is that four world powers, hostile to

God's people, have scattered them throughout the earth. It is difficult to specify *which* four nations are meant here; it is best to take them as a whole, where "four" means that they *are* the world. The craftsmen (or smiths; carpenters) are other powers sent by God to "terrify" these hostile nations. In other words, for every challenge brought to God's people by the world, God responds with those who will conduct His judgment against such nations—in this case, His "craftsmen."

<u>**Zech. 2:1-5**</u> In the **third vision**, Zechariah sees a man with a measuring line (or, cord; lit., ball of string) who has been commissioned to "measure" Jerusalem. As mentioned above, to "measure" something is to establish, bless, and protect it. Thus, this is God's symbolic way of saying that He will build up Jerusalem and preserve it. However, "Jerusalem" here is itself a symbol in the vision, for the divine prophecy cannot be limited to the actual city itself. God is not preserving a *city*, but His *people*—and He will not protect His people with a city wall, but with His own divine presence ("a wall of fire") (2:5). Thus, "Jerusalem" is used in a *spiritual* context, not a literal one, and has ultimate reference to the Messiah and His people (church). The "young man" (2:4) is most naturally the prophet Zechariah; never is an angel referred to as a "young man." Also, the message is intended for the prophet and his people, not for an angel.

<u>**Zech. 2:6-13**</u> In an interlude, God calls to His people to come out of the lands to where they have been dispersed, and to come with joy into this *new* Jerusalem. "[T]he north" (2:6) is the direction (out of Palestine) of Assyria; this alludes to the Israelites exiled there. Those in Babylon (2:7) are Jews who still reside in that place since the captivity began. In other words, God is calling for the *regeneration* and *restoration* of His people, but in a new and unprecedented context. He is not merely saying, "Come back to Palestine," but instead, "Come to where I will dwell in your midst"—indicating a *spiritual* reunion, not a literal one. This speaks (again) of the messianic era in which *all* faithful Jews will assemble in the New Jerusalem (see Heb. 12:22). "The promise here overreaches the fate of earthly Jerusalem. and applies gloriously to the Church of Jesus Christ," in which the Holy Spirit will indwell God's people. Not

only this, but "Many nations will join themselves to the LORD in that day" (2:11)—this invitation begins with the Israelites, but is ultimately extended to people of every nationality (see John 10:16, Rom. 1:16, and 11:25–32).

In a statement similar to Hab. 2:20, all the earth is told (in the vision) to "be silent," since the Lord's presence is near, and His work among men is a sacred one.[221] In other words, "Things were about to change; the indifference indicated by the report of the horsemen (1:11) was about to be altered. The heathen nations would be judged, Jehovah would build and inhabit the new Zion, and He would fulfill His promises concerning Jerusalem."[222]

Zech. 3:1–5 The **fourth vision** deals with the reinstatement of the high priesthood, symbolized by Joshua's appointment as the high priest. This was necessary because the priesthood prior to the captivity was corrupt and dysfunctional. The priests' failure to teach, warn, and even rebuke the people is partly what led to the seventy-year Babylonian exile in the first place. The priests are among the pathetic "shepherds of Israel" (see Ezek. 34:1ff) that saw to their own interests at the expense of the "flock." Now, however, God wants His priesthood reinstated, according to the proper lineage of the high priest. "Satan" [lit., adversary; accuser] is traditionally thought to be the devil himself, yet this conclusion is unwarranted and unnecessary. "The term 'the Satan' is used here as a title of an accuser before Yahweh rather than as a personal name. 'The fuller development of the doctrine of a personal and devilish opponent of God is a feature of the New Testament,'"[223] and one that comes about especially in response to the incarnation of God's Son.[224]

In any case, "Satan" (in the vision) accuses Joshua of being *unfit* to hold the office, or that the office is too honorable for *any* sinful man to hold. "A nation so guilty and so punished could no longer be the holy and priestly nation [compare Exod. 19:5–6]: its priests could no longer be priests; nor could its high priests be high priests any more"[225]—such was the accuser's implication. God bluntly dispenses the accusation ("The LORD rebuke you, Satan [Adversary]!"—3:2). Joshua/the priesthood has been through the fire of testing and adversity, namely, the seventy-year captivity; that process has refined the priesthood of the corruption that once plagued it. A "brand [or, firebrand]" (3:2) is a small stick or log in a fire; God has *saved* the priesthood from its fiery ordeal. "Satan" insinuates that God is unaware of the sins of the priesthood; God responds that not only is He fully aware of its sins, but that the priesthood has undergone sufficient punishment for its crimes against Him.

Even so, "Joshua" (in representing the entire priesthood) is not yet *prepared* to fulfill his role as a high priest (3:3–5). His "filthy garments" represent both the sins of the priesthood as well as the sins of the people (Jews) (see Isa. 64:6). The garments of the high priest are, according to the Law, *supposed* to be beautiful, clean, and highly ornamented (see Exod. 39). The high priest is to wear a turban with a plate of fine gold fastened to it with the inscription, "Holy to the LORD" (Exod. 39:27–31). God's order to remove the filthy garments proves "that it is not on the ground of His people's righteousness that He accepts them," but on the basis of God's own gracious forgiveness.[226] The call for a "clean turban on his head" (3:5; compare Luke 15:22–23) appears to come from the prophet Zechariah himself, no doubt caught up in the ecstasy of this vision.

Zech. 3:6–10 At this point, the "angel of the LORD," through whom God speaks, gives a message intended personally for Joshua. (These words are in the vision *about* the priesthood, but the message is for the actual high priest, Joshua.) God promises Joshua "free access among those who are standing" in the vision, the angelic beings that serve in God's presence. In other words, God will have fellowship with Joshua and allow him to intercede for the rest of the Jews. But all this is conditioned upon Joshua's own moral character and his obedience to "My ways" (3:6–7). God also foretells the coming of "the Branch [lit., Sprout]" (3:8), so named because He will be a descendant of the "root of Jesse" (Isa. 11:1), specifically, of the house of David (Jer. 23:5, 33:15).[227] "My Servant" indicates that this "Branch" will come to serve God's will (Isa. 42:1, 49:3, 52:13, 53:11, and Ezek. 34:23–24). This is a direct messianic prophecy about Jesus Christ who will both *come* into the world of His own volition and be *sent* into the world to do the will of His Father (Heb. 10:5–10). The "stone" (3:9) is yet another reference for the Messiah, specifically, the "chief cornerstone" (Psalm 118:22, Isa. 28:16; see Dan. 2:34–35) of a new and spiritual temple of God (Eph. 2:19–22). The "seven eyes" symbolize the omniscience of this "stone," since He is a Divine Being, the Son of God. The Lord also promises to "engrave an inscription on it [i.e., the stone]," no doubt a reference to the "Holy to the LORD" inscription on the turban of the high priest.

Through the mediatory work of this Divine Being/Eternal High Priest—namely, His blood sacrifice on the cross—God will "remove the iniquity of that land in one day"—the "land" really being *the entire world* (John 1:29, 1 John 2:1–2). In one day, through one act of perfect self-sacrifice, the Messiah will provide the means by which *all* men can be saved in His name (Acts 4:12). "In that day" (3:10) indicates that this is a distant-future event, but that everyone will benefit from it ("all the families of the earth will be blessed" through Christ—Acts 3:25).

Zech. 4:1–14 The **fifth vision** involves a golden lampstand and two olive trees. Zechariah begins this vision by saying that he had to be awakened, as if he had fallen into a deep sleep after the fourth vision (4:1). We are not to suppose that this was *literal* sleep, but rather (it appears) the exhausting effects of a series of visions upon his human spirit.

The prophet Zechariah is now shown a "lampstand [or, candlestick; Heb., *menorah*]" with seven lamps on it—similar in design to the *menorah* that stood within the tabernacle (Exod. 25:31–40, 37:17–24). Zechariah's lampstand, however, has a "bowl" (i.e., lamp oil reservoir), seven "pipes" for conducting oil to each lamp, and "olive trees" on either side of it (4:2–3). The lamps of the tabernacle *menorah* have seven separate lamps, all lit individually; this visionary lampstand has seven lamps all lit by one common source (the golden "bowl"), the oil of which comes directly from the two "olive trees" (4:12). The *menorah* that stood in the tabernacle/temple was to provide light throughout the night (being lit every evening at twilight), symbolizing God's presence among the people of Israel. Here, this visionary lampstand carries a similar message, though the message is *messianic*, not practical (i.e., for spiritual illumination, not to provide a physical light). In John's *Revelation*, it is Christ Himself who walks among the lampstands of the churches, taking the symbol to an entirely new (and spiritual) plane.

The message here—which is initially meant for Zerubbabel, as the one who has overseen the rebuilding of the temple in Jerusalem—is: this work (the rebuilding) will not be accomplished solely by human effort, because God is behind it. Zerubbabel has been facing years of opposition and interference from the Samaritans (recall earlier citations in *Ezra*) and is no doubt frustrated by all this. Zechariah's vision shows him that this project *will succeed*, that God's Spirit *will make it so*, and therefore no man or human obstruction will be able to stop it (4:6). God will level mountains, if necessary, to get it done (4:7).

This message is to encourage Zerubbabel to finish what he started (4:8–10). "[T]hese seven" (4:10) refers to the "seven eyes" in 4:9 and allude also to the heavenly mission of the four horsemen that have patrolled the earth, watching over the kingdoms of men (recall 1:10). While the new temple seems a "small thing" in comparison to the original Solomonic temple, it is important, needed, and part of God's overall plan. The idea of Zerubbabel holding the "plumb line [or, plummet]"—a string with a weight on the end, for determining the exact uprightness of a wall—indicates that God has put him in charge of this holy project and will embolden him to complete it. In time, the "top stone" of the building will be set amidst much rejoicing (4:7).

The last part of the vision finally returns to the two "olive trees": they are two "anointed ones [lit., oiled ones; sons of oil]," but remain unidentified. Under the

Law of Moses, the two anointed offices were the high priest (Exod. 30:30) and the king (1 Sam. 10:1). These two offices represented the spiritual (or religious) and earthly (or civil) government within the theocracy of Israel.[228] The "anointed ones" in the vision, however, remain obscure; we only know for certain that they carry out the Lord's will over "the whole earth"—indicating something *beyond the scope of* Israel.[229] Being in the context of a vision, it is not even required that these be two *men*, but—as we will see in 6:12–14—are actually *one* Man (the Messiah) in whom *both* offices are fulfilled.

Zech. 5:1–4 The **sixth vision** involves a "flying scroll" and its message. God shows the prophet Zechariah a scroll or parchment that is fully open (unrolled) "flying" (or floating?) through the air. It is *large*: twenty by ten cubits (which, based on a standard eighteen–inch cubit, is thirty feet by fifteen feet) (5:1–2). This is the same size of the porch of the original Solomonic temple (1 Kings 6:3). This scroll carries two messages, one on each side: one side condemns all who steal; the other, all who swear falsely (or lie, especially to misrepresent a situation or destroy the character of an innocent men). Swearing falsely "by My name" (5:3) indicates a condemnation against anyone who claims to represent God but whom He has not commissioned as His prophet (Lev 19:12, Deut. 6:13, and 18:20–22). Likewise, God has condemned thievery in His law (Exod. 20:15).

The implication here is that the people who have returned from captivity have been careless to keep the laws of God, and yet are engaged in the holy work of rebuilding the temple and representing God to the rest of the world. God's message is: He will bring a curse upon any person (and his home) who treats His laws or His name with disrespect. The curse—symbolized by the flying scroll—will be as one who enters that man's home and "consumes" (as in, devours or destroys) it (5:4). Stealing and lying may have been among the predominant sins to which God refers; it may also be that these two sins characterize all other sins against God. In other words, the scroll may symbolize the entirety of divine law. The fact that it is "flying" indicates the full disclosure of His law: no one can claim he did not know of it; the laws of God (among His people) are as unavoidable as would be a large scroll flying overhead. This is true about the people's sins, too: they are not hidden from God, since the law (as portrayed in the vision) "sees" all things and pronounces a curse upon those who practice sin.[230]

Zech. 5:5–11 The **seventh vision** is of an ephah and a woman. The angel that has been accompanying Zechariah on his series of night visions now tells the prophet to look upon yet another unusual sight: an "ephah going forth." An ephah is a dry unit of measurement roughly equal to that of a modern bushel, or about eight gallons of dry goods. In the present case, the "ephah" refers not to its capacity, but to the container itself, like a large basket. This basket has a circular cover (or lid) made of lead—a most unusual material for this—but is open so that the prophet can see inside of the ephah/basket. He sees "a woman sitting inside the ephah"—another very unusual expectation.[231] The angel suddenly identifies the woman as "Wickedness" (5:8) and slams the lead cover of the ephah down upon her, to keep her contained within.

Then Zechariah sees two other women flying through the air, both having the wings of a stork, and they lifted up the ephah to carry it away (5:9). (The use of a stork in this vision seems only to involve a bird strong enough to carry a heavy weight.) Zechariah asks the angel where these two women are taking the ephah (5:10), and the answer is: "To build a temple [lit., house] for her in the land of Shinar" (5:11). "Shinar" is the ancient designation of the land of Babylon (Gen. 10:10–11), and for all human history has been synonymous with a kingdom that has stood opposed to God and (later) His people. In the vision, "Shinar" *represents* this kingdom; it is not to meant literally. This kingdom (and the "house" or temple being built) belongs to the satanic realm, which provides a "pedestal" in the world for wickedness to reign. No timeframe is associated with this vision, but it corresponds to the messianic prophecies given earlier. As the Messiah establishes His kingdom throughout the world, as represented in each citizen (Christian) of that kingdom, Satan establishes his own kingdom *of* the world, as represented by all who give allegiance to him (John 8:44, Rev. 13:16–17, 14:9–10, and 19:20). The implication is: while God is carrying out His work among His people, Satan is carrying out wickedness and mischief among *his* people. Even so, *the two peoples* must remain separate for God's work to remain holy (see 2 Cor. 6:16—7:1).

Zech. 6:1–8 In the **eighth (and final) vision**, Zechariah is shown four chariots drawn by horses of assorted colors. These horses and chariots come riding toward Zechariah (and the angel that has been accompanying him) between two "bronze mountains." Some think that these two mountains are Mt. Moriah (the "mountain" upon which the temple was built—2 Chron. 3:1) and the Mount of Olives. This latter mountain faces the Jerusalem temple from the other side of the Kidron Valley (also known as "the valley of Jehoshaphat"—Joel 3:2) where God sits "to judge all the surrounding nations" (Joel 3:12).[232] Others think these mountains to be merely symbolic in nature, "as two lofty elevations of the vision, which serve as pillars between which the chariots must come.[233] In any case, we must remember that the entire scene *is* a vision, and thus is not to be taken literally.

Each chariot has different colored horses pulling it: red, black, white, and dappled (or, spotted; grizzled)—the latter of which are also called "strong" (6:2–3).[234] The horses and their chariots are together described as "the four spirits of heaven" which go into the world to carry out God's purpose, whatever that may be (6:4–7; compare Jer. 49:36). The "strong" horses, in particular, "were eager to patrol the earth"—i.e., to keep things where they need to be for the Lord's will to be executed. The black horses came from "the land of the north" to where they had been sent to appease God's wrath (6:8; recall 1:15). This refers to the direction of Assyria and Babylon: the route to these nations from Israel was to the north, through Mesopotamia (a.k.a. the Fertile Crescent). God had exercised His judgment against Assyria, then Babylon, for their roles in punishing His people. His punishment of these two heathen nations was for their brutal and inhumane treatment of His people, which deserved divine justice in response. South of Israel (from whence the "dappled" horses came) was Egypt, Ethiopia, and Edom, all old enemies of Israel at one time or another. Thus, God's judgment has gone out into the world against all those who had afflicted His people.

Recap of the eight visions:

- **First (1:7–17):** horses and riders that have patrolled the earth, portraying God's survey of the world of men, and what yet needs to be done for His people.
- **Second (1:18–21):** four "craftsmen" whom God will send out into the world to break the peace among the secular nations to bring about His will.
- **Third (2:1–5):** "Jerusalem" (ultimately, the church in prophecy) is "measured," symbolizing the protection and preservation of God's people.
- **Fourth (3:1–5):** the reinstatement of the Levitical priesthood, with Joshua appointed as the high priest.
- **Fifth (4:1–14):** the two offices of leadership and priesthood (represented by Zerubbabel and Joshua) are sanctified by God's Holy Spirit, which is the "olive oil" that supplies them both.
- **Sixth (5:1–4):** a "flying scroll" that condemns lying and thievery (which represent all sins against His law), indicating God's full knowledge of when these sins are taking place among His people (and that they must stop).
- **Seventh (5:5–11):** a wicked "woman" in a large basket is carried away from Judah into the land of Babylon, symbolizing that the Jews have paid for their sins (so to speak) in captivity.
- **Eighth (6:1–8):** four chariots pulled by four different colored horses, symbolizing God's war against those nations which have afflicted His people over the last several centuries.

<u>Zech. 6:9–15</u> This next section does not appear to be yet another vision, given the literal manner in which it is introduced. The prophet Zechariah is relating what God has told him to do, not describing something shown to him in a vision. He is told to take silver and gold from three men who have recently come from Babylonian exile—Heldai, Tobijah, and Jedaiah—who, it appears, have transported these precious metals from the storehouse of articles that had once been taken from Judah by King

Nebuchadnezzar (see Ezra 7:14–16, 8:26–30, and Jer. 28:6).[235] If so, then this silver and gold is not their own possession, but belongs to the house of the Lord.

God tells Zechariah to make a crown from these two metals and to place it on the head of Joshua, the high priest (6:11; recall 3:1–5). (It appears that this is a two-tier crown, or a single crown made of an interweaving of the two materials.) A two-tiered crown—representing the union of two offices—is unprecedented in Israel: only in the dual office of Melchizedek (Gen. 14:17–20; see Heb. 5:9–10 and 7:1–17) do we see a priest of God also serving as a king (which is what the crown symbolizes). Yet, this crowning of Joshua is merely ceremonial, not binding. It is also prophetic, in that it really does not speak of Joshua at all, but one called "Branch" who will come in the distant future (see comments on 3:8).[236] The prophecy reveals several features of this "Branch" figure:

- "He" is a person, not an idea, concept, or mere symbol ("Behold, a *man* ..."—6:12). God speaks of an actual, historical, flesh-and-blood Person who will fulfill this prophecy.
- His name is "Branch [or, Sprout]"—i.e., this is His identity in the prophecy. Whenever God names someone in the context of fulfilling His will, He has a specific mission for that person (as in 1 Kings 13:2, Isa. 44:28, Luke 1:13, and 1:31).
- "He will build the temple of the LORD" (6:13)—this is said while the physical temple of the Lord was already in the process of being built, so it refers to something other than that. Jesus Christ is the cornerstone for a *spiritual* temple (Eph. 2:19–22, 1 Peter 2:4–9), and He is most certainly the identity of "Branch."
- "Branch" will reign as both High Priest *and* King, which is what is meant by combining "the honor [or, glory]" of ruling "on His throne" as king (6:13), *and* "He will be a priest on His throne." Since one Man ("Branch") occupies both offices, there is "the counsel of peace between the two offices." "The Messiah, who unites in Himself royalty and priesthood, while counsel and promote peace of His people."[237]

- Christ alone, in all of God's revealed word, will be crowned with many crowns ("on His head are many diadems"—Rev. 19:12). This indicates the unprecedented, supreme, and transcendent royalty that He alone possesses as the King over all of God's Creation.

Again, the crown is merely symbolic and ceremonial, not something Joshua is to wear upon his head (6:14). It is to remain "in the temple" as a reminder of God's instruction given through the prophet Zechariah. Furthermore, "Those who are far off" will also be involved in the building of this spiritual temple of the Lord (6:15)—an expression that has no other reference than to the Gentiles whom Christ will invite into His "temple" or church. (See Acts 2:39 and Eph. 2:13, 17, where the "far off" phrase has specific reference to Gentiles.) When all this happens—even though it will be well beyond the lifetimes of Zechariah and those who first received his prophecy—it will prove that the prophet's words were truly of God. All this will take place only for those Jews who "completely obey the LORD your God"—i.e., those Jews who give full submission to His Servant ("Branch") will be part of this ethereal temple.

The second division (7:1—8:23)

Zech. 7:1-7 This next message came to Zechariah "in the fourth year of King Darius"—i.e., ca. 518 BC, two years after all the previous oracles (recall 1:1). The "ninth month" corresponds to our December/January time. Certain men have been sent from Bethel with a question for the prophet Zechariah (7:1-3). Bethel is the ancient city where King Jeroboam erected a golden calf in the southern part of the land of Israel, after the division of the kingdom (1 Kings 12:28-29); King Josiah later destroyed the altar there (2 Kings 23:15). These men ask Zechariah to seek a ruling from God as to whether they are to continue the fast of the fifth month—the month in which Nebuchadnezzar destroyed Jerusalem (2 Kings 25:8-11, Jer. 52:12). This fast, then, was to memorialize this destruction, and to mourn the great devastation brought upon their nation.

God's response is less than sympathetic (7:4–7). He says that they did not fast to draw near to *Him*, but only to mourn their *own* loss—i.e., it was not a holy fast, but a self-serving one.[238] Thus, the Jews fasted for themselves or for their own sorrow, then ate and drank for themselves; in neither case did they do so to honor Jehovah. They had forgotten the words of the prophets that foretold the destruction of Jerusalem and its temple (7:7)—if they (the Jews in general) had listened to those prophets, there would have been no need for this destruction, their exile, or their mourning over these things. They acted, then, as though the destruction of Jerusalem and its temple was something that simply happened *to* them rather than something they brought upon themselves through the sins of their people.

Zech. 7:8–14 This passage explains to Zechariah more fully God's response to the envoy from Bethel, although it applies to all the generations of Jews prior to the fall of Jerusalem. God told His people to practice justice, kindness, and compassion, and to take care of those who had no one else to take care of them—namely, the widow and orphan (7:9–10; see Isa. 1:16–17, Mic. 6:8, etc.). Then He cites four things that they did instead: they refused to give serious attention to His commandments; they made themselves stubborn against the word of the Lord; they stopped listening to Him altogether; and they hardened their hearts ("like flint") so that they no longer had any regard for the truth. *This* is why God poured out His wrath upon the people; and *this* is why they should have mourned and fasted—not because they suffered the loss of their city and livelihood, nor for the death of Gedaliah, but because they repeatedly offended their God (i.e., the kind of "mourning" Jesus called for in Mat. 5:4). Just as they would not listen to His Spirit when He (the Spirit) called to the people through the voice of the prophets, so God did not listen to His faithless people when the foreign invaders came upon them. Instead, He scattered them—"them" here (7:14) having a broad reference to *all* Israelites—throughout the nations in exile into Assyria and then Babylon. "This places on the shoulders of the people the responsibility for the land's desolation."[239]

This sums up God's response to the delegation from Bethel, who wondered if they should continue a fast that *they* initiated in the first place. The message from God is: "Obedience is better than fasting. God is pleased by obedience, not by self-imposed fasts!"[240]

Zech. 8:1–8 Rather than sustaining His anger against Jerusalem, however, God makes it clear that He has made provision for its *great success*. His "exceeding" jealousy (8:2) refers to His passionate desire for His people; this is also accompanied with "great wrath [or, fury]" against those who oppose them. Instead of a city devastated by divine judgment, invasion, and conquest, the New Jerusalem will be "the City of Truth" (8:3)—i.e., where truth dwells; from whence truth goes out into the world. It will also be called "the Holy Mountain"—the place where God dwells among His people. Such language is messianic in context (see Isa. 4:2–6, Heb. 12:22), and speaks not of the literal city of Jerusalem but of Christ's church.

The picture of old men sitting in city squares *and* children playing in the streets gives the idea of peace, prosperity, longevity, and the perpetuation of life (from one generation to the next). This is set in great contrast to all the horrors and deprivations the Jews have endured in the past seventy-plus years. God asks rhetorically: just because the remnant (that has returned from exile) cannot make this happen, do they think that *He* cannot? (8:6; recall 4:6; see Jer. 32:27). God is fully capable of performing where human power fails. Instead of invasion and devastation, God now speaks of regathering His people from all over the world so that they can live in peace, and He can dwell among them (8:7–8). Once again, the great theme of the entire Bible resurfaces: "They shall be My people, and I will be their God" (see Jer. 31:33, Ezek. 37:23, 27, 2 Cor. 6:16, etc.). All this points forward to the reign of the Messiah over the kingdom of God, and the church age in which all believers are united as "one new man" (Eph. 2:13–22).

Zech. 8:9–17 Having given the prophet a glimpse into the distant future, God now returns to Zechariah's present-day scenario: the rebuilding of the physical temple in Jerusalem. (It should be noted that sixteen times in this chapter alone, the prophet declares that the source of his information is "the LORD of hosts.") God wants the work on the temple to continue until it is completed (8:9). It has been about eighteen years since they laid its foundation, and two years since they had resumed work on it. Previously, in the time between the laying of the foundation and the work being resumed, God withheld prosperity and success from the people (8:10; see Hag. 1:2–11); from this time forward, as long as the work continues, He will bring prosperity and abundance to His people (8:11–12). Instead of being the object of a curse, they will be the recipients of His blessing (8:13). Thus, "Do not fear; let your hands be strong."

God also reminds the people (through Zechariah) that their ancestors provoked His anger, and thus He brought harm upon them as a punishment (8:14). But, if the present generation will listen to and obey Him, He will bring about good for them (8:15; see Jer. 18:7–10). Thus, what He told the pre-exile generation, who refused to listen to Him, He now tells these people: do what is right; speak the truth; do not "devise evil" against each other; and do not be false witnesses (liars), since He hates these things (8:16–17; recall 7:8–13; see Prov. 6:16–19 and Hos. 4:1–6).

Zech. 8:18–19 The four fasts mentioned here occur in: the tenth month (when Nebuchadnezzar laid siege against Jerusalem; 2 Kings 25:1); the fourth month (when the Babylonians breached the city wall; 2 Kings 25:3); the fifth month (when the Babylonians destroyed the temple; 2 Kings 25:8); and the seventh month (when Gedaliah was murdered; 2 Kings 25:23–25). These are not fasts required by the Law of Moses, or by God Himself, but are what the people observed by their own volition. However, *all* such fasts (really, the genuine *purpose* of fasting itself) will take on new meaning when the people devote their hearts to "truth and peace" in a favorable relationship with God. When their hearts are right, their fasts will be pleasing to God.

Zech. 8:20–23 "Peoples" and "inhabitants" refers to non-Jews (Gentiles) from foreign lands. Upon hearing of all that God has done for

His people, God-fearing foreigners will desire to "entreat the favor of the LORD" as well. "In those days" (8:23) provides a historical timestamp. This refers to the distant future (from the perspective of Zechariah's lifetime) but speaks ultimately of the dispensation of the Messiah's reign. The benefits of His reign will initially begin with the Jews but will then extend to people of *every* nation (Acts 2:39, 10:34–35). "[T]en men" indicates a full number, or a full representation or sampling of a given people. "[A]ll the nations" in 8:23 is, in the Hebrew text, "all languages of the nations" (compare Isa. 66:18 and Rev. 7:9). That these people will "grasp the garment of a Jew" is "the gesture of suppliant entreaty as to a superior,"[241] indicating their strong desire for what the Jew is already privileged to have received. In the context of the messianic reign, "the Jew" here is symbolic rather than literal. God's people in Christ's church are known collectively (and spiritually) as "the Israel of God" (Gal. 6:16), or the spiritual descendants of Abraham (Gal. 3:28–29).

Questions on *Zechariah* (chapters 1—8)

1.) Why do you suppose the book of *Zechariah* is written in such a symbolic or even cryptic manner? What purpose does this serve?

2.) What are some major themes of *Zechariah*? Are these themes relevant for us (in the church) today, or were they limited to the ancient Jews?

3.) What do the visions of the horsemen and their chariots (1:7–11 and 6:1–8) say about God's oversight of the entire world? (There are several answers.)

4.) Zerubbabel (the governor of Judea) and Joshua (the high priest of Israel) are two key characters in chapters 3, chapter 4, and 6:11–13. Why is special attention given to them?

   a. What does the oil symbolize in the vision of the two olive trees?

   b. What is the significance of the crowning of Joshua, as this symbolic event relates to the future "Branch" (Messiah)?

5.) Chapter 8 is an uplifting chapter that speaks of the coming peace and prosperity of Judah. This picture finds its ultimate fulfillment, however, not in the physical people of Judah, but in the spiritual people of God (i.e., Christ's church).

   a. As you see it, does the church today experience this peace and prosperity? If not, why not? If so, how so?

   b. Should Christians see themselves as those "Jews" whose garments other people will grasp (so to speak) in 8:20–23? Before we should expect this reaction, however, what kind of people ought we to be? (Consider Mat. 5:13–16, Col. 4:5–6, and 1 Peter 3:15, for example, in your answer.)

The third division (9:1—14:21)

The third division of the book is itself divided into two parts, both introduced as "the burden [or, oracle] of the LORD" (9:1 and 12:1). Thus, chapters 9—11 comprise the first "burden"; chapters 12—14, the second "burden." These divisions, however, do not correspond exactly with the subject matter. Chapters 9 and 10 deal with prophecies against foreign nations; chapters 11—14 deal with the struggle between "the shepherd" (Messiah) and unbelieving Jews who resist Him ("the flock doomed to slaughter"—11:4, etc.).

This entire third division of the book is regarded as prophetical, that is, it has nothing to do with rebuilding the temple, the Jews living in Judah in Zechariah's day, or anytime in their near future. Rather, it has to do with what will happen in (what we call) the intertestamental times, and up to the time of Christ (Messiah). Because of this, some commentators think that someone other than Zechariah wrote this section (a so-called "deutero-Zechariah," where "deutero-" means "second"), since it deals with things of which he could not have known. But such a constraint undermines the entire *description* and *purpose* of a prophet, who speaks, among other things, of what has not yet happened (Deut. 18:21–22, Jer. 28:9, Lam. 3:37, Ezek. 33:33, etc.). The unity of the book of *Zechariah* has been maintained for some 2,500 years, except for the relatively recent criticism of liberal-minded scholars. Our present study honors this unity since these scholars have not provided any substantive and objective-minded reason why it should be otherwise.

Zech. 9:1–10 God opens this "burden"—i.e., an utterance or solemn declaration that He places upon the prophet to deliver to others—with prophecies concerning foreign nations. "Hadrach" (9:1) is a province of Syria (near Damascus), the nation to the north of the ancient land of Israel.[242] "The eyes of men ... are toward the LORD" means: God-fearing men look to God to bring about judgment upon those who have afflicted them with great harm. "Hamath" is to the north of Syria and is the gateway into Palestine from the north, the direction from which all invaders from the east have come. Thus, it is possible that this prophecy is not against Syria itself but is against (symbolically) all those who have invaded Israel and Judah. If this is the case, then this is a broadly applied prophecy of God's divine judgment against *all* foreign invaders from the east who have contributed to the suffering of His people.

"Tyre and Sidon" (9:2b–4) are the two sister-cities (or, city-states) of Phoenicia, the nation on the Mediterranean coast to the northwest of Israel and south of Syria. Tyre, in particular, built an island fortress about a half–mile offshore of the seacoast and established itself as a powerful commercial trading center. This was connected to the mainland by a manufactured land bridge that was some 2500' feet long and 27' wide. Ezekiel 27—28 provides considerable detail of Tyre's arrogance, as well as prophecies concerning its downfall. Nebuchadnezzar had laid siege against Tyre and destroyed the (then) mainland part of Tyre, but was unable to conquer the island itself. However, in his conquest of Palestine, Alexander the Great (*ca.* 330 BC) took the ruins of the old city from the mainland and used them to build a 200' wide causeway to the island fortress of Tyre, which he besieged for seven months. Finally, the city fell to him, and he destroyed it completely—and vengefully.

> [The ancient historian] Diodorus Siculus records that he [Alexander the Great] massacred 6,000 to 8,000 of her [Tyre's] men, crucified 2,000 of her men, and sold from 13,000—30,000 into slavery. All of her weapons of warfare and the testimonies of her wisdom were cast into the sea, and in the final humiliation fire was set to the remains of the city. The words of God's prophets Ezekiel (some one hundred years earlier) and Zechariah were abundantly fulfilled in the greatest detail.[243]

Ashkelon, Gaza, Ekron, and Ashdod are four of the five city–states of Philistia, the coastal nation to the south of Phoenicia (9:5–7). These cities will "see" the destruction of Tyre and will realize that they are next in line for disaster. In previous conquests, invading armies would leave the nations relatively intact and would only require them to pay annual tribute (to ward off complete devastation). Alexander the Great's policy was different, and he removed the kings of foreign nations so as to impose his Hellenistic (Greek-oriented) culture upon the defeated people.[244] Ashdod's city will be replaced by a "mongrel race" (9:6)—a reference to one born out of wedlock, or in a forbidden marriage; i.e., a foreign people.

> When Gaza fell, following a two months siege, ten thousand of its inhabitants were killed; and the rest were sold to the slave merchants who followed in the wake of Alexander's armies. Their 'king' was tied with two thongs through his feet to Alexander's chariot and dragged through the city in one of the young conqueror's characteristic fits of revenge against one who resisted his forward march.[245]

The Philistines regularly sacrificed animals to their idols and consumed these with the blood—an abomination to God (Lev. 17:10–11)—but God will put an end to this practice when He brings an end to their nation (9:7). Even so, God will allow such heathens to enter the spiritual "Israel" of the future (under Messiah), so that the two (Jews and foreigners) will become as one (Eph. 2:15, "one new man"). On "Jebusite," see Josh. 15:63 and 2 Sam. 24:18ff; "like a Jebusite" indicates similarity, not exact identity.

All said, God will surround His people with divine protection (9:8–10).[246] "[A]n army" and "him who passes by and returns" refers to any invading army (or king); when the Messiah begins to reign, no foreign invader will be able to destroy His people anymore. This is reason to rejoice, even though it speaks of the distant future (i.e., it is not fulfilled until the church age). "Zion" and "Jerusalem" carry double meanings: they symbolize the faithful *Jews* in the literal city of Jerusalem, but also God's faithful *people* everywhere. The idea of a King entering the city on a donkey colt indicates the humble, peaceful, and completely *unexpected* nature of a royal personage. Jesus fulfilled this prophecy literally when He rode into Jerusalem on a young donkey (Mat. 21:1–5, John 12:12–16). Under the otherworldly rule of Messiah, there will be no wars—no chariots, horses, or bows; His will be a peaceful but powerful reign (Isa. 9:6–7). His "dominion" will not be limited to Palestine but will be worldwide.

Zech. 9:11–17 This entire section poetically and metaphorically describes God's redemption of His people—initially, this means the literal faithful remnant of Israel, but ultimately it takes in *all* those who call upon His name—from shame, reproach, captivity, and oppression (from war and foreign invaders).[247] God presents Himself as a mighty warrior who fights for His people, to balance the scales (so to speak) for all the suffering, indignation, and captivity they have had to endure. (The deliverance of the Israelites from exile compares to the deliverance of the captives of sin; see Acts 26:16–18, Eph. 4:8, 2 Tim. 2:24–26, etc.) God will stir up the "sons" of Zion against the "sons" of Greece—no doubt referring to the Jews' resistance of Grecian oppression, most notably in the Maccabean Revolt (2nd century BC), but also in the first-century Jews' resistance of Grecian (Hellenistic) culture, philosophy, and religion that opposed Christian teachings (Acts 17:16–32, 2 Cor. 10:5, Col. 2:8, etc.).[248] The imagery of God's people as *victorious* over the secular forces is viewed with prosperity, abundance, health, and joy (9:16–17). Whether this was ever fulfilled in the literal sense cannot be determined, but most certainly it has been fulfilled in the spiritual sense, as Christianity reigned supreme over all the pagan and idolatrous world of the Gentiles.

Zech. 10:1–7 Chapter 10 seems to further expound on what has already been revealed in the previous chapter. God (through the prophet Zechariah) encourages His people to pray to Him for rain—a critical necessity for an agrarian society. The same God who makes "the storm clouds [or, thunderbolts]" in times of divine anger to *ruin* crops (as in 1 Sam. 12:16–18) can also provide "showers" of rain for the *benefit* of men and their crops. In other words, God wants His people to ask *Him* for blessings without ever again turning to idols for answers (10:1–2). "Teraphim" refers to small household statuettes (Gen. 31:19, 34, and 2 Kings 23:24) to which the people bowed and sought deliverance. "Diviners" are those who claim to predict the future, either (falsely) in God's name or by their own ability; all they really see are "false dreams" (Isa. 44:25, Jer. 14:14, 23:32, Ezek. 13:7, 22:28, etc.). False dreams produce nothing but false hope; instead of bringing the sheep (people) of Israel together, they contribute to their being scattered (compare Mat. 9:36). Furthermore, God is opposed to all the "shepherds" and "male goats" of Israel (10:3a)—i.e., the leaders and rulers of the Jews who have exploited His people for their own gain, and to their (the people's) own destruction (see Ezek. 34:1–10 for an explicit exposition of this).

God's prophecy specifically cites Judah as the tribe from which will come "the cornerstone"—the primary and key block of stone that orients and establishes the foundation of a building—for His kingdom (10:3b–7). This is undoubtedly a prophecy about Christ, since He is described as the "cornerstone," even in His own words (Psalm 118:22–23, Isa. 28:16, Mat. 21:42, 1 Peter 2:4–5, etc.). Even though God seems to refer to several key people whom He will use to fulfill His purpose, clearly these imageries and symbolic references are all summed up in Christ: He is the "tent peg," "bow of battle," "ruler," etc. He, together with His people (Christians), "will be as mighty men" in battle and will be victorious through the strength of God.

The reunion of Judah and Ephraim (a name often used to stand for all the northern tribes of Israel), resulting in *all* Israelites fighting side-by-side against a common enemy, can only be fulfilled in the spiritual context of the church.[249] In this case, they are brought together to fight against "the world forces of darkness" which declare war against Christ's church (Eph. 6:12). This means the identity of God's people it is not merely Jews/Israelites (in this prophetic view), but people of *every* nation. In Christ's church, there is *no distinction* between Jews and Gentiles (Acts 11:12, 15:8–9, and Rom. 10:12); the two groups are united into "one new man, thus establishing peace" between them (Eph. 2:15).

Zech. 10:8–12 The great regathering of Israel—a people once dispersed into foreign exile because of their sins—will happen only by God's purpose and leadership. **First**, He will be the One who summons them to return—not to the literal land of Israel in Palestine, but *to Him*, through their obedience to the Messiah. **Second**, they will be *able* to return because He will make provision for this. The "sea of distress [or, affliction]" (10:11) alludes to when Israel passed through the Red Sea in their exodus out of Egypt (Exod. 14:13–31). In other words, whatever stands in their way, even an obstacle that is humanly impossible to overcome, God will deliver them through it. A sea, the Nile River, etc.—there is nothing too difficult for God to overcome (compare Jer. 32:17, 27, and Mat. 19:26). (The reference to the drying up of the Nile may also indicate the end of Egyptian power, especially given the verses that follow.) Historically, both Egypt and Assyria have brought all kinds of trouble upon the northern tribes of Israel, but they will no longer be of concern. Instead, His people will walk by God's strength and in His name (10:12).

Zech. 11:1-3 Lebanon is the country to the north of ancient Israel, to the northwest of Damascus (in Syria). It is famous for its fine cedar trees which have been used in many notable building projects in the past, including Solomon's temple. Bashan is east of the Sea of Galilee and has long been a coveted region because of its fertile pastures and beautiful landscape. But if "fire" (judgment) destroys the cedars, then the lesser "trees" will not be able to stand; and if the land is ruined, then the land's rulers ("shepherds") will mourn, and natural predators ("lions") will return. This passage figuratively describes some kind of devastation (the result of divine judgment), but the *object* of that judgment is unstated. Some think it is Syria, which is in the direction of Lebanon; others think Bashan, which is on the other side of the Sea of Galilee from Syria. Perhaps both places suggest a northerly entrance into Palestine—thus, the direction from which many invaders have entered Palestine in ages past. If this is the case, then Judah is the object of this dreadful picture. It is possible that this speaks of what will happen when, during the Greek Empire, an assault against Judah will come from a Seleucid invasion from the north.[250]

(Upon his death, Alexander the Great's empire was divided among four of his military generals. The dynasty of these generals/kings later went to war against each other, battling over land, resources, and supremacy. One king, Ptolemy, occupied Egypt and most of Palestine; another king, Seleucus, occupied northern Palestine and Syria. These two kings used Judah and vicinity as their battleground, bringing great devastation and trouble to the Jews. Antiochus, one of the Seleucid kings, attempted to stamp out the Jews and their religion altogether, forcing the Jews to resist with warfare. This struggle is recorded in *Maccabees*, in the Apocryphal writings [non-biblical literature of Jewish history] and is alluded to in Dan. 8.) Hailey, for one, thinks Zechariah's vision concerns the end of the Jewish state after the Romans decimated it in AD 70. It is possible, through a combined effort, that God describes both events telescopically, albeit obscurely. In other words, Zechariah's message is that Judah will eventually fall to one foreign power or another—it is a "flock doomed to (the) slaughter" (11:4)—ultimately because of the Jews' failure to recognize their own Messiah [the shepherd, the role of which Zechariah himself assumes for the sake of this prophecy].)

Zech. 11:4–14 There is little doubt that the unnamed shepherd in this prophecy—personified *by* the prophet Zechariah, but not referring *to* him—is Jesus Christ. The "flock doomed to slaughter [or, the flock of slaughter]" (11:4, 7) is most certainly Judah, or the Jewish state. The Jewish people, over the next centuries, will be harassed, invaded, and persecuted by one heathen ruler after another; because of this, the Jewish people will suffer dearly. Eventually, the Romans will destroy the Jewish state, level the temple in Jerusalem, and level Jerusalem itself. In that event, many thousands of Jews will be killed outright or captured as prisoners of war (and worked to death or executed later). God will not prevent this from happening, since it is He who called for it in an act of divine vengeance (see Luke 19:11–27, particularly verses 14 and 27). In fact, the Romans will justify their slaughter of the Jews as being ordained by God and will make themselves rich at the Jews' expense (11:5–6).

In this sense, God will send His Son to the Jews to restore and reunite them (11:7–8). Restoration will come through "Favor [or, Graciousness; Beauty]" the name of one of the symbolic staffs of the Shepherd; reunification will come through "Union [or, Binding; Bands]," the name of the other symbolic staff. Favor is what God extends to His people, if they honor their covenant with Him and receive His Son; Union will be the result of this wise and beneficial decision.[251] The Shepherd—in essence, the *Chief* Shepherd (1 Peter 5:4)—has shepherds under Him; likely, these refer to the Jewish rulers who oversee the Jews during Jesus' day. But, instead of cooperating and obeying, these other shepherds will contend with the Chief Shepherd (e.g., Luke 11:53–54), and thus they were "annihilated [or, cut off; eliminated]" by the Lord (11:9). To "eat one another's flesh" in this context may be figurative, referring to the way evil people often destroy each other in pursuit of personal ambitions (Gal. 5:15). But if we think of the historic Roman destruction of Jerusalem, the Jews trapped in the siege of Jerusalem did practice cannibalism in a desperate attempt to survive.[252] (We should not press the imagery here, nor the number "three." Likely, "three" symbolizes a witness against the Shepherd—in this case, a *false* witness [Deut. 19:15]; "in one month" simply means a very short period of time.[253]) The Chief Shepherd has no patience for these men; and they, in turn, hold the Chief Shepherd in contempt.

The Shepherd, having been rejected by His own flock, refuses to shepherd them anymore (11:8–11). The flock's action constitutes a rejection of God Himself—thus, a rejection of the divine favor He offered them. They have made their own decision; now they can suffer the awful consequences of that decision (Luke 19:41–44). Disease, war, and famine will descend upon them, and God will no longer defend or spare them. At this point, the Shepherd breaks the staff called "Favor," demonstrating the annulment of God's covenant with His people.[254] (It is likely that Zechariah, playing the role of the Shepherd, acts this out in the presence of witnesses.)

Now the Shepherd addresses the rest of the flock (not the "afflicted"): He asks that they decide what they will give Him ("as my wages") for having shepherded them (11:12). All they are willing to give to Him is "thirty shekels of silver," the price for which: Joseph was sold into slavery (Gen. 37:28); a slave's life is compensated when killed by another's animal (Exod. 21:32); Jesus was betrayed by Judas (Mat. 26:15).[255] In other words, this is a huge slap in the face to the Messiah, who had come from heaven to bring them Favor and Union. God instructed the Shepherd (played here by Zechariah) to "Throw it [the money] to the potter" (11:13)—a prophecy about what Judas would do with the money he was paid to betray Jesus (Mat. 27:3–10).[256] The "thirty pieces"—a pathetic and insulting demonstration of what the unbelieving Jews thought of God's Son—was not only demeaning to Jesus, but to God Himself. Thus, the Shepherd destroys the second symbolic staff ("Union"), thereby destroying any hope that the brotherhood of the Jews (or the Jewish nation in covenant with Jehovah) will survive. "As they had rejected Him, He now rejects them. No longer will He seek to hold the nations united as one."[257]

Zech. 11:15–17 Now the prophet Zechariah is told to give shepherding equipment (a bag, staff, etc.) to a "foolish shepherd"—a mere man, not the Christ—to shepherd His people. This "foolish shepherd" will be raised up by God, but he will not actually care for his sheep (God's people); instead, he will exploit and destroy them. It is unclear (historically) as to the identity of this "foolish" or "worthless" shepherd, or whether it is a single man or a man–made government. Whoever (or whatever) it is, he (or it) represents what the Jews deserve after rejecting God's covenantal protection.[258] The "right eye" symbolizes wisdom or good judgment; "right arm" symbolizes strength and protection. This "foolish/worthless" shepherd will have neither, and all those who are under him will suffer greatly as a result.

Zech. 12:1–5 This "burden [or, oracle]" most certainly concerns Israel (12:1), but in the context, "Israel" is not an ethnic or national group of people, but the *new* "Israel"—God's people under the *new covenant* (i.e., Christians). First, God reminds the reader of who He is: His sovereign power, creative ability, and supremacy over "man" (human beings) (12:2). A distinction is made between "Jerusalem" and "Judah" (or "the clans of Judah"). While this is admittedly a difficult passage to interpret, *considering the context*, "Jerusalem" seems to refer to God's church, and "Judah/the clans of Judah" to those Jews who join themselves to that church. When unbelievers besiege "Jerusalem" (the church), they also besiege the faithful Jews who have identified themselves with this symbolic city. "It will come about in that day" (12:3) indicates a prophecy of the distant future, which supports this explanation.

While men may think that destroying the church is an easy thing to do,

God will not permit it (12:2–3). They think it is a goblet to drink down quickly; God says it is a large basin filled with drink that makes men "reeling" (or, mad). They think that His church is a small stone to pick up and carry away; God says that whoever tries to lift this stone will only bring harm to himself. God promises to personally "watch over the house of Judah"—i.e., to take care of the remnant of Jewish believers who have entered a new covenant with Him—so that no one can defeat them (12:4). They will recognize this divine help (12:5) and be very grateful for it.

Zech. 12:6–9 God will not glorify Jerusalem *instead* of Judah—i.e., He will not give divine protection only to Gentile believers, but not Jewish—but will protect them both (12:6–9). While the enemies of God's people come to destroy them, it is the enemies who will be destroyed instead. The picture here must be viewed as a *spiritual* battle more so than a *historical* one, although it is true that the spiritual struggle does manifest itself among real, flesh-and-blood people. The fact that Jehovah "will save the tents of Judah *first*" (12:7, emphasis added) is another indicator that "Judah" refers to the faithful remnant of Israel and not all Jews (Acts 3:26, 13:46, and Rom. 1:16). Thus, the faithful Jewish remnant will unite with the faithful Gentile remnant (the new or spiritual "Jerusalem"). Even the seemingly weakest member of God's people will be strong like King David in his glory (12:8), because of his faith in God's deliverance. Indeed, "the house of David"—God's church, led by His Son, the King—will be strengthened like "an angel of the LORD." Whatever person, government, or entity comes against God's people will find themselves fighting against *God Himself* and will be destroyed by Him (12:9; see Ezek. 39:1–8 and Rev. 20:7–10, in principle).

Zech. 12:10–14 The "Favor" that the Jews rejected (recall 11:7–10) will be lavished upon His people (the church) (12:10). This will be the Spirit (or, a spirit) of "grace and supplication"—i.e., of divine favor and a willingness to receive their petitions. The "mourning" here (12:11–14) refers to the humble and penitent sorrow that they—those redeemed by the blood of the One "whom they have pierced" (see Rev. 1:7)—have for their sins, and all the grief and trouble their sins have caused God and His Son (Mat. 5:4). The idea seems to be that *every* soul redeemed by Christ's blood has also had a part in His *death*: He did not die for innocent, righteous souls, but for those who have sinned against the Father. Thus, all believers will recognize the price that has been paid for them—"precious blood, as a lamb unblemished and spotless, the blood of Christ" (1 Peter 1:19)—and the sacrificial death that brought about the *shedding* of that blood, and all for *their* redemption. "Hadadrimmon in the plain of Megiddo" (12:11) likely refers to the actual place where the good king Josiah was killed (2 Chron. 35:20–25)—a prefigure of Christ's own death. The repeated phrase, "and their wives by themselves," likely has to do with the very *personal nature* of this "mourning." It is not a national mourning, and not necessarily even a family mourning (since not all members of a family may be Christians), but an intensely *personal* one.

Zech. 13:1–6 "In that day" puts a timestamp upon the fulfillment of this prophecy: it does not concern the immediate situation (Zechariah's day, the rebuilding of the temple, or any time soon), but the distant future. The opened "fountain" illustrates an abundance of water for cleansing—or, in this case, *blood* for the cleansing of sin, enough to cleanse the *entire world* of its sin (1 John 2:1–2). This passage has no natural reference other than Christ Himself, who was "pierced" (recall 12:10) and then bled for the remission of "sin and for impurity" (the "purification of sins"—Heb. 1:3).

Also "in that day," the cursed idolatry that had so plagued both Israel and Judah for centuries will no longer be present—at least, not among those who call upon the name of God (13:2; see 13:9b). Idols, false prophets, and unclean spirits have defiled Israel and Judah, leading to their punishments and exiles; these will not be allowed in Christ's church. This is not to say that all these elements will disappear entirely, or that Christians (and their churches) will not have to deal with them. Rather, this speaks of the character of the Messiah's church, versus what was historically true about the congregation of Israel. Those who *do* prophesy falsely are worthy of death because they do not honor Christ or the Father—parallel to a son who refuses to honor his parents (Deut. 18:20–22, 21:18–21).[259]

This will not stop false prophets from arising, however (13:4). Putting on a "hairy robe [or, mantle]" alludes to the garment that Elijah wore that identified him as a prophet of God (2 Kings 1:7–8); later, John the Baptist dressed similarly (Mat. 3:4). Yet, such men will not be able to deceive the saints through *outward* appearance, because their "fruits" will reveal their *inward* nature (Mat. 7:15–20). The false prophet, trying to evade detection for who he really is, will lie about his profession (13:5), or about the "wounds" (marks; scars; distinctive identifying characteristics) that he bears. (Such wounds are inconsistent with what happened to Christ; this passage [13:3–6] is not talking about Christ, but those who are unable to deceive God's people as they had done in the past.)

Zech. 13:7–9 Here, the context changes: now, the passage *is* talking about Christ, for indeed Jesus quoted this passage concerning His own situation (13:7; see Mat. 26:31, Mark 14:27). The "sword" implies military might (or governmental authority; Rom. 13:4), not a literal weapon to kill God's Shepherd. God does, however, call upon this might or authority to *be active* (or activated) to fulfill His will. "My Shepherd" and "My Associate [or, Fellow]" are terms used to indicate that this Man (Christ) is in league with God; "He is of the very essence of God and is identical in purpose with Him."[260] The "sheep" and "little ones" (as, children; Mark 10:24) refer to those whom the Shepherd was leading when the "sword" came against Him. All this poignantly and accurately foretells the occasion of Jesus' arrest in the garden of Gethsemane and His disciples were allowed to escape (Mat. 26:56, Mark 14:48–50, and John 18:4–9). To "turn [His] hand" in this case means to dismiss His disciples, not to strike them.

What follows the striking of the Shepherd will be judgment and upheaval, including a refining of "the land" (i.e., Judea) (13:8–9). Two parts will be destined for destruction (death); one third will be spared, but it also will be brought through the fire (of persecution; see 1 Peter

1:6–9). This latter part (or "third") is God's people—Christians—because it is only these who call upon God for salvation *and* whom God will answer through His Son. The latter part of 13:9 is yet another citation of the theme of the entire Bible (in so many words): "I will be their God, and they will be My people" (recall 8:8).

Zech. 14:1–8 In keeping with the prophetic theme of the context (which began in 12:1), "Jerusalem" here does not refer to the actual city in Judea, but *the church* (14:1–2). The Romans did come against the actual city, but they did not spare half of the city (the half not "exiled"); they destroyed the *entire* city, and *everyone* was sorely affected. This passage instead speaks of a great persecution that will come upon the church—what appears to be a "capture" of the church by imperial powers (Rev. 13:7). In that figurative context, many Christians will be severely affected—even killed—but not all of them. God has always preserved a faithful remnant as a representation of His people upon the earth, until the earth is no more.

God will, however, step in and fight for His people (14:3); whatever was taken *from* them will be returned *to* them (14:1). The "Mount of Olives" is a hill just to the east of Jerusalem, on the other side of the Kidron valley. However, just as "Jerusalem" is symbolic, "Mount of Olives" must also be symbolic. Splitting the Mount of Olives in half—part moving north, the other, south—indicates *divine intervention* in saving God's people from a complete destruction (through the persecution of their enemies).[261] "You will flee" (14:5) indicates *a way of escape* from being overwhelmed by what is happening to them (1 Cor. 10:13, 2 Peter 2:9). "Azel [or, Azal]" is an ancient site near the east gate of the city of Jerusalem, as one would use to go toward the Mount of Olives. The reference to the historical earthquake in the days of King Uzziah of Judah (only mentioned in Amos 1:1) is simply to say: as you fled *then*, so you will be given opportunity to flee *in the future*.[262] "You" here refers back to those who have called upon the name of the Lord (recall 13:9; see Acts 2:21, 22:16)—i.e., *Christians*.

A day without light (14:6) indicates a time of great distress (Joel 2:2, 10), as does the dwindling light of "luminaries" (i.e., cosmic lights; planets and stars) (Isa. 13:10). It will not be *complete* darkness (indicating hopelessness), but a "unique day" in which is "neither day nor night"—i.e., an *unnatural* time for those who witness it, but not one that is outside of God's control (14:7). Even so—in the midst of all of this—"living waters" will flow toward the "eastern sea" (i.e., the Dead Sea) and the "western sea" (i.e., the Mediterranean Sea). If "Jerusalem," "Mount of Olives," and this "day" are all figurative, then so are these "living waters." The "waters" represent the life-giving message of salvation through the gospel of Christ (John 4:13–14, 7:37–39) which will continue to flow to *the entire world* as Christians continue to preach it and maintain their faith in it, despite persecution. These "waters" will flow—i.e., the message will be preached—"in summer as well as in winter"—i.e., in every season (2 Tim. 4:2).

Zech. 14:9–11 "[I]n that day"—the same "day" as when all the above prophecies will take place—God will rule over all the earth as King (14:9). He will do this through the reign of His Son, who sits at His right hand (Acts 2:33) and to whom He has given His kingdom (Mat. 28:18, John 18:36–37, and Rev. 11:15–18). That "the Lord" (Jehovah) will be "one" underscores what has been said since the days of Moses (Deut. 6:4): Christ's reign as King does not interfere with this, but is an expression of the seamless unity between Him and His Father (John 10:30, 17:20–23). It also means that God's people will call upon no *other* god but *Him.*

God promises to make "all the land" around (symbolic) Jerusalem like a plain—i.e., a route to the city of God that is easy to travel, with no insurmountable obstacles (14:10). Everyone can come; no one will be hindered; no one who calls upon the name of the Lord for salvation will be denied (Rom. 10:11–13). As for "Jerusalem" (the church) itself, it will remain *above* the "plain," not only as a place easy to see from a distance, but also a state of being that transcends the rest of the world (parallel to when Jesus walked *on top of* the sea—Mat. 14:22–33). "Geba" is about six miles to the north of Jerusalem (1 Kings 15:22); "Rimmon" is the city's southern boundary (Josh. 15:32, 19:7); "gates" indicate access points. All this symbolizes not multiple *methods* of salvation, but multiple *opportunities* for it, regardless of which direction (so to speak) one comes. Those who dwell in the city—i.e., those who find spiritual refuge in Christ's body, the church—will no longer be under the curse of God's condemnation for sin (Rom. 8:1).

Those who go to war against Jerusalem—i.e., who declare war against (or are persecutors of) Christ's church—God will strike with a "plague" (14:12–15). This cannot be a literal plague, just as "Jerusalem" here is not a literal city; but it is a *spiritual* malady that causes all kinds of dread, moral confusion, spiritual torment, and even physical suffering. Such suffering is described here figuratively, but the suffering will be *real*, nonetheless. Not only will this "plague" affect people, but also their animals (14:15)—an extension of the people's wealth and well-being. "Judah" again refers to the literal Jews who have chosen to become Christians (recall 12:2–9); these will fight for the church, since they are united in identity and cause *with* the church (14:14). The "wealth of all the surrounding nations" will try to destroy Christ's church, but this campaign will not be successful.

Zech. 14:16–21 Those who are "left of all the nations" (14:16) most naturally refers to a remnant of believers who come out of the original assailants of Christ's church. In other words, these are people who have reconsidered and are converted to Christianity. The possible reason for their change of heart may that they want what they have seen in faithful Christians: a belief system and a Savior so powerful that they are worth dying for (recall 8:20–23). The "King" here is Christ, who is the "exact representation of" God (Heb. 1:3), the "Lord of hosts." "Feast of Booths [or, Tabernacles]" refers to the joyful feast of thanksgiving at the end of the summer harvests that symbolizes God's care and provision for His people (Lev. 23:39–44). Thus, *all* those who "go up to Jerusalem" (i.e., come to Christ) will celebrate together; they will all be as "one new man" (Eph. 2:15) and thus be at peace with God and one another.

Those who refuse to honor Christ as King, and to identify as His people, will be as those upon whom no rain will come—a perpetual and agonizing drought (14:17), which will be regarded as a plague (14:18). This drought is *spiritual* in nature, but it will affect the physical lives of those who endure it, taking an awful toll on them. "Egypt" symbolizes an ancient enemy of God's people, a place of bondage, captivity, and oppression. It is not meant to be taken literally here but represents all those who have long opposed God, just as Pharaoh once opposed God repeatedly (to his own great harm) prior to Israel's exodus. Whatever happens to "Egypt" will happen to anyone who follows its example (14:19).

"In that day" *everything*—meaning, *every Christian*—will be dedicated to God (14:20–21). "Holy to the LORD" is what was inscribed on the plate attached to the turban of the high priest (Exod. 28:36–38). But "in that day," *every Christian* will be holy to the Lord (1 Peter 1:16), and *every Christian* will be a priest of God (1 Peter 2:9, Rev. 5:9–10). Horses and cooking pots indicate common elements of everyday life; bowls before the altar are utensils set apart for the holy ministry of the temple. But God is saying through Zechariah: *every Christian* will be as important as the next; He will regard no believer as common or expendable. In the Christian dispensation, there is:

- no sacred gender ("there is neither male nor female" in Christ—Gal. 3:28).
- no sacred language (God's *truth* is the language of the church—Acts 2:4–11).
- no sacred place ("neither in this mountain nor in Jerusalem"—John 4:21)
- no sacred dress or clothing ("the fine linen [of the Bride] is the righteous acts of the saints"—Rev. 19:8).
- no sacred station in life ("there is neither slave nor free man"—Gal. 3:28).

"Canaanite" (14:21) refers to the original inhabitants of Palestine whom God cursed because they were unclean, impenitent, and thus devoted to destruction (Deut. 7:1–5, 20:16–18). Christ will not identify with any such people. Again, this does not speak of any actual nation or individuals but speaks to the unholy *character* that will not be allowed in Christ's church.

Questions on *Zechariah* (chapters 9—14)

1.) In 9:9, God promises to deliver the Jewish nation by a King who will be "humble, and mounted on a donkey" colt—something completely *unexpected* and (from a human standpoint) *underwhelming* or *disappointing*. Yet, what is God's message to the people through this depiction of their Redeemer?

2.) God scattered His people into exile yet promises to bring them back together at the appointed time *and* under the proper context (10:4–12). What does this say about:

   a. God's power and authority?

   b. His supremacy over the idols in which the Israelites once put their confidence?

   c. His supremacy over anything or any person(s) that might stand in the way of this holy regathering?

   d. His promise to overcome His people's doubts, fears, and discouragement?

3.) In chapter 11, the doomed "flock" represents the Jewish nation that would reject the leadership of Christ, God's "Shepherd" (see John 10:1–30).

a. Given the shepherd–flock relationship, how *should* they have regarded Him? What *should* that nation have done?

b. Given the *church's* relationship with the "Chief Shepherd" (1 Peter 5:4), how are *we* (Christians) to regard Christ? What should *we* be doing?

c. What happened to the Jewish nation when they refused to listen to their Shepherd? (What will happen to any Christian who also refuses?)

4.) In chapters 12—14, God promises to fight to save His people from their enemies, and false prophets especially. The repeated "in that day" phrase clearly looks beyond a physical battle but refers instead to a much more sinister one—a battle between satanic forces and Christ's church.

a. Is this describing a "battle" in our own future, or do you think that battle is already raging? If we are presently in that battle, then is God fighting for us?

b. What must every *Christian* do to survive such a battle with his faith (and soul) intact? (Consider Eph. 6:10–18 in your answer.)

5.) God promised Abraham that in his seed "all the families of the earth will be *blessed*" (Gen. 12:3, emphasis added). We see this promise fulfilled in Christ and His salvation (Acts 3:25–26). But in Zech. 14:16–19, "all the families of the earth" that refuse to listen to Christ will be *cursed* (Acts 3:22–23).

   a. What insight do we gain from the fact that God spoke of this division of "all the families of the earth" some five hundred years before Christ came in the flesh? (There are several answers.)

   b. Has God provided sufficient time, opportunity, and reason for "all the families of the earth" to choose between blessing and curse? Please explain. (Consider Deut. 30:15–20 and Rom. 2:5–8 in your answer.)

Introduction to *Malachi*

Authorship: "Malachi"—which may be an abbreviation of Malakiah, "messenger of Jehovah"—is not mentioned anywhere else in the Bible except in Mal. 1:1.[263] Some think "Malachi" is a name given to an otherwise anonymous prophet (based upon the meaning of the name), but there is no good reason to believe this. No prophetical book has thus far been written by or credited to an anonymous writer, to our knowledge. Such a conclusion based only on the meaning of the prophet's name alone is unwarranted.

Date and Place of Writing: Malachi is the last of the recorded prophets—and quite likely the *last prophet* until the time of John the Baptist. The situation he describes seems to correspond with the conditions of the Jews during the time of Nehemiah, which would place its date of writing in the mid-400s (mid-5th century) BC. The first wave of exiles from Babylon began returning ca. 536 BC, under the leadership of Zerubbabel (as discussed in "Introduction to Haggai"). Later (*ca.* 458 BC), Ezra came to restore an understanding of the Law of Moses and to teach it (Ezra 7:10). The Persian emperor Artaxerxes I (ruled 465–425 BC) allowed Nehemiah to go to Jerusalem to rebuild the wall around the city, and to serve as its governor on two different trips (between 444–425 BC). Nehemiah confronts a people who have been lax about taking care of God's work, which corresponds to the lax attitude of those whom Malachi confronts. It is impossible to know where Malachi wrote his message, but he must have spoken it in person (or sent it in writing) to the people of his generation, rather than simply providing a prophetic record for an unknown audience.

Purpose and Character of Writing: The style of writing in *Malachi* is like that which became popular among Jewish rabbis in the intertestamental period, the era of the Jewish synagogue. "In this type of teaching an assertion or charge is made, a fancied objection is raised by the hearers, and a refutation to the objection is presented by the speaker."[264] On multiple occasions, "You say ... ," "But you say ... ," or similar expressions are used to interrupt the speaker (Jehovah), indicating a defensive and argumentative people who are unafraid to challenge God with their own "take" on things. Even so, Jehovah responds to such arguments and provides an *accurate assessment* of things, despite what the people say. The repeated appeal to Jehovah ("[thus] says the Lord of hosts") counters the teaching, conclusions, or sheer indifference of the people, and the priesthood in particular.

At the time of writing, exiles from Babylonian captivity have been in their native land for nearly a century. An earlier generation rebuilt their temple (1:6–7, 3:10), yet the present generation's attitude toward the Lord shows a decline from that earlier time rather than an improvement. God has done everything He could do for them, but they show no genuine appreciation for this. The worship of Jehovah is no longer intermingled with idolatry as before the exile; now it is mixed with disdain, tiredness (1:13), and general apathy. The people's disregard for their covenant with God also spills over into their disregard for their marriage covenants; the same treachery they exercise toward their sacrifices (1:6–8), they also show toward their wives (2:14–16). They have little regard for God's laws, so He has withheld from them rain, prosperity, and freedom from pestilence (3:8–12).

> The great prophecies [concerning Israel's future, and particularly the reign of Messiah] are not yet fulfilled, and the people of Israel become disillusioned and doubtful. They begin to question God's providence as their faith imperceptibly degenerates into cynicism. Internally, they wonder whether it is worth serving God after all; and externally, these attitudes surface in mechanical observances, empty ritual, cheating on tithes and offerings, and crass indifference to God's moral and ceremonial law. Their priests are corrupt and their practices wicked, but they are so spiritually insensitive that they wonder why they are not being blessed by God.[265]

The people seem to be following the example of the priests, which is why much of the discourse in *Malachi* addresses the priests (as the source of the problem) rather than the general populace. "There is a kinship between the book of Malachi and that of Nehemiah," since both deal with several of the same issues: social and religious abuses; money issues; divorce and mixed marriages; etc.[266] It is very likely, then, that the two men lived concurrently.

Overall, *Malachi* is a depressing read. Yet, like nearly every book of the minor prophets, it is punctuated with glimmers of hope, renewal, and encouragement to do well. The book closes with the ominous promise of the coming of "Elijah" who will be the forerunner to the Messiah's own appearance in the world (4:4–6), and for the next 400 years of prophetic silence, this is what faithful Jews anticipated with great eagerness.

Overview of *Malachi*

Mal. 1:1 "Oracle [or, burden]," as in previous prophetical books, indicates a message or judgment from God laid upon the people, but also one borne by the prophet himself (as His messenger). That the oracle is addressed to "Israel" rather than Judah (or, the Jews) is interesting, and indicates that by this time Israelites scattered from the Assyrian exile as well as Jews from the Babylonian exile have begun to repopulate the land of Judah.

Mal. 1:2–5 God begins by reaffirming His love for His people: everything He has done for them has been an act of love (seeking their best interest). Instead of reciprocating that love, however, the Israelites dispute it, thinking perhaps that a loving God would never have sent His people into exile (or other moral accusations). "In all the centuries since creation the human heart has not changed—it always questions what God affirms."[267] They forget, of course, that God's actions were forewarned in the Law of Moses, and that He simply responded to their persistent sinful behavior rather than acting maliciously on His own.

God, in His divine patience, offers two proofs of His love. **First**, He chose "Jacob" (Israel) over "Esau" (the Edomites) as heirs of the Promised Land, even though this countered every natural expectation (Gen. 25:21–23).[268] This decision was made before the nation of Israel ever existed, so it was completely dependent upon God's sovereign choice (Rom. 9:6–16). **Second**, He preserved Israel over and above the Edomites, even though the Edomites vowed to regroup and rebuild after every invasion or form of destruction they endured. They are a wicked people, and therefore God will be against them always; but He has always sought Israel's well-being, since within Israel there has always been a remnant of believers. God's response is, "You should have seen all this happening and *thanked* Me, rather than question My love for you" (paraphrase of 1:5).

Mal. 1:6–14 In particular, the priests' disrespect for God violates all natural and social expectations. If a son is to respect his earthly father, and a servant his master, then *how much more* should an Israelite priest respect the God to whom he ministers (1:6)? God is then specific as to how they have shown their disrespect: they offer Him defiled (or, corrupted; blemished; unfit) sacrifices—animals that are blind, lame, or sick (1:7–8). The Law called for perfect specimens of animals (Lev. 22:17–33), but they chose to overlook this out of neglect, indifference, or to get rid of unwanted animals. This is an offense that they would dare not even commit against their own governor of the land!

Despite having offended God in this way, the priests wonder why their entreaties (prayers) have gone unanswered—why God has not been "gracious" toward them (1:9). The problem is obvious: the fault lies with the people's defiled hearts, not God's inability to answer and perform. God longs for at least *one person* to stand up for Him—like in the days of Phinehas during Israel's sin with the Moabite women (Num. 25:10–18)—someone to "stand in the gap" between God and unfaithful men (Ezek. 22:30–31), but no one will speak for the Lord. God says, in so many words, it is better not to have an altar at all than to allow it to be disgraced with useless sacrifices.[269] In due time, it is prophesied (1:11), "the nations" will present an offering to God far better than what these Jews are offering Him (Isa. 66:19–23).

As it is, the Jews profane His altar (1:12), treating it with disdain and boredom, as though the entire process of offering sacrifices to the God of Israel was a great burden to them (1:13).[270] "Instead of their worship being one of joy growing out of gratitude for the Lord's having chosen them to such an exalted honor, they found their work a boresome chore. Here might be found a lesson for preachers, elders, and teachers of the Lord's service in the present dispensation."[271] Not only did this justify (in their minds) the offering of lame or sick animals, but also ones that were stolen or taken by force ("robbery")—i.e., those that did not cost them anything (compare 2 Sam. 24:24).

Yet God deserves not merely a *placeholder* sacrifice, but the very *best* one has to offer Him (1:14). If a man offers a vow to God, but sanctions it with a faulty sacrifice, this invalidates his vow and deeply offends the One to whom he made it. (The Hebrew text calls such offerings a *cheating* and a *corruption*.²⁷²) Thus, all those who participate in profaning His altar are "cursed"—they are promised to received divine punishment for their carelessness and disregard. "[F]or I am a great King…and My name is feared [or, revered] among the nations"—such contempt is no way to treat a great King, and will not go unpunished. This passage also looks ahead to what is coming under the leadership of the Messiah. "The Mosaic system was seen by Malachi as about to be transcended, as indeed it was in the sacrifice of Christ. Through this sacrifice those who were strangers to the covenants of promise [i.e., Gentiles] would be reconciled to God."²⁷³

Mal. 2:1–9 God had chosen the tribe of Levi to minister to Him—a privilege that should have been received with honor, dignity, and obedience. Yet, the priests (Levites) in Malachi's day are doing little to honor God's name, and thus bring dishonor upon themselves (2:1–2). Not only this, but they bring a curse upon themselves, their work, and their "offspring [or, seed]" (2:3). God refers to *their* feasts—not His—because they had so defiled the festivals they claimed were done in His honor. While all the defilement of sin was to be taken outside the camp for disposal, God promises, in essence, to rub their faces in it instead. The idea of smearing "refuse" [lit., dung; vomit] upon the faces of the priests is to utterly humiliate them—a humiliation that they have brought upon themselves. Such humiliation is not meant to destroy them, however, but to lead them back to what they should have been doing in the first place (2:4).

God further explains (2:5–7) that His agreement ("covenant") with the tribe of Levi was never supposed to be one of disgrace and judgment, but "one of life and peace." Instead of the Levites (priests) showing contempt for God, they were to show reverence and stand "in awe of My name." The Levitical priesthood (here personified as a single "he") was supposed to enlighten the people with knowledge of God, not set a terrible example for them; they were to serve as a messenger of God, not invite divine curses upon the people. Such was the original intent; the priests of Malachi's day failed to honor that holy charge. Instead, they "turned aside" from what God had commissioned them to do (2:8); instead of being a source of righteous instruction, they made themselves a stumbling block to the people. In all, they "corrupted the covenant of Levi" (i.e., God's agreement with the tribe of Levi—Num. 3:1–10). In response, God will humiliate, debase, and dishonor these men before the people.[274] They have corrupted their sense of justice and fairness; thus, as it stands, they are unfit to fulfill their duty to the Lord (2:9).

Mal. 2:10–12 Since God is the "father" of their covenant with Him (in that He created it), and this covenant necessarily requires justice and faithfulness between all those who are in covenant with Him, it stands to reason that there is *no excuse* for any treachery toward God *or* one another (2:10). The problem described in this passage is that Jewish men are marrying non-Israelite women ("the daughter of a foreign god," the worshiper of a heathen deity), and thereby corrupting the purity and integrity of the nation of Israel (see Deut. 7:1–6). God did not make a covenant with foreigners, but only with the people of Israel (Exod. 19:5–6, 24:8). God will "cut off" or judge harshly every man who corrupts this covenant, from the one who has *done it himself* ("awakes and answers") to the one who attempts to *sanction this practice* through offering a grain offering to the Lord on that man's behalf.[275]

Mal. 2:13–16 Not only are Jewish men marrying idolatrous women, but they are leaving their Jewish wives to do so. These divorced women's weeping and tears cover (figuratively) God's altar—i.e., they are tearfully pleading for God's help and intervention—and that, because of their weeping, God is not accepting the offerings of their former husbands. (This is reminiscent of 1 Peter 3:7: failure to treat one's spouse as a "fellow heir" of God hinders that man's prayers to Him.) In a sense, their tears douse the fire that would receive their husbands' sacrifices—but those men seem oblivious to this ("For what reason?"—2:14).

God Himself stands as a "witness between you and the wife of your youth" (i.e., the wife whom you originally married) that they have dealt treacherously toward these women. They have violated the covenant they made with their wives; in doing so, they have also violated their covenant with God. "The wife who had been the companion of a sacred covenant, who had borne children to her husband and who had shared his joys and sorrows, his hardships and days of darkness, now was being rejected for a heathen woman, a worshiper of foreign deities."[276]

A man who would do such a thing clearly did not do so with the right "spirit" (2:15). Likewise, if he wanted to bring up godly offspring (or, "seed"), he could not do so through divorcing his wife and marrying a heathen woman. The idea is that holy (or sanctified) children cannot by the outcome of an unholy union involving one who is already in covenant with a holy God. Or: treachery and covenant–breaking will not lead to a godly family. "For I hate divorce" (2:16)—God could not be clearer on the subject—but He also hates all the treachery, lack of compassion (toward the "wife of [one's] youth"), and violence toward one's marriage covenant that leads *to* divorce. Thus, even if marital treachery and destructive behavior do not lead to an actual divorce, God condemns these actions all the same. "Such a vigorous warning and exhortation from the Lord in a former decadent and permissive age should not be silenced; its principle should be heralded to the ends of the earth in our own time."[277]

Mal. 2:17 This verse seems to introduce the remainder of Malachi's prophecy. It is general in nature but shows the overall disrespect that the people had toward God and His laws. Instead of honoring His word, they "wearied" God with their "w`ords" (i.e., with their reasonings and false conclusions). **First**, they claimed that God regarded Jewish men who did evil as "good" in His sight—i.e., they praised what God condemned. **Second**, they claimed that God "delights" in such men—an indirect way of saying that God's laws have *led* them to do such things, making Him responsible for wicked men. **Third**, they asked, "Where is the God of justice?"—this is either asked bewilderingly (as in, "Why isn't God doing something about all the injustice?") or sarcastically (as in, "If these things are truly wrong, then why doesn't God do something about it?"). In the context, the latter sentiment seems more plausible. And yet, Malachi's scathing prophecy describes God doing something about it.

Mal. 3:1–7 In response to, "Where is the God of justice?" (recall 2:17), God promises to send His "messenger"[278]—the "Elijah" of 4:5–6 (3:1; see Isa. 40:3–5). All four of the gospel accounts agree that this refers to John the Baptist (Mat. 3:3, Mark 1:3, Luke 3:4, and John 1:23, where John the Baptist says this *himself*). Jesus later confirmed this as well (Mat. 11:10–14 and 17:10–13). This "messenger" will be the herald of the Lord who comes after him. This fits with typical ancient protocol: before a king would enter a city, his messenger(s) would go ahead of him to announce his coming. This was so that the people would properly prepare themselves *and* the city so as not to offend the king and face his wrath. "The messenger of the covenant, in whom you delight" (3:1) refers to a *different* "messenger" than the first. Both are "messengers" in that Jehovah has commissioned them; but each one has a different role or function.[279] "But who can endure ... His coming?" (3:2a)—a prediction of the potency and far-reaching implications of Jesus' message. It will be difficult to accept; some will *not* accept it (John 6:60–66); others will run away from it in fear (John 3:19–20, Acts 24:25, Rev. 6:17, etc.).

The people waited expectantly for their Messiah ("the messenger of the covenant, in whom you delight"), but God warns that He (Christ) will not fulfill their expectations of Him (3:2b–3). A "refiner's fire" refers to a smelter that heats up raw ore to extract precious elements from the useless rock (as in 1 Peter 1:6–7). A "fuller's soap" refers to one who washes clothing with a strong and cleansing lye soap to rid it of all its dirt and uncleanness. These are not two different actions, but are the same action described differently. God's people need to be *purified* and *cleansed*, since they presently are *unprepared* to enter a new covenant with God through His Messiah. ("[S]ons of Levi" specifically refers to the priests, but, as said earlier, the priests set the example for the rest of the people. Thus, it is natural and fitting to single them out here.) Instead of offering bulls and goats, the people will offer to God "[grain] offerings of righteousness" in the new covenantal system. God is ignoring their present offerings because of their treachery (recall 2:13); but "then"—in the future dispensation—their offerings will be "pleasing" to Him, after He has refined and cleansed the people (of their sins) (3:4). New types of offerings also imply a new priesthood, and wherever the priesthood has changed, so does law (Heb. 7:12).

At that time, God will not be a Judge *against* His people, but *for* them (3:5). All those who take delight in lawlessness—those who dabble in the occult, adulterers, false witnesses, oppressors of the innocent, oppressors of the helpless (widows and orphans), those who refuse to help strangers, and those who "do not fear Me"—God will expose such people and openly condemn them (compare John 3:18–21 and Eph. 5:7–13). These will have no place in the coming kingdom of God since they will have judged themselves unworthy of eternal life with Him (Acts 13:46). Just as God does not change, so His moral laws do not change. As God condemns those who violate His justice *now* (in Malachi's day), so He will condemn such people in the age of His Messiah. But God will not end His covenant with His people until that time; because of His mercy toward them, they will not be "consumed" before the Messiah appears. He does charge them, nonetheless, with having "turned aside" from Him (3:7; compare Josh. 1:7). He calls for their repentance, but they are unwilling to admit (in this figurative exchange) that they have done anything wrong.

Mal. 3:8–12 Besides all the crimes He has already laid at the feet of this people, God adds one more: robbery (3:8). The people act incredulous, thinking they have not *taken* something from God; but God explains that they have robbed Him in what they have *withheld* from Him—namely, "tithes and offerings." Such gifts were to honor Him as the Source of all income and prosperity; to withhold them is to deny this rightful acknowledgment. In response, God has visited them with "a curse" upon their crops, harvests, and vineyards (3:9). This curse has come in the form of pestilence (worms; caterpillars; locusts) and wasting disease (causing the vines to drop their fruit prematurely) (3:11; see Amos 4:9 and Hag. 2:17).

The tithe was given *to* the people but *belonged* to God. "It was holy unto the Lord (Lev. 27:30–33). God had commanded it to be given, not because God needed to receive it, but because men needed to pay it."[280] God challenges the people: if you bring the food tithes into "the storehouse"—the designated places where the tithes were collected for the Levites (Num. 18:24–32) and the helpless (Deut. 14:22–29)—then He will bless those who bring them with overflowing prosperity (3:10). While God calls upon the people to "test" *Him* in this, it is really a test of their own *faith* in Him since they need to give up something first. When the testing (or, proving) has shown to be successful, and God blesses them with great abundance, then all the foreign nations will call them "blessed" and "a delightful land" (3:12).

Mal. 3:13–18 But instead of putting their faith in God's provision, the people have spoken arrogantly against Him (3:13). ("Arrogant" here means strong, hard, harsh, or violent.[281] The implication is: they have not simply criticized God, but have done so bitterly, forcefully, and accusatorily.) Specifically, they have decided that it is "vain [or, useless; unprofitable]" to serve God, since they feel that they have not gained any advantage from doing so. Keeping His "charge" (commandments) or "mourning" (fasting) before Him seemed a waste of time (3:14). It is like they have been doing God a big favor but are tired of continuing it. Their thinking is warped, convoluted, and twisted (as in Isa. 5:20). Instead of reveling in their privileged role as God's people, they praise wicked people who do whatever they want and still prosper (3:15).

God does not answer these accusations immediately, however—not because He is unable, but because, given all that He has done for them, it is pointless to do so. He has already made His case; His verdict is already decided: God has always been faithful to His people, but His people have—and continue to—snub their nose at Him in deep disrespect. However, there are those in Malachi's presence—possibly listening to his prophecies, or at least aware of them—who fear God and seek His favor (3:16). These men speak with one another and seem to make an agreement amongst themselves to be faithful to God. They write down this agreement in a "book of remembrance" that serves as a record of their decision to honor the Lord.

This book catches the Lord's attention, and He is pleased with those who wrote it (3:17). "They will be Mine" indicates not only these men, but also anyone who has the same kind of heart as they have, as He says elsewhere ("'To this one I will look, to him who is humble and contrite of spirit, and who trembles at My word'"—Isa. 66:2b). In the time when His Messiah will appear, it is such people whom God will make His own "possession [or, treasure]" (compare Titus 2:13–14). While the wicked will face divine judgment, these humble men will not only be spared that judgment but will be richly blessed by God. In this way, He will distinguish the righteous from the wicked (3:18): He will welcome the righteous into His kingdom as sons, while casting away the wicked into the outer darkness of judgment (see Mat. 8:11–12 and John 8:34–36).

Mal. 4:1–6 God ends this prophecy—and, in effect, the entire OT—with a sobering warning: the "day [of the Lord]" is coming, and no one will be able to stop it or escape its effect (4:1, bracketed words added). This "day" will be like a devouring fire to those who persist in arrogance and wickedness, and "will set them ablaze" (compare Mat. 3:10, 12, Luke 3:9, 16–17, John 15:6, etc.). His judgment will leave such people with "neither root nor branch"—i.e., once He has destroyed them, it will be as if they had never existed. They will have no praiseworthy legacy, and no one will remember them.

But God makes several promises to those who fear Him (4:2–3): **First**, they will enjoy the "sun" (meaning: warmth; comfort; illumination) of righteousness—the fruits of dwelling in God's favor. This pristine existence will bring spiritual healing and peace. **Second**, they will be joyful and full of life, as depicted by young, frolicking calves released from the stall into the open meadow. **Third**, they will "tread down the wicked," which indicates a complete victory over them. The wicked will be destroyed by fire; not only will the righteous *not* be destroyed, but they will triumph over those who tried to destroy *them*. All this, God is "preparing" for His people: it is a promise, yet to be fulfilled (to those in Malachi's day), but one that *has* been fulfilled for all those who are redeemed by the blood of the Messiah.
Meanwhile, until that "day" comes, God makes it clear what He wants His people to do: "Remember [i.e., obey] the law of Moses My servant ..." (4:4). This is the same thing Abraham told the rich man concerning his five brothers: "They have Moses and the Prophets; let

them hear them" (Luke 16:29). No one will be the recipient of God's promises of righteousness, joy, and triumph who refuses to obey the commandments He has already given him. And, until the Messiah perfectly fulfills God's covenant with Israel, its laws are still in full force (Mat. 5:17–19). "Horeb" is another name for (Mount) Sinai, where God originally gave the Law of Moses (Exod. 19—20).

Again, God's messenger—dubbed "Elijah," because he will finish what the actual prophet Elijah started—will be sent ahead of the Messiah (4:5). Just as "David" (Messiah) is not the literal David the king of Israel, so this "Elijah" is not the literal prophet Elijah. John the Baptist will not be a city–dweller, but (like Elijah) will remain in the wilderness; he will dress in much the same way as Elijah (compare 2 Kings 1:8 and Mat. 3:4); he will live off the land as Elijah did; etc. Elijah left the world in a unique way—being carried to the sky by chariots of fire (2 Kings 2:11–12)—but he will, in a prophetic sense, re–enter the world in a unique way as well. John the Baptist will be the only prophet whose own birth is prophesied, and who will be born in the context of a miracle (i.e., being born to aged parents, his mother being barren; see Luke 1:5–25).

The role of "Elijah"/John the Baptist will be to "restore [or, turn] the hearts of the fathers to their children" (4:6)—i.e., the adults would humble themselves like children, which is a necessary precursor for obedience to God (Luke 1:16–17). But also: "…and the hearts of the children to their fathers"—i.e., the children will be taught the ancient, ancestral importance of God's covenant with His people. In both cases, the people's hearts are to be *turned back to God*, as indicated by John's baptism that symbolized God's forgiveness of their sins (Luke 3:3).

If this did not happen—or, for those who refused to humble themselves so that this *could* happen—God promises to "smite the land with a curse [or, a devotion to destruction]." This is exactly what the gospel accounts record: while many Jews were baptized by John, most Jews rejected the One whom John foretold, namely, the Messiah (Jesus Christ) (John 3:28–36). This brought upon Judea, and Jerusalem in particular, an awful curse, as Jesus predicted (Luke 19:41–44, 21:20–22).

In AD 66, Jewish extreme nationalists (zealots) provoked the Roman government by declaring war on it and murdering Roman soldiers in the military garrisons throughout Judea. This was met by the full strength of the Roman army, which besieged Jerusalem and then, when its wall was breached, leveled that city to the ground. Many, many Jews lost their lives; others were taken as prisoners of war to foreign countries (including Italy) where they were either executed or literally worked to death. God's promise of judgment upon His people was not an empty one, even though it spoke of things hundreds of years in Malachi's future.

Hailey provides a most appropriate summary not only for the book of *Malachi*, but for the entire study of the minor prophets:

> The Book of Malachi serves as a fitting close to God's ancient revelation to His people. A final appeal is made to the people to purge out the wickedness found among them and to render to Jehovah an acceptable service. A final warning is given of inevitable judgment upon the wicked. And a final promise is made of Jehovah's righteousness to be provided in Him who would be the personal bond of unity between Jehovah and His people. There was no more that Jehovah could say or do; therefore no word was heard from Him until the silence was broken by the messenger [John the Baptist] who would introduce the Messiah.[282]

Questions on *Malachi*

1.) What overall or overarching impressions does the book of *Malachi* leave upon you?

    a. Why do you think the Jews struggled so much to be faithful to God, after all He had done for them?

    b. Is this book relevant for Christians today? If so, why? If not, why not?

2.) One commentator wrote: "One of the problems of Malachi's day was the blurring of moral and theological values. No one seemed to be able to distinguish right from wrong, or the righteous from the wicked." Is this still happening today? Please explain.

3.) The book of *Malachi* provides a series of disputes between the Jews and God. What is often the source of these disputes? Do some Christians, like the Jews in Malachi's day:

    a. still question whether God loves them (1:2–5)? If so, what is such questioning often based upon?

    b. offer (in essence) blind, lame, or otherwise unfit offerings to God, and then wonder why He does not answer their prayers or relieve their suffering?

c. refuse to "take it to heart to honor give honor to [God's] name" (2:2), and then wonder why they are not growing spiritually or enjoying God's fellowship?

d. enter covenant–binding relationships with those who are not Christians, and then wonder why their marriages and households are filled with tension, strife, and division (2:10–12, in principle)?

e. deal treacherously with their spouse—in *any* context, regardless of whether this leads to divorce—and then wonder why they experience God's judgment upon them?

f. weary God with their own rationalizations, self-righteousness, and clever justifications for their sinful behavior (2:17), and then wonder why they never amount to much of anything as a man or woman of God?

g. rob God by withholding from Him whatever offering, sacrifice, or contribution is rightfully His—by virtue of what they *promised* Him in their baptism—and then wonder why nothing ever goes well for them?

h. say in their heart, "It is vain to serve God" (3:14), because they see no advantage in doing so above their arrogant and wicked friends or peers (3:15)?

i. need to have *their own hearts* "turned back" or restored to the Lord and His word to avoid a divine curse in their future (4:5–6)?

4.) While Malachi's overall message is dark and depressing, he does provide some excellent promises for those who take God seriously and "fear [His] name" (3:16–18, 4:2–3).

a. What are these promises? Are these promises conditional or unconditional?

b. Do *faithful Christians* have such promises? (Consider Rom. 8:16–17, 2 Cor. 6:17—7:1, Eph. 1:13–14, and 1 Peter 1:3–5 in your answer.)

Sources Used for This Study

Allen, Matthew. *The Minor Prophets: Mighty Messengers of God*, vol. 1 and 2. Summitville, IN: Spiritbuilding Publishing, 2007.

Coffman, James B. *The Minor Prophets, vol. 1: Joel, Amos, and Jonah.* Abilene, TX: ACU Press, 1981.

_____. *The Minor Prophets, vol. 2: Hosea, Obadiah, and Micah.* Abilene, TX: ACU Press, 1981.

_____. *The Minor Prophets, vol. 3: Nahum, Habakkuk, Zephaniah, and Haggai.* Abilene, TX: ACU Press, 1982.

_____. *The Minor Prophets, vol. 4: Zechariah and Malachi.* Abilene, TX: ACU Press, 1983.

Dobson, Edward G.; Charles L Feinberg; et al. *Bible Commentary.* Nashville, TN: Nelson Reference and Electronic, 2005.

Driver, S. R. *An Introduction to the Literature of the Old Testament.* New York: Meridian Books, 1956.

Gordon, Cyrus A., and Gary A. Rendsburg. *The Bible and the Ancient Near East*, 4th ed. New York: W. W. Norton & Company, 1997.

Hailey, Homer. *A Commentary on the Minor Prophets.* Louisville, KY: Religious Supply, Inc., 1993.

Holman Illustrated Bible Dictionary (electronic edition). © 2003 by Holman Bible Publishers; database © 2014 by WORDsearch Corp.

International Standard Bible Encyclopedia (electronic edition). © 1979 by Eerdman's Publishing Co.; database © 2013 by WORDsearch Corp.

Jamieson, Robert; A. R. Fausset; and David Brown. *Commentary Critical and Explanatory on the Whole Bible* (electronic edition). Database © 2012 by WORDsearch Corp. (originally published 1871).

Keil, C. F. *Introduction to the Old Testament*, vol. 1, trans. by G. C. M. Douglas. Peabody, MA: Hendrickson Publishers, 1991.

Keil, C. F. and F. Delitzsch. *Commentary on the Old Testament, vol. 10: Minor Prophets.* Peabody, MA: Hendrickson Publishers, 1996.

Smith, Ralph L. *Word Biblical Commentary*, vol. 32. Waco, TX: Word Books, 1984.

Stuart, Douglas. *Word Biblical Commentary*, vol. 31. Waco, TX: Word Books, 1987.

Thomas, Robert L., gen. ed. *NASB Hebrew–Greek Dictionary* (electronic edition). © 1998 by The Lockman Foundation.

Wilkinson, Bruce, and Kenneth Boa. *Talking Thru the Old Testament*, vol. 1. Nashville, TN: Thomas Nelson Publishers, 1983.

Endnotes

1   Consider this same application to Jesus: "Therefore Jesus answered and was saying to them, 'Truly, truly, I say to you, the Son can do nothing of Himself, unless it is something He sees the Father doing; for whatever the Father does, these things the Son also does in like manner. For the Father loves the Son, and shows Him all things that He Himself is doing ...'" (John 5:19–20).

2   Homer Hailey, *A Commentary on the Minor Prophets* (Louisville, KY: Religious Supply, Inc., 1993), 14.

3   "The English word 'prophet' is from two Greek words that mean 'speak for.' This emphasizes the role of these people as divinely chosen spokesmen who received and related God's messages, whether in oral, visual, or written form" (Bruce Wilkins and Kenneth Boa, *Talk Thru the Old Testament, vol. 1* [Nashville, TN: Thomas Nelson Publishers, 1983], 185).

4   Certainly, one could make the argument that Jesus revealed God to us in Himself even more—and more personally—than did any of the OT prophets (see John 1:17–18, 5:19–20, 14:7–10, Col. 2:9, Heb. 1:3, etc.). But considering only the human factor of the prophets themselves (and not the divine factor that Jesus adds), God has revealed Himself far more through the prophets than He has anywhere else.

5   A. A. MacRae, "Prophets and Prophesying," *The Zondervan Pictorial Encyclopedia of the Bible, vol. 4*, Merrill C. Tenney, gen. ed. (Grand Rapids: Regency Reference Library, 1976), 876.

6   G. V. Smith, "Prophet; Prophecy," *International Standard Bible Encyclopedia* [*ISBE*] (electronic edition) (© 1979 by Eerdman's Publishing Co.; database © 2013 by WORDsearch).

7   Smith, "Prophet; Prophecy," *ISBE*.

8   C. F. Keil, *Introduction to the Old Testament, vol. 1*, trans. by G. C. M. Douglas (Peabody, MA: Hendrickson Publishers, 1991 [originally published in 1869]), 267–268.

9   MacRae, 897; bracketed words are mine.

10   "Although the prophets had a ministry of foretelling future events, their primary role was that of forthtelling. This demanded spiritual insight as well as foresight, because they proclaimed the consequences of specific attitudes and practices of their day. They dipped into the past for lessons and exhortations concerning the present. And they spoke of the need of present reforms to avert future judgment" (Wilkinson and Boa, 186).

11   Smith, "Prophet; Prophecy," *ISBE*; bracketed words are mine.

12   MacRae, 885.

13   Matthew Allen, *The Minor Prophets: Mighty Messengers of God*, vol. 1 (Summitville, IN: Spiritbuilding Publishing, 2007), 7.

14   MacRae, 880.

15   Randy Hatchett, "Prophecy; Prophets," *Holman Illustrated Bible Dictionary (electronic edition),* Chad Brand, Charles Draper, and Archie England, gen. eds. (© 2003 by Holman Bible Publishers; database © 2014 by WORDsearch Corp.).

16   Hailey, 12.

17   *Daniel* may be classified with the major prophets, the minor prophets, or as a third category. The so-called "apocalyptic" prophets include *Ezekiel, Daniel,* and *Zechariah*; it is from these books that much of the symbolism in *Revelation* is drawn.

18   Keil, 364.

19   "The Hebrew name Obadyah means 'worshiper of Yahweh' or 'servant of Yahweh.' The Greek title in the Septuagint is Obdiou, and the Latin title in the Vulgate is Abdias" (Wilkinson and Boa, 251).

20   Such are the educated opinions of both Homer Hailey (*Minor Prophets,* 28–9) and James B. Coffman (*The Minor Prophets,* vol. 2 [Abilene, TX: ACU Press, 1981]), 241. Also, the ancient Hebrew organization of the OT also placed it prior to the Babylonian subjugation of Judah (Coffman, vol. 2, 242; C. F. Keil and F. Delitzsch, *Commentary on the Old Testament,* vol. 10 [Peabody, MA: Hendrickson Publishers, 1996], 228). Douglas Stuart disagrees, saying that Obadiah belongs to the period during the Judean exile (after 586 BC), but offers nothing conclusive to substantiate this claim (*Word Biblical Commentary,* vol. 31

[Waco, TX: Word Books, 1987], 404). The Jewish Talmud maintains that Obadiah, the writer of the book that bears his name, is the same Obadiah that lived during the time of Ahab, which Stuart mentions (ibid., 406–407), but then quickly dismisses as speculation.

21   Edward G. Dobson, Charles L Feinberg, et al, *Bible Commentary* (Nashville, TN: Nelson Reference and Electronic, 2005), 1027.

22   Hailey, 30; bracketed word is mine.

23   Keil and Delitzsch, 251; bracketed words are mine.

24   Coffman, vol. 2, 248; bracketed words are mine.

25   Hailey, 30.

26   Coffman, vol. 2, 250; Keil and Delitzsch, 239.

27   "On the other hand, the Israelites are always commanded in the law to preserve a friendly and brotherly attitude towards Edom (Deut. 2:4–5); and in Deut. 23:7 it is enjoined upon them not to abhor the Edomite, because he is their brother" (Keil and Delitzsch, 241).

28   Hailey, 36–37.

29   "The Hebrew name Yo'el means 'Yahweh is God.' This name is appropriate to the theme of the book, which emphasizes God's sovereign work in history. The courses of nature and nations are in His hand. The Greek equivalent is Ioel, and the Latin is Joel" (Wilkinson and Boa, 240).

30   Robert Jamieson, A. R. Fausset, and David Brown, *Commentary Critical and Explanatory on the Whole Bible, electronic edition* (database © 2012 by WORDsearch Corp.; originally published 1871), on "Introduction to Joel."

31   Some commentators suggest that the locust swarm is allegorical, not literal. But there is no good evidence to support this theory. The mere use of heightened poetic imagery, as what Joel uses, does not constitute an allegory. "An allegory must contain some significant marks of its being so. Where these are wanting, it is arbitrary to assume that it is an allegory at all" (Keil and Delitzsch, 113).

32   *Bible Commentary*, 1002.

33   "In view of its small size, it is almost incredible how this small

prophecy has been quoted and referred to by so many" (James B. Coffman, *The Minor Prophets, vol. 1* [Abilene, TX: ACU Press, 1981], 7).

34   "Locusts look like large grasshoppers and mature desert locusts have a four-inch wingspan and bodies around three inches long. James Smith [*The Minor Prophets*, 67] writes that what 'typically distinguishes a true locust from a large grasshopper is behavior. When conditions are right, grasshoppers that normally act as solitary individuals begin to swarm. Great clouds of insects will rise during daylight hours in search of moist green vegetation. The sky can be blackened to an altitude of five thousand feet over tens of square miles. A swarm can contain over a billion creatures that altogether can weigh more than three million pounds. When a species of grasshoppers exhibits this type of behavior, they are called locusts'" (Allen, vol. 1, 18; bracketed words are added from Allen's footnote).

35   "These four stages of the locust's development are often taken as prophetic of the Babylonian, Persian, Grecian, and Roman empires, which subsequently overran and controlled Judah. The parallel, however, is probably more coincidental than designed" (*Bible Commentary*, 1004). On the other hand, nothing God does is "coincidental," so there is nothing wrong with seeing this as a foreshadow or prefigure of what is to come. Even so, the prophecy remains focused on this specific insect invasion, not future (or military) invasions.

36   Stuart, vol. 31, 241.

37   "[Sackcloth is a] garment of coarse material fashioned from goat or camel hair worn as a sign of mourning or anguish, also marked by fasting and sitting on an ash heap (Isa. 58:5). ...The shape of the garment could have been either a loose–fitting sack placed over the shoulders or a loincloth. The word "sack" is a transliteration of the Hebrew word rather than a translation" ("Sackcloth," *Holman Illustrated Bible Dictionary, electronic edition* [© 2003 by Holman Bible Publishers; database © 2014 by WORDsearch Corp.]; bracketed words are mine).

38   Keil and Delitzsch, 123; bracketed word is mine.

39   Hailey, 48.

40   It is assumed that "northern" (in 2:20) refers to the direction from which the locust invasion will come. "But locusts never (or scarcely

ever) enter Palestine from the north; so that (unless the occasion was one of the exceptions) 'the northern one' [or "northern army"—the word 'army' being supplied by the translators] would be an unsuitable designation for them; hence by some the term is considered to be descriptive of a human foe [i.e., a an army of men, not a swarm of locusts]" (S. R. Driver, *An Introduction to the Literature of the Old Testament* [New York: Meridian Books, 1956], 308; emphases are his; bracketed words are mine).

41 Jesus promised to baptize with the Holy Spirit and fire—two separate "baptisms," one relating to salvation and the other to the destruction of Jerusalem and the Jewish state (Mat. 3:11–12; see Luke 19:41–44). Thus, the "day of the Lord" in Acts 2 ushers in both salvation and judgment: salvation to those who call upon the name of the Lord (Acts 2:21) and judgment upon that people which rejected their Prophet, God's Son (3:22–23); cf. Rom. 11:22.

42 "People of these regions [i.e., Philistia and Phoenicia] were seafaring traders whose markets for slaves around the Mediterranean fueled their interest in both buying captured Israelite prisoners of war and capturing some themselves for sale elsewhere, especially to the Greeks along the northern Mediterranean coast" (Stuart, vol. 31, 267; bracketed words are mine).

43 "The figure of a great battle between the nations and the warriors of God is joined to that of the nations gathered around before the judge of al the earth" (Jacob Myers, quoted in Coffman, vol. 1, 61).

44 JFB, on 3:14.

45 Stuart, vol. 31, 431.

46 Credit goes to Coffman (vol. 1, 254), from whom this list was assembled.

47 *Ibid.*, 256.

48 "The purity of the language implies the antiquity of the book, and the likelihood of its being Jonah's own

writing. Indeed, none but Jonah could have written or dictated such peculiar details, known only to himself" (JFB, "Introduction to Jonah").

49 *Bible Commentary*, 1034.

50   Hailey, 62–63.

51   Driver, 324; bracketed words are mine.

52   Stuart, vol. 31, 434; bracketed word is mine.

53   Consider Ezekiel's vision of the valley of dry bones in connection with this thought (Ezek. 37:1–14).

54   While Nineveh had long been the palace-city of Assyrian rulers for a millennium prior to Jonah, it did not officially become the capital of Assyria until that nation's rise to an imperial power, specifically during the time of Sennacherib (ruled 705–681 BC). He "enlarged and beautified the city with temples, broad streets, and public gardens. Unique in the Near East were the dimensions and design of his aqueduct, which by its system of dams brought fresh water into the city from the mountains to the east. The king also built massive walls and fortifications around the city for protection against his enemies. Only Babylon in the ancient world surpassed Sennacherib's capital in magnificence and beauty" (C. T. Fritsch, "Nineveh," *ISBE*). Stuart also provides a scholarly defense to Nineveh's prominence in the days of Jonah (vol. 31, 441–442).

55   Wilkinson and Boa, 258.

56   Hailey, 68.

57   Stuart, vol. 31, 459–60.

58   "Attempting to run away from God is like fleeing light and falling into darkness, relinquishing wealth and welcoming poverty, abandoning joy and receiving sorrow, or giving up peace in order to have chaos and confusion!" (Wm. Banks, quoted in Coffman, vol. 1, 284).

59   In the Hebrew Bible, Jonah 1:17 is the beginning of chapter 2 (2:1). Thus, all the verses in chapter 2 are off in the Hebrew Bible by one verse when compared to our modern biblical text.

60   The Hebrew word for "appointed" here, in the context in which it is being used, "does not mean to create, but to determine, to appoint. The thought is this: Jehovah ordained that a great fish should swallow him [Jonah]" (Keil and Delitzsch, 269).

61   Allen, vol. 1, 31–2.

62   "Ancient writers believed that 'Greater Nineveh' was a complex of several cities and their suburbs, in the shape of a parallelogram and about sixty miles in circumference. Modern writers think Greater Nineveh was in more of a triangular shape, but about the same distance around" (Hailey, 67).

63   Since there is nothing in the Assyrian state record concerning this prophecy, or the Ninevites' response to it, some Bible critics have concluded that it did not happen. But "The silence of the official Assyrian records on the preaching of Jonah *per se* is quite understandable. It was hardly incumbent upon archivists to keep lists of visiting prophets! Moreover, official records tend to be as sycophantic [i.e., flatteringly] toward the royalty as possible" (Stuart, vol. 31, 490; bracketed word is mine).

64   Allen, vol. 1, 30.

65   List is cited verbatim from Coffman, vol. 1, 324; bracketed word is mine.

66   "But however deep the penitential mourning of Nineveh might be, and however sincere the repentance of the people, when they acted according to the king's command; the repentance was not a lasting one, or permanent in its effects. Nor did it evince a thorough conversion to God, but was merely a powerful incitement to conversion, a waking up out of the careless security of their life of sin, an endeavour [sic] to forsake their evil ways which did not last very long. …The repentance of the Ninevites, even if it did not last, showed, at any rate, a susceptibility on the part of the heathen for the word of God, and their willingness to turn and forsake their evil and ungodly ways; so that God, according to His compassion, could extend His grace to them in consequence" (Keil and Delitzsch, 277).

67   Stuart, vol. 31, 502.

68   Coffman, vol. 1, 337.

69   Stuart, vol. 31, 507.

70   "The sycamore tree [produced] a fig of poor quality, being a cross between a fig and a mulberry; and it was eaten for food by only the poorest of people" (*Bible Commentary*, 1010, bracketed word added).

The fruit was "slightly sweet and watery, and somewhat woody in its nature. It … had to be pinched or bruised before it would ripen" (Hailey, 82-3), thus Amos' self-description as a "nipper" of figs (7:14, margin reading).

71 Keil and Delitzsch, 158; bracketed words are mine.

72 Stuart, vol. 31, 283.

73 Coffman, vol. 1, 76.

74 Hailey, 83.

75 *Bible Commentary*, 1012.

76 M. Liverani, "Tyre," *ISBE*.

77 It can also symbolize the utter debasing of a person's life, as seen in Josiah's burning of the bones of the priests who led Israel into idolatry (1 Kings 13:2, 2 Kings 23:13-16).

78 Stuart, vol. 31, 322.

79 The full title of God—"the LORD [Jehovah] God, the God of hosts [lit., Sabaoth]" (3:13)—is found nowhere else in Amos. "The Lord of Sabaoth means the Lord of Hosts and is found some 300 times in the OT. The imagery of 'the Lord of Sabaoth, i.e., Lord of Hosts' is that of the ruler over an organized host, such as a great army, or all of the angels of heaven" (Coffman, vol. 1, 119).

80 *Biblical Commentary*, 1018.

81 JFB, on 4:2; see also 2 Chron. 33:10-11. "The Assyrian illustrations depict such scenes with captives being led with hooks through their noses or mouths, and Amos was no doubt familiar with this barbaric practice" (J. Keir Howard, quoted in Coffman, vol. 1, 129).

82 Hailey, 104.

83 *Ibid.*, 106-7. Amos speaks this prophecy in the present tense, even though the event has not yet happened; this is similar to Rev. 18:2, in which "Babylon" is prophesied as already "fallen," even though its "fall" had not yet taken place. The idea here is: so certain is Israel (or "Babylon") to fall, it can be regarded as something that is already happening.

84 This passage is so similar to Isa. 1:10–17, it is possible that one prophet borrowed from the other, or that God simply provided the same essential message to both prophets. It is also interesting to note that sin offerings are not mentioned in this passage, implying that the people did not acknowledge their own sins, but offered offerings of consecration and peace instead, as though they could appease God without taking responsibility for their crimes.

85 Stuart, vol. 31, 356.

86 "Sikkuth was no doubt a portable shrine, in which the image of the deity was kept. Such shrines were used by the Egyptians … ; they were small chapels, generally gilded and ornamented with flowers and in other ways, intended to hold a small idol when processions were made, and to be carried or driven about with it" (Keil and Delitzsch, 196).

87 "In the original Hebrew these gods are called Sikkuth and Kiyyun. The names of these gods were known to the people as Sakkath and Kaiwan. Note that the spelling of the names of both is changed from 'a' to 'i' [sound] in the text. The names of pagan gods were deliberately misspelled in Hebrew literature to mock the idols and further illustrate their shamefulness" (Allen, vol. 1, 49; bracketed word is mine).

88 Arnold C. Schultz, quoted in Coffman, vol. 1, 187.

89 Allen, vol. 1, 44.

90 *Bible Commentary*, 1026.

91 *Ibid.*, 980.

92 Hailey, 127.

93 Keil and Delitzsch, 18; bracketed words are mine.

94 Wilkinson and Boa, 236.

95 Coffman, vol. 2, 12.

96 Fausset says "Gomer" and "Diblaim" are "symbolical names; literally, 'completion, daughter of grape cakes'; the dual expressing the double layers in which these dainties were baked. So, one completely given up to sensuality" (JFB, on 1:3, emphases are his). But while the names may be symbolical, the people are not: Gomer is a real person, and so is her father, and so are the children she bears to Hosea.

97   This study maintains that this marriage is a literal one, and not a figurative or allegorical one. "Some have tried to get rid of what they call the 'moral problem' involved in God's commandment for Hosea to marry a 'wife of whoredom and children of whoredom' [KJV text], by making the whole thing some kind of a parable or allegory; but if such a marriage cannot be allowed in real life, it is equally unacceptable in a parable or an allegory" (Coffman, vol. 2, 6; bracketed words are mine).

98   "'Jezreel' became in Israel a kind of byword for 'decisive battle' alongside 'Midian' in Isa. 9:4 and 10:26 and Ps. 83:9. The fact that the great defeat of Midian by Gideon took place at Jezreel (the valley) reinforces the similarity in usage of the two words" (Stuart, vol. 31, 30).

99   In the Hebrew Bible, 1:10–11 is the beginning of chapter 2 (2:1–2).

100 "That which Hosea had experienced in his unfaithful wife, Gomer, Jehovah had experienced in the unfaithful nation, Israel. [In 2:2,] Jehovah is the husband; Israel is the wife; and the children are individuals of the nation. 'Contend with your mother.' Let the individuals not addicted to idolatry—the better minded among them—contend with the mother, the nation, that she [would] change her ways" (Hailey, 141; bracketed words are mine). Incidentally, I will refer to Israel in this section as "she," since that is how God refers to Israel here.

101 "'Some evidence suggests that women who broke marriage vows were first stripped naked before they were executed (Smith)'" (quoted in Allen, vol. 1, 60).

102 "[The nation of Israel] places the true God on the level of the Baals, either by worshiping other gods along with Jehovah, or by obliterating the essential distinction between Jehovah and the Baals, confounding together the worship of God and idolatrous worship, the Jehovah-religion and heathenism" (Keil and Delitzsch, 42; bracketed words are mine).

103 Coffman, vol. 2, 57.

104 *Ibid.*, 54.

105 Stuart, vol. 31, 66.

106 *Ibid.*, 68.

107 "The prophet mentions objects connected with both the worship

of Jehovah, and that of idols, because they were both mixed together in Israel, and for the purpose of showing to the people that the Lord would take away both" (Keil and Delitzsch, 48).

108 This "New Jerusalem" (Heb. 12:22) will be the adopted family of Israel, the "woman" (compare Gal. 4:26, 31, and Rev. 12:17, where "the rest of her children" refers to the church on earth). God keeps Israel in seclusion, so to speak, but brings forth from her—spiritually-speaking—His own Son (Rev. 12:1–5), and then prepares a bride (the church) for Him from the spiritual descendants of the promise once given to Abraham (Gal. 3:26–29).

109 Hailey, 150.

110 JFB, on 5:7. Hailey suggests, with equal plausibility, that the "new moon" reference has to do with the time in which the Israelites made sacrifices to their false gods for deliverance, even though this would bring them destruction instead (*Minor Prophets,* 153).

111 The crescendo of troubles is defined by the speed in which these maladies take their toll: a moth, for example, can bring about complete ruin to a garment, but takes time to do so; a lion can kill a man in an instant; and whatever lies in–between these two timeframes or scenarios.

112 Hailey, 165; bracketed word is mine.

113 This is a comparative analogy, not an exact repeat of what happened to Sodom and Gomorrah. Isaiah says, "Unless the Lord of hosts had left us a few survivors, we [Israel] would be like Sodom, we would be like Gomorrah" (Isa. 1:9, bracketed word added). God would certainly punish Israel for their sins just as He punished Sodom and Gomorrah for their sins, but He will not wipe Israel off the face of the earth as He did these other cities. Since the world's Redeemer will come through Israel, God will preserve that nation as part of His "eternal purpose" (Eph. 3:11).

114 *NASB Hebrew-Greek Dictionary (electronic edition),* Robert L. Thomas, gen. ed. (© 1998 by The Lockman Foundation), H2617a.

115 Stuart, vol. 31, 220; bracketed words are mine.

116 JFB, "Introduction to Micah."

117 Wilkinson and Boa, 264.

118 Coffman, vol. 2, 274–5; bracketed word is mine.

119 Hailey, 186.

120 Coffman, vol. 2, 269.

121 Bible Commentary, 1043.

122 Ralph L. Smith, *Word Biblical Commentary*, vol. 32 (Waco, TX: Word Books, 1984), 10.

123 "The diction soars poetically, and is rhythmically rounded off [i.e., it has a certain beat, rhythm, or cadence to it]; and the language is classically pure" (Keil, Introduction, 405; bracketed words are mine).

124 "Those who might have expected Micah to produce a smoothly written treatise in the best traditions of rhetorical and grammatical excellence are certain to be disappointed. Sometimes, he did not even bother with complete sentences. There is characteristic roughness and kaleidoscopic effect throughout, as doom and hope, exhortation and condemnation, threat and promise follow each other in rapid–fire succession" (Coffman, vol. 2, 274).

125 Smith, vol. 32, 35; bracketed words are mine.

126 Some think that Micah meant "Assyria" here instead of "Babylon," since Israel—the northern ten tribes to whom he preached—would soon be defeated by Assyria and sent into exile, not Judah/Jerusalem. But Israel would not be "rescued" from their exile, whereas Judah would be rescued after a 70-year exile (2 Chron. 36:17–23). Thus, Micah sees far past the Assyrian invasion and prophesies of yet another powerful nation that would subjugate Judah—a nation (Babylon) that, in Micah's time, was itself a vassal state to Assyria and not yet a world empire.

127 *Bible Commentary*, 1052.

128 Hailey, 209–210.

129 "Asherim" (plural of Asheroth, a.k.a. Ashteroth or Asherah) is a Canaanite goddess, "the worship of which was characterized by the grossest form of licentiousness" (Hailey, 212). It is a fertility goddess of the Phoenicians and the Canaanites, allegedly the mother of Baal (James Newell, "Asherim," *Holman*). The Israelites were supposed to eradicate all the images of Asherim from the Land of Canaan (Exod. 34:13), but

instead adopted the worship (and cultic lifestyle) of this goddess; the people "built for themselves high places, and sacred pillars and Asherim on every high hill and beneath every luxuriant tree" (1 Kings 14:23).

130 Hailey, 212.

131 *Ibid.*, 214.

132 See Neh. 1:5–10 and Dan. 9:4–13 for similar prayers of confessions of sin on behalf of the righteous remnant.

133 James B. Coffman defends this position with much greater detail (*The Minor Prophets, vol. 3* [Abilene, TX: ACU Press, 1982], 120–121).

134 *Bible Commentary*, 1077.

135 *Ibid.*

136 Hailey, 226.

137 Coffman, vol. 3, 127.

138 *Ibid.*; bracketed words are mine.

139 Smith, vol. 32, 131.

140 Hailey, *Minor Prophets*, 228; bracketed words are mine.

141 In the Hebrew text, 1:3b reads: "I will cut off mankind ['adam] from the face of the earth ['adamah]," thus making man's sin responsible for the destruction of the land, birds, fish, and animals (F. E. Eakin, cited in Coffman, vol. 3, 130).

142 Hailey, 230.

143 *Bible Commentary*, 1080.

144 "Stagnant in spirit" is literally rendered (from the Hebrew) "thickening [or, settling] on their lees" (NASB margin reading). "[This] is a metaphor from the treating of wine. In making the best wine the liquid is poured from vessel to vessel, separating the wine from dregs or settlings. If allowed to remain too long on its lees [i.e., the solid waste that settles to the bottom in the winemaking process] the wine became harsh and syrupy (cf. Jer. 48:11–12)" (Hailey, 232; bracketed words are mine).

145 "Modern men reject any conception of an eternal judgment, but in doing so they overlook one thing. Christ, the sovereign head of our holy religion, emphatically endorsed and expanded the very conception

that is found here in Zephaniah and in the other prophets. The reason for the universal destruction accompanying that day is the rebellion of men against the God and Creator. In rejecting the very reason for which they were created, men, as a result, lose all cosmic and eternal value" (Coffman, vol. 3, 142).

146 Hailey, 233.

147 Smith, vol. 32, 136; bracketed word is mine.

148 Wilkinson and Boa, 281.

149 *Bible Commentary,* 1083. But Coffman says: "However, God certainly knew the word for the Egyptians, and our view is that if He had meant that, He would have said it. The reference [in 2:12] is to the most southern kingdom that was known by the world of that period; and it is Zephaniah's purpose of including the south in this universal montage of judgment which forms the fabric of his prophecy in this chapter" (vol. 3, 153). We will leave the conclusion for each student to decide for himself or herself. In the end, to decide between Egypt itself or an Ethiopian-controlled Egypt does not seem to affect the outcome of the prophecy.

150 Cyrus A. Gordon and Gary A. Rendsburg, *The Bible and the Ancient Near East,* 4th ed. (New York: W. W. Norton & Company, 1997), 249.

151 J. M. Powis Smith, quoted in Coffman, vol. 3, 155.

152 "The Hebrew word *nahum* ('comfort, consolation') is a shortened form of Nehemiah ('comfort of Yahweh')" (Wilkinson and Boa, 267).

153 Coffman, vol. 3, 3.

154 A. van Selms, "Elkosh," *ISBE.*

155 Hailey, 249–50.

156 George Adam Smith, quoted in Coffman, vol. 3, 7.

157 Hailey, 249.

158 Bible Commentary, 1059.

159 F. W. Farrar, *The Minor Prophets* (147–8), as quoted in Matthew Allen, *The Minor Prophets: Mighty Messengers of God, vol. 2* (Summitville, IN: Spiritbuilding Publishing, 2007), 26.

160 Wilkinson and Boa, 268.

161 Coffman, vol. 3, 25.

162 Smith, vol. 32, 68; bracketed words are mine.

163 JFB, on 1:4.

164 Keil and Delitzsch, 359.

165 Paul quotes this verse (1:15a) in Rom. 10:15, with reference to the general profession of preachers of God's word throughout the ages.

166 Smith, vol. 32, 82.

167 "The shields are reddened ... not with the blood of enemies who have been slain, but either with red colour [sic] with which they are painted, or what is still more probable, with the copper with which they are overlaid. ... The fighting dress of the nations of antiquity was frequently blood-red" (Keil and Delitzsch, 365).

168 *Bible Commentary*, 1063. Hailey, however, says that "there is no indication from the Babylonian monuments that their chariots were equipped with rotating blades on the wheels or with blades protruding from the sides of the chariots" (*Minor Prophets*, 260).

169 Bible Commentary, 1063.

170 "The wall about Nineveh was seemingly impregnable, being about 60 miles in length as it surrounded the city and having some 1,500 towers, each about two hundred feet high" (*Ibid.*, 1064).

171 Hailey, 263; bracketed word is mine.

172 Coffman, vol. 3, 34; bracketed words are mine.

173 *Ibid.*, 47.

174 Hailey, 250; Smith, vol. 32, 63–4. An inscription from the Assyrian king Ashurbanipal, discovered in 1878, relates in detail how he attacked and destroyed the city of Thebes (No-Amon), and carried away "heavy booty" including many captives, and then returned to Nineveh (*Ibid.*, 64).

175 Lubim may refer to "the Libyans, whose capital was Cyrene; extending along the Mediterranean west of Egypt (2 Chron. 12:3; 2 Chron. 16:8; Acts 2:10). As, however, the *Lubim* are always connected with the Egyptians and Ethiopians, they are perhaps distinct from the Libyans. The *Lubim* were probably at first wandering tribes, who afterwards were settled under Carthage in the region of Cyrene, under

the name Libyans" (JFB, on 3:9).

176 *"Habaqquq* is an unusual Hebrew name derived from the verb *habaq,* 'embrace.' Thus his name probably means 'one who embraces' or 'clings.' At the end of his book this name becomes appropriate because Habakkuk chooses to cling firmly to God regardless of what happens to his nation" (Wilkinson and Boa, 273).

177 *Bible Commentary,* 1068.

178 Keil and Delitzsch, 388–9. However, the reference in 2 Kings 21:10–14 is a general statement covering a broad period. Habakkuk is most certainly one of these prophets mentioned there; however, when he prophesied cannot be determined from this passage.

179 While we commonly interchange "Chaldeans" for "Babylonians," there is a distinction between the two. The Chaldeans are Babylonians, but not all Babylonians are Chaldeans. "Chaldeans" is from the Hebrew word "Kasdim," and the Assyrian word "Kaldu." This refers to a tribal area in the southernmost region of Babylonia. "The people lived in loosely organized tribal groups and were fiercely independent of each other and especially of the major cities to the north, such as Babylon and Nineveh. They were natural enemies of all urbanized societies" (Smith, vol. 32 101). This depiction of the Chaldeans makes God's message to Habakkuk even more incredible, since it would not seem that a coalition of tribal people could take over all of Mesopotamia, Palestine, and Egypt—but they did.

180 Hailey, 272.

181 Wilkinson and Boa, 273.

182 Coffman, vol. 3, 63–4.

183 *Bible Commentary,* 1069.

184 Hailey, 278.

185 This battle took place *ca.* 605 BC and is described in Jer. 46:3–12.

186 Coffman, vol. 3, 72.

187 "However terrible and prostrating the divine threatening may sound, the prophet draws consolation and hope from the holiness of the faithful covenant God, that Israel will not perish, but that the judgment will be only a severe chastisement" (Keil and Delitzsch, 396).

188 Coffman, vol. 3, 76.

189 Smith, vol. 32, 107.

190 Hailey, 286.

191 "Not satisfied with robbing men and nations, and with oppressing and ill-treating them, the Chaldeans committed wickedness upon the cedars and cypresses also, and the wild animals of Lebanon, cutting down the wood either for military purposes or for state buildings, so that the wild animals were unsparingly exterminated" (Keil and Delitzsch, 412).

192 This passage calls to mind Phil. 2:9–11, when all of Creation will be made to bow before God's Son and recognize Him as having "all authority" (Mat. 28:18). In honoring God the Son, one must also honor God the Father who gave Him this authority.

193 N. C. Ridderbos and P. C. Craigie, "Psalms (Technical terms)," *ISBE*.

194 Coffman, vol. 3, 112.

195 *Bible Commentary*, 1087. "The etymology and meaning of haggay is uncertain, but it is probably derived from the Hebrew word hag, 'festival.' It may also be an abbreviated form of haggiah, 'festival of Yahweh.' Thus, Haggai's name means 'festal' or 'festive'" (Wilkinson and Boa, 283).

196 Hailey, 297.

197 *Bible Commentary*, 1087.

198 This is not the same Darius the Mede that is mentioned in *Daniel* (beginning in Dan. 5:31); rather, it is Darius the Medes' son, also known as Darius I Hystaspes (ruled 521–486 BC). He left behind an autobiography which was known to the infamous Greek historian Herodotus, giving us a great deal of information concerning his rise to the throne, his conquests, and his rule. Cyrus' son, Cambyses, was to succeed his father on the throne of Persia, but when this transfer of power was to take place, Cambyses was busy conquering Egypt. A man named Gaumata, posing as Cambyses' brother, took the throne instead; Darius led a conspiracy against this impostor and overthrew him, taking the throne of Persia for himself (even though he had no legal claim to it). Darius then had to put down revolts in Persia, Media, Babylonia, and the

Far East. A prolonged conflict with the Scythians resulted in the capture of Thrace and Macedonia. His confrontations with the Greeks, however, was difficult, and his Persian army was defeated by them in the battle of Marathon (490 BC). His son and successor, Xerxes I, would continue this battle against the Greeks (D. J. A. Clines, "Darius," *ISBE*).

199 Keil and Delitzsch, 469.

200 Hailey, 298. Driver adds: "The style of Haggai, though not devoid of force, is, comparatively speaking, simple and unornate. His aim was a practical one, and he goes directly to the point" (*Literature*, 344).

201 Coffman, vol. 3, 179.

202 Hailey, 300–1; bracketed words are mine.

203 *Bible Commentary,* 1089.

204 Part of the reason for this was that the Jews simply did not have the financial resources that Solomon had at his disposal for the building of the first temple. It is estimated that the amount of gold and other precious metals used in the construction of Solomon's temple would be in the billions of dollars in today's money; the gold on the ark of the covenant alone was equivalent to many millions of dollars. The Jews who returned from exile faced hard times as it was, so they could not duplicate what had been done in the extraordinarily prosperous days of Solomon.

205 Keil and Delitzsch, 484.

206 Hailey, 310–1.

207 "The nation, in its attitude towards the Lord, resembles, on the one hand, a man who carries holy flesh in the lappet [or, fold] of his garment, and on the other hand, a man who has become unclean through touching a corpse. 'Everything that Israel takes hold of, or upon which it lays its hand, everything that it plants and cultivates, is from the very first affected with the curse of uncleanness; and consequently even the sacrifices which it offers there upon the altar of Jehovah are unclean' (Koehler)" (Keil and Delitzsch, 492; bracketed words are mine).

208 Coffman, vol. 3, 210–1.

209 *Bible Commentary,* 1093.

210 *Ibid.,* 1094.

211 "Zerubbabel is seen as a type of Christ in that, 'He led the people out of Babylonian bondage, as Christ would lead his people out of the bondage of sin. Also, he built a temple, as Christ built the far greater Temple of his church' (Clinton R. McGill)" (Coffman, vol. 3, 218).

212 It is possible, however, that Jesus was referring to a different Zechariah than the one mentioned in 2 Chronicles or the Zechariah—one who was only known in Jewish tradition. Otherwise, the "son of Berechiah" identification in Mat. 23:35 is puzzling, since the Zechariah killed in 2 Chron. 24:20–22 is clearly the son of Jehoiada the priest.

213 James B. Coffman, *The Minor Prophets, vol. 4* (Abilene, TX: ACU Press, 1983), 5.

214 "[A]ll the parts of the book hang closely together; and the objection which modern critics have offered to the unity of the book has arisen … partly from the dogmatic assumption of the rationalistic and naturalistic critics, that the biblical prophecies are nothing more than the productions of natural divination, and partly from the inability of critics, in consequence of this assumption, to penetrate int the depths of the divine revelation, and to grasp either the substance or form of their historical development, so as to appreciate it fully" (Keil and Delitzsch, 503).

215 Wilkinson and Boa, 289; bracketed words are mine.

216 Many of the symbols and visions used in OT apocalyptic literature are carried over, in a sense, to the vision that the apostle John is given (a.k.a. *Revelation*). One who understands the symbols in their OT context will have the "key" necessary to decipher the same kind of symbols in *Revelation*.

217 Hailey, 325.

218 Compare these four horsemen with those described in Rev. 6:1–8. In both cases, the color of the horses corresponds to a different part of the message, and/or to different events of the future.

219 Keil and Delitzsch, 514; bracketed word is mine.

220 Coffman, vol. 4, 44; see 1 Cor. 6:19–20 and Eph. 2:19–22 regarding the indwelling of the Holy Spirit, both in the individual believer and in Christ's church.

221 The "rousing" (KJV, "waking") of Jehovah "is an idiomatic expression. We may not suppose that any prophet of God ever believed that God would go to sleep and neglect His people while taking a nap" (*Ibid.*, 47). The idea instead is that God would act to be with His people, in contrast to His having allowed them to go through their time of indignation (in exile), which some assumed to be a time when God was indifferent toward them.

222 Hailey, 332.

223 Smith, vol. 32, 199–200.

224 Compare this with 2 Sam. 24:1 (and 1 Chron. 21:1) where "Satan" indicates an adversary of any kind rather than the devil by name. We tend to impose our NT understanding of Satan on such OT passages, but the Satan of the NT is the avowed enemy of God's Son—and, when this fails, God's church—rather than the nation of Israel (see Rev. 12:3–8, 17). I cover the idea that the "Satan" in the OT is not necessarily the "Satan" identified in the NT in my book, *This World Is Not Your Home* (Spiritbuilding Publishers, 2022); go to www.spiritbuilding.com/chad.

225 Keil and Delitzsch, 526.

226 JFB, on 3:3.

227 "'Branch is a technical term in the prophets to portray the coming Davidic Prince [Messiah]…who would rise to become the builder of the Temple [His church], and combine in Himself the offices of priest and king. Joshua knew that he could not be the Branch because he was not of the Davidic line; and Zerubbabel, the civic head, was not present, neither was he a priest, so he did not qualify for the office'" (R. E. Higginson, quoted in Coffman, vol. 4, 57–58; bracketed words are mine).

228 Keil, for what it is worth, believes that these "anointed ones" are Zerubbabel and Joshua (Keil and Delitzsch, 543). However, the vision's full understanding remains obscured, so that it seems best to speak in general terms rather than try to assign specific identities. Coffman claims that these are the Old Testament and the New Testament (vol. 4, 72), yet his argument is not convincing.

229 In Rev. 11:4, the "two witnesses" of John's vision are identified (symbolically) as "the two olive trees and the two lampstands that stand

before the Lord of the earth"—apparently a direct allusion to Zechariah's vision. The problem is that both scenes are visionary, and it is not wise to interpret a symbolic picture in one vision with the same picture used in another vision. Such a comparison does not provide interpretation, but only a connection between the two: they both symbolize the same things, but we are not told what these are.

230 Coffman sees a direct connection between the "curse" and God's covenant with Israel (vol. 4, 77)—i.e., the Jews' sins are not merely against "law" in general, but specifically are violations of covenant—and for what it is worth, I believe he is correct. This does not take away, however, from a general application of this vision, namely, that God's moral laws are evident to all men, as Paul argues in Rom. 1:18—2:16.

231 "That a woman could be crouching in the ephah indicates that it was larger than a bushel basket; therefore the word was used only to designate the shape of the container and not its size" (Hailey, 345). Coffman, however, says that either the bushel must be bigger than it really is, or the woman must be smaller than an actual human being. Thus, he concludes, this "woman" is "one of the popular female goddesses of the day. Ishtar or Ashteroth [sic] could have been meant. This certainly avoids what seems to us the error of making womanhood to be the essence of personification of sin" (vol. 4, 82). But the vision does not make "womanhood" the personification of sin; it says in essence that this "woman" (in the vision) represents the sins of God's people. In like manner, Paul's "man of lawlessness" in 2 Thess. 2:3–7 does not make all males "lawless," but only that man of whom he spoke. We must be careful not to stretch our interpretations of visions beyond what the context in which they were intended.

232 *Bible Commentary*, 1111.

233 Hailey, 347.

234 Compare to the similar colored horses described in the vision given to John in Rev. 6:1–8. In John's vision, white horses mean victory; red, bloodshed; black, grief or famine; and "ashen," death; compare also to Ezek. 5:16–17, 14:21. It is not clear, however, if the horses in Zechariah's vision serve these exact same purposes.

235 "The names of the returnees given here were deeply religious names carrying these affirmations of faith in God: Hildah = the Lord's world; Tobijah = the Lord is good; and Jedaiah = the Lord knows" (Coffman, vol. 4, 92).

236 "Peace will be provided by the Branch holding the twofold office of king and priest" (Hailey, 354).

237 Keil and Delitzsch, 555.

238 The only fast that God required by the Law of Moses was for the Day of Atonement in the seventh month; see Lev. 23:27. However, it does not appear that the people were fasting in the seventh month for this reason, but possibly for Gedaliah, the governor of the land of Judah whom Nebuchadnezzar appointed, who was murdered shortly after he took this position; see Jer. 41:1–3.

239 Hailey, 359.

240 *Bible Commentary,* 1115.

241 JFB, on 8:23. "How incredible must this prophecy have seemed to the enemies of Israel. Who could have believed that a little handful of despised returnees would yet see the whole world turn to one of them for redemption and salvation? Yet it has been gloriously fulfilled" (Coffman, vol. 4, 125).

242 Hailey (and others) propose that it has reference (in the etymology of "Hadrach") to the Medo–Persians, all of which entered Israel from the north via the Mesopotamian "Fertile Crescent"; see Hailey, 367–368.

243 *Bible Commentary,* 1121; bracketed words are mine.

244 "One source states that the king of Gaza was brought alive to Alexander who had him bound to a chariot and dragged through the city [of Gaza] until he was dead"—effectively fulfilling the prophecy stated here in 9:5 (*Bible Commentary,* 1121; bracketed words are mine).

245 Clinton R. Gill, quoted in Coffman, vol. 4, 134.

246 This happened literally in the case of Jerusalem being spared of Alexander the Great's destruction of it. Alexander called for Jerusalem's surrender while he was besieging Tyre, but the Jews refused. On his way to the city to destroy it, he was met by Jaddua, the high priest, fully

clothed in his high priestly garments. Alexander, seeing the name of Jehovah on the priest's turban, bowed in reverence to him and asked the meaning of this confrontation. Jaddua told him that he had a God-given dream that Alexander would be successful in his campaign against Asia and told him of the prophecies concerning him in the book of Daniel. Thus, Alexander offered sacrifices to God and extended great privileges to the Jewish people (Coffman, vol. 4, 137).

247 The "waterless pit" [lit., cisterns in which there is no water] (9:11) indicates a state of being in which there is no blessing, kindness, or deliverance by God (see Jer. 2:13). More generally, it indicates the realm of sin and moral darkness, a state of being in which the soul's thirst remains unquenched and the soul itself in a miserable condition (contrast with John 4:13–14).

248 The Maccabean Revolt refers to the Jewish resistance against the Seleucidan (Grecian) oversight of Palestine in the 2nd century BC, during the intertestamental period. "Maccabee" ("the hammer") is the nickname given to Judas, the son of Mattathias, who defended the Jewish temple and its rites against the Grecian sacrilegious defilement of it (by Antiochus IV Epiphanes). By extension, Judas' lineage was referred to as the "Maccabees." For an explanation of this entire situation, see H. W. Hoeher, "Maccabees, *ISBE*.

249 On this reunion of the two tribes as one people, see Ezek. 37:15–28. It is conspicuous that in the NT there is no distinction between the two nations of Israel—the northern tribes and the southern tribe of Judah—but describes all "Jews" as a unified people.

250 Some commentators think that, because the temple was made of the cedars of Lebanon, this passage speaks of the destruction of that temple (Coffman, vol. 4, 159–161). Others believe that what is described here is a Roman invasion of Palestine (JFB, on 11:1–3). Given these two choices, the latter scenario fits much better. Thus, it may mean that, since Jerusalem (the most distinguished city of the region—the "cedar" here) will fall, then so will all the lesser cities ("cypresses" or firs). This also fits the "doomed flock" context: having rejected their Shepherd, the Israelite nation will be destroyed by an inferior shepherd (the Roman Empire), which in turn will also be judged and destroyed.

251 Matthew Henry points to the two staffs mentioned in David's psalm: "Your rod and Your staff, they comfort me" (Psalm 23:4). One staff (or "rod") was for correction or redirection; the other was for support (adapted from Coffman, vol. 4, 164–165).

252 *Ibid.*, 166.

253 On the other hand, it is hard to ignore what happens in the gospel accounts. The scribes (Mosaic lawyers), Pharisees, and Sadducees gave Jesus a great amount of grief and resistance, which is why He levels a strong denunciation of them (e.g., Mat. 23; see also John 8:37–59). These three groups may indeed be the "three shepherds" of which this prophecy speaks.

254 While the text uses "breaking" or (margin) "annulment," the technical language is that the covenant was fulfilled by Christ, thus allowing for a new covenant to be made. God provided a probationary or transitional period (40 years) for the Jews throughout the world to hear the terms of this new covenant (i.e., the preaching of the gospel). Yet, because of the Jews' persistent and widespread rejection of His Son's kingship, God finally ended His relationship with the Israelite nation once and for all (in the destruction of Jerusalem [AD 70]; see Jesus' parable about them in Luke 19:11–27). It is in this sense that God "broke/annulled" His covenant with Israel. It is impossible, in any context, for a covenant between two parties to be upheld by only one of them. Christ's fulfillment of God's covenant with Israel legally freed God from any binding obligation to it; even so, God extended kindness and priority to Israel by inviting them into a new and superior covenant with Him through His Son. Keep in mind that all this speaks of what happened between God (and His Son) and the Israelite nation, not individual Jews.

255 There is a very dark aspect to this allusion. The Law stated that if an ox gored a slave, then the owner of the ox would have to pay 30 pieces of silver to the owner of the slave. If the "slave" is Jesus, and God is (for all intents and purposes) His "owner," then the owner of the "ox" is the Jewish leaders (see John 11:47–53 and 19:11), and the "ox" itself is, in effect, the city of Jerusalem (Luke 13:31–35). According to the Law, after the payment has been made, the ox is to be put to death by stoning. Thus, the Jewish leaders sealed the fate of their own city through this

exchange of money. This is doubly incredible by the fact that Zechariah foretold all of it.

256 In the reference given (Mat. 27:3–10), it is said that "Jeremiah" spoke this prophecy, when clearly it is a prophecy of Zechariah. The best answer is that the works of Zechariah were contained in the volume (or, roll) of prophecies headed by Jeremiah, and so to refer to "Jeremiah" is simply to cite the volume from which the prophecy came, not the literal prophet who spoke it (JFB, on Mat. 27:9).

257 Hailey, 384.

258 The most natural identity of this "foolish" or wicked shepherd is Rome, which would not only rule over the Jews in the decades after Jesus but would also destroy them in the end (AD 66–70). This would also serve as God's fitting but chilling response to the Jews' claim during Pilate's presentation of Jesus before the people: "We have no king but Caesar" (John 19:12–15).

259 In my opinion, a *literal* execution is not being called upon here (in 13:3), but the passage illustrates one who is worthy of death. Nowhere in the NT are Christians called upon to execute false prophets—or anyone else—in the name of God.

260 Hailey, 393.

261 Modern Premillennialists, and many others, think this refers to a yet-future event in which the Mount of Olives will literally be split in half and moved apart. This will allegedly happen sometime during the holy war ("Armageddon") between Christ and the heathen powers of the earth at the end of the world. Such literal conclusions are nullified, however, by the context of the passage, which is both visionary and symbolic.

262 In the literal sense, Jesus warned His disciples to flee from the city of Jerusalem when they saw the signs of its impending doom; see Mat. 24:15–22. In the figurative sense, God has always provided His people with a "way of escape" (1 Cor. 10:13) from whatever would overwhelm their ability to follow Him in faith.

263 Hailey, 401; *Bible Commentary,* 1138. "Malachi might have been the personal name of this prophet or it might have been a title, Malachi =

'my messenger'" (Smith, vol. 32, 298).

264 Hailey, 402.

265 Wilkinson and Boa, 297; bracketed words are mine.

266 Smith, vol. 32, 298.

267 *Bible Commentary,* 1140.

268 In *Malachi*, God is not speaking of the two brothers (Jacob and Esau), but of the nations that came from each of them (the Israelites and the Edomites). "Loved" and "hated" must be seen in this context: God showed His love for the one, but He also showed His contempt for the other. When God says that He "hated" Esau, He does not mean that He loved Esau less than He did Jacob. Rather, He hated what Esau (i.e., the Edomites) had become, which followed in the footsteps of their patriarch, Esau. They were a worldly, unspiritual, vengeful, and bitter people—all defining characteristics which God hates because they are in contrast with His own moral nature. "With the same intensity that Jehovah loves the right and good, He hates the evil and bad. His attitude toward Edom had been demonstrated by His giving Edom into the hand of Nebuchadnezzar (Jer. 49:7ff, 25:9, 21) and not restoring them to their land as He had Jacob" (Hailey, 406). This was not based upon God's choice alone, but by what kind of people each nation chose to be. Absolutely nothing in the text, or anywhere in the Bible, speaks to the spiritual destiny of either Jacob or Esau personally; this is irrelevant to the development of God's ushering in His Son through the nation of Israel.

269 It is hard not to see a direct connection between what is being said here (in 1:10) and what is happening in churches today. Simply put: it would be better not to go through the motions of a "worship service" at all than to have one that is lacking in zeal, reverence, or sincere devotion to God (compare Isa. 1:11–17, for example).

270 To "sniff at" the sacrifices "is a metaphor taken from cattle that do not like their fodder. They blow strongly through their nose upon it; and after this, neither they nor any other cattle will eat it" (Adam Clarke, *A Commentary and Critical Notes: The Old Testament,* vol. 4 [New York: Abingdon-Cokesbury Press, no date], 800).

271 Hailey, 410.

272 Keil and Delitzsch, 644.

273 Joyce G. Baldwin, quoted in Coffman, vol. 4, 251.

274 "Since they had shown their contempt for God, He would make them contemptible; and since they had shown such a low regard for God, God would make them low in the estimation of men" (*Ibid.*, 261).

275 While there are numerous explanations in the commentaries on 2:12, what is written here seems the easiest and most natural interpretation.

276 Hailey, 416.

277 *Ibid.*, 417.

278 The Hebrew word for "messenger" here can also be translated "angel," and so it reads in the margin (NASB). However, it is better to say that all angels of God are messengers than to make John the Baptist into some kind of angelic figure. Clearly, God is speaking in figurative language throughout this passage (3:1–4), not literal.

279 We see this further explained when John the Baptist is asked if he is "the Prophet," which he denies, although in fact he is a prophet; see John 1:19–23. Jesus, on the other hand, says clearly that He is the Prophet who has been sent by the Father (see John 8:42, 16:28, 17:8, etc.).

280 Coffman, vol. 4, 283.

281 Strong, H2388.

282 Hailey, 426; bracketed words are mine.

283 Smith, vol. 32, 338.

www.ingramcontent.com/pod-product-compliance
Lightning Source LLC
Chambersburg PA
CBHW040303170426
43194CB00021B/2869